Organizing Justice Church

Organizing Justice Church

PAUL KITTLAUS
Foreword by Randi Jones Walker

RESOURCE *Publications* · Eugene, Oregon

ORGANIZING JUSTICE CHURCH

Resource Publications
An Imprint of Wipf and Stock Publishers
199 W. 8th Ave., Suite 3
Eugene, OR 97401

www.wipfandstock.com

PAPERBACK ISBN: 978-1-6667-7648-5
HARDCOVER ISBN: 978-1-6667-7649-2
EBOOK ISBN: 978-1-6667-7650-8

09/23/23

I dedicate this book to:

Our children and their families—Mark, Adam, Ann, Aaron, and Ben.

Genie Holmes who shared the earlier part of the story.

Janet Vandevender, who shared the experiences in the latter part of the story. She picked me up and carried me and my stories across the finish line in the last six months. Her love, good cooking, and laughter created a wonderful environment in which to work.

And Joe Hough who wanted to live long enough to read my book. I needed a month more than he had available. Thanks for the push, Joe. Sorry I missed the deadline.

Contents

Foreword

MY FIRST ENCOUNTERS WITH Rev. Paul Kittlaus came when I was a young pastor in the Southern California Nevada Conference of the United Church of Christ. I was ordained and began my ministry when he was pastor of the First Congregational Church of Santa Barbara, UCC. He had been in ministry almost as long as I had been alive, having been ordained the year I started the first grade. To me he was one of the pastors I admired, and I was not sure I had the courage for the kind of ministry he and the other Young Turks had practiced. The Young Turks were a legend in their time. The same year he left Southern California for Wisconsin, I left to join the faculty at Pacific School of Religion in Berkeley. There I taught, among other things, a course on the History and Theology of the United Church of Christ.

As I worked to frame the history of this complex denomination, I found the attention of the available textbooks focused on the founding of the denomination in the 1950s and the histories of the constituent denominations before that. Having been a pastor during the 1980s and now a seminary professor, I constantly ran into a background lament about what the church had lost, how it was in decline, how more conservative churches were growing, presumably doing something right that the mainline liberal Protestant churches were doing wrong. The turning point had come, according to the usual narrative, in the "sixties." So that my students and I could be clear about what had happened during that decade in the face of this lament of lost vitality and direction, I set out to explore that decade in depth. What constituted the decade seemed to have a long life, beginning somewhere just before or during World War II and ending sometime in the late 1970s, the "long sixties" one might call it.

In that nearly twenty-five year "decade," all the religious groups in the United States confronted a series of challenges from the culture around them holding up a mirror to show the difference between the religions' teachings and what they actually did about racism, poverty, hunger, nuclear weapons, war, gender inequalities, threats to the environment from pesticides, human overpopulation of the earth, fear of homosexuality, anxiety about immigration, and misgivings about the growing power of multinational corporations vis-à-vis democratic government and a growing public split among churches and other religious groups over the authority of certain readings of sacred texts and theological orthodoxy. These issues had completely overwhelmed the ecumenical enthusiasm which led to the formation of the United Church of Christ and the optimistic liberal view of American mainline Protestantism, rooted in the beginnings of the twentieth century, that Christianity was an obvious force for good in the world and by century's end historians could call it the Christian Century. There was even more going on under the surface of European and American Christianity than I can sketch here, much of it rooted in the already long history of Christian engagement with modernity, but these few issues concentrated as they were in time and space, radically altered the face of US mainline Protestant Christianity.

This book is the story of one pastor and his colleagues as they waded into the times determined to live out the Christian gospel as they understood it and to shape the life of the United Church of Christ and the congregations they served by this gospel. They stand out because they did not abandon the attempt to engage this host of issues and revert to a traditional style of pastoring, providing a comfortable place for people to nurture individual spirituality and stability, leaving the engagement with injustice to others. They stand out because they did not abandon the church and seek secular avenues of confronting injustice, destruction, and fear. Nor did they withdraw with a few kindred spirits into a small but perfect community. They chose to engage these issues from the context of UCC congregations, a choice fraught with ambiguous feelings, uncertain results, internal tensions, and second-guessing. Paul Kittlaus, in these pages, allows us to see the struggle, the cost in false hope and despair, and the moments of transcendence. As I have read these pages, I think of the metaphor of moving a battleship moored at a pier, that all it takes is for people to lean against it long enough and it will move. Here and there in Paul's story, I think I have felt the battleship move. This book is an invitation to wade into our times, armed only with the age-old Christian gospel and its even longer prophetic roots and each other's love and support. Kittlaus and his colleagues, the Young Turks, leaned into the injustice of their times and ours and moved that battleship a little way.

RANDI JONES WALKER
Professor Emerita, Pacific School of Religion

Preface

I FINALLY FIGURED OUT why I am writing this book. I want to recruit and encourage leaders of the church to join in building the justice church. I want to increase the capacity of the church to do its justice work. By justice I mean actions more challenging and dangerous than works of charity. I mean addressing the conditions that cause poverty and hunger.

A radical assertion is at the heart of Frederick Herzog's book *Justice Church*. He is reporting on the work of several theological commissions appointed by the World Council of Churches and by national and denominational teams of theologians seeking to faithfully respond to the challenges raised by liberation theology in the Global South. He writes,

"The gospel pertains to the liberation of the poor as well as to the salvation of the soul."[1]

"Responsible Christian theology is always an effort to give an account of the continuing activity of Messiah Jesus in his community. Just what that activity is can ultimately not be settled abstractly by theologians talking to each other, but only by Christians struggling together in the praxis of history. . . . We are zeroing in on the church immersed in the struggles of history."[2]

My book is basically my memoir focusing on how I understood my work as a minister during the struggles of history from the late 1950s to the end of the century.

The first half of this time were years of turmoil and challenge to the political and cultural status quo. The last half were years of a relative calm resting on a new status quo.

My undergraduate and seminary education was based on assumptions of the fifties. These gave way to forces and energies that required massive resistance or creative adaptation to keep the church and the gospel relevant to the new, evolving ethos.

---

1. Herzog, *Justice Church*, 3.
2. Herzog, *Justice Church*, 5.

I was ordained in the fall of 1959. The following decade challenged expectations and pushed me into experimenting with church organization and liturgy, developing plans for exploring the neighborhood, and partnering with secular and religious groups for various campaigns. There were uprisings in the society and the culture and in the political life of the country.

I found I needed new skills. Especially helpful were the skills in the field of planned social change and community organizing and those at the urban training centers.

It is the accumulation of these skills and the experience of special ministries that bring me to the confidence of leadership in helping the church to be transformed by taking on a new function, liberating the poor. I know some of the processes by which we could explore causes and potential solutions to poverty.

I hope you can see the bits and pieces of experience that helped shape my way of being and my skills. I hope you challenge yourself to define the issues of your time so you can help the church become even more engaged in its justice work. I hope you can find mentors and colleagues who teach you to recognize your gifts and develop the skills needed for your work.

Acknowledgments

As I wrote, I walked again in memory with so many friends who touched my heart, who gave me courage, who set me straight, who gave me meaningful work to do, who taught me magic, who held my hand to keep me from falling, and who restored me to my proper size when I got inflated (often with some sharp-edged sarcastic remark). I thank you all.

This book has been in the background of my mind. I have kept files of papers, newspaper articles, letters, agendas, and notes everywhere I worked. Since I retired, I've written bits and pieces after consulting these files and letting them take me back to reflect, sometimes unknowingly writing the same stories years apart. Two years ago, I decided to get serious about the project and began to assemble all of it to see how many of the stories have been told and which ones were missing. Some periods of serious writing followed. I pictured a self-published book. After some encouragement I filled out the proposal for a book application on the Wipf and Stock Publisher website. A month later I was sent a contract and their author's guide. With that encouragement I drastically reduced my involvement in my abstract painting, my newest form of self-expression. I love the painting. All I must do is spin my chair 180 degrees around and I'm sitting before my easel, a palate of glorious paint and brushes and a terrible painting I'm going to cover over with a new one, and I'm lost in an ocean of creativity. But I'll finish the book first.

I have worked always to build the church's capacity to do its justice work. I consulted. I collaborated. I experimented and improvised. I risked, I organized, I challenged, I screwed up, I got fired. And I wouldn't change a thing. I'm grateful to the United Church of Christ for educating me, ordaining me, and putting me to work. I am not the only one going around working to bring the church into our moment of history. I'm grateful for the company in the UCC and various ecumenical and interfaith teams I have been a part of.

I had readers who read the stories as I wrote them, readers who criticized, suggested, pushed me to do better. I thank Dick Fernandez, Speed

Leas, Ann Kittlaus, Harvey Peters, and especially Randi Walker. Randi and I have talked a lot about the significance of what we were doing in the sixties, how the Young Turks and similar groups around the country challenged the UCC to face the big issues and work them through: the war, racism and civil rights, homophobia, women's rights, the environment, and poverty.

I thank Janet. This is not the first time we risked our marriage to partner on a project for which we felt passion and to which we brought our conflicting perspectives and processes. This memoir is much closer to what I wanted it to be after her rigorous editing.

Thanks to all of you.

Paul Kittlaus
Summer 2023

For photographs of many of these stories see https://paulkittlaus.art

Chapter 1

Seeking a Church Engaged in the World

TOM BURST THROUGH THE front door of my home into the midst of the Bible study group I was leading for elderly adults. He was big. He had red hair and a beard. And he was holding high a magnum of chilled champagne.

Tom and the class did not know what to make of each other.

"Congratula . . . oops! Wrong house!" And with that he exited as quickly as he had arrived.

Tom sat in his truck parked in front of my house until the class was over. Then he came in and we popped the cork to celebrate that I had become a new dad. Genie had given birth to our son Mark earlier that day.

That night, Tom showed me the fastest mind ever.

That experience—an explosive disruption, the need to step back to find a workable plan, essential camaraderie in times of excitement and challenge, risk taking or acting according to existing norms or expectations, and recognizing the importance of the current reality—served as a metaphor for my ministry.

Some periods of history are relatively calm. Life moves forward on a stable foundation. Other times the foundations crack and rumble like an earthquake. I remember the 1971 Sylmar quake that measured 6.5 on the Richter scale. Just before sunrise the house began to roll as if it were on a wave that surfers would love. We dashed to our kids' rooms to be sure they were safe. Around us fifty-eight people died. There was $500 million in damage.[1] Earthen dams threatened to break. The aftershocks went on for two weeks, recharging our adrenaline each time. Rumors of greater, bigger quakes spread. It was very unsettling, and any plans were no longer relevant.

---

1. Sweeney, "Unit Formed to Coordinate."

An inflection point is a time when an organization must respond to disruptive change in the environment effectively or face deterioration. An inflection point, in general, is a decisive moment, event, or situation that marks the start of significant change. Such a time had arrived for the church.

I lived and engaged in ministry during one such inflection point in our history, the sixties and seventies. And I pastored in a calmer period during the eighties and nineties. I share here how I worked in my times.

I was ordained into the ministry of the United Church of Christ (UCC) in October 1959 at the Kensington Community Church UCC in San Diego. I was a midwesterner who was moving to the West Coast because that's where I found the best job; I was seeking to discover who I was and what ministry would mean during that time. The next two decades were filled with the civil, political, and cultural earthquakes of the sixties and seventies: the massive anti-war marches, the civil rights march on Washington, the police riots in Watts. And the blows to our sense of hope in the assassinations of Jack Kennedy (1963), Malcolm X (1965), Martin Luther King Jr. (1968), and Bobby Kennedy (1968). My work was giving leadership to our church, which seemed largely to prefer ignoring the turmoil of the time. In the following decades my ministry was serving in the national setting of the church and rediscovering local church ministry. All required shifts as the world and my assignments changed.

In 1962 the Rev. Albert G. Cohen, the Rev. Tom Lasswell, and I agreed that, with very few exceptions, the churches were trying to avoid the turmoil of the world in which they were set. Al served as campus pastor at California State University in Fullerton in Orange County. Tom was campus pastor at California State University in Northridge. I was pastor of a church in Pacoima, a poverty area in the northeast section of the San Fernando Valley of Los Angeles. From our social locations in ministry, the college campus, and the ghetto and barrio, we could feel the rumbles of a new generation seeking to create a new world: of people who were poor seeking expression for the rage for being left out, pushed down, and deprived of meaningful choices for their lives and families, and of students who would not conform to the limits on free speech and were energized for work for change.

We felt that the church had a role to play but we found very little evidence of it doing so.

Al suggested that we be the research and development department for the United Church of Christ. This conversation led to a lifelong commitment to each other to work for change in the church and the world. And it began friendships in which we accompanied each other through many ups and downs, loves and losses, triumphs, and failures in our ministries and lives.

We shared the view that the church must get immersed in the struggles of its time in history. Seeing nothing like we felt was needed in the church, we agreed it might be up to us to get things started. We were convinced that the church needed some new theological work and a new praxis, new ways of being present in the troubled world.

There was a ton of both arrogance and ignorance in our vision that it might be up to us. But we did feel creativity and innovation. Strengthened together, we were sure that ahead of us lay the breaking of old established patterns. This analysis and commitment gave us a sense of vocational purpose. This became for me the answer to a long-held question: Why am I here? I knew now that I was here to help build something new in my church. To call the church into engagement with our moment in history. To build the justice church. I did not have a clear vision of what needed to be done but was ready to find the beginning of the path and follow where it took me.

In a way, this memoir is a report card on this commitment. My hope is to encourage new generations of clergy and laity who might feel the rumble of social change under their feet, who sense in their times a call to work for justice and peace, and who might wonder how others responded as the world was in turmoil around them. I felt a call to social change ministry in and for the church and the world.

In the last years of my ministry, I read Frederick Herzog's book *Justice Church: The New Function of the Church in North American Christianity* (1980),[2] which in an amazing way suggested the path that I had taken in my efforts to understand how the church was to be engaged in the life of the world. Herzog was an American theologian who devoted his work to the challenges that arose in liberation theology in Latin America and to letting those challenges help restate some new understandings of the nature and purpose of the church. I will reflect at the end how the concept of *Justice Church* formulated by Herzog helps clarify what I was about and what might be helpful to a new generation.

2. Herzog, *Justice Church*.

Chapter 2

Developing Values and Skills

How did I know what courses to sign up for at the university if I didn't know what I planned to do with my life? Wasn't I just spinning my wheels if I didn't have direction? I felt a lot of grief from my dad.

He used my friend, Dan, as the example of how it was supposed to work. Dan seemed to know from birth that he was going to be a forest ranger. His path through the various levels of education was Interstate 10 across the Mojave. My path was more like driving Lombard Street in San Francisco.

Dan's clarity about his lifework, his life vision, was strange to me. I had no clue what lay ahead or what I wanted. I did not know what I was here for. Dan was piling up bits and pieces of knowledge, language, and courses that affirmed his work in the forests. My Dad wanted me to have that kind of clarity, which I did not. I wanted it. He regularly asked me where I was headed with my life, and I could not satisfy his question.

I felt a sense of disapproval from him. He saw me as aimless. I did not feel aimless. I was curious about a lot of things. In grade school I was interested in the skills and talents of my classmates. I was envious of Bobby because he could draw. He would put a few lines on a page, and I would guess which of our classmates he was drawing. I wished I had that gift. I was envious of Carl because he was tall, good looking, and at ease with the girls. I was none of those things. Wished I was. I was envious of Corky because he could stand up and lie to the teacher with a stone face when the whole class knew he was lying. I wanted to be able to hide my emotions, but they seemed to show up out of my control. Larry could hit the softball further than any of us and he didn't even look like an athlete. He held the bat way at the end even with a couple fingers off the bottom. I could run the bases much faster than Larry but seldom had the opportunity. I felt down because

I wanted to do all those things but could not. I felt average in everything. They were stars and I was not.

Each of those gifts carried a suggestion about a possible future. They were natural gifts that might be developed, that suggested a life as an artist, an actor, a baseball player. I was cut out to be average in a lot of things and none of them provided a vision of what I might want to be and do in life. How do you pick a college based on that data? Sorry, Dad.

I was mostly quiet and easy with myself when I was alone. I had a circle of friends on my block on Oleatha Avenue in southwest St. Louis. Our childhood was during World War II. We structured our playtime doing basically two things. We dug trenches in the vacant lot just up the street. We were fighting the war in Europe. We put boards over the trenches and covered them with dirt so no one could tell that there were tunnels and that we were lurking down there.

And we played hundreds of hours of cork ball. This was a St. Louis thing, cork ball. When I went to the University of Missouri in Columbia, no one other than those of us from St. Louis knew what cork ball was. It was a scaled down version of baseball and was played by four players, two on each team. I could not throw a curve and my hits were seldom. Of course, we saw ourselves as various current members of the St. Louis Cardinals. I had the best Stan Musial batting stance. Unmistakable.

I got to know Stan Musial and his wife, Lil. They rented my grandpa's house for three baseball seasons in the late 1940s. At grandpa's request I was responsible for lawn upkeep. I mowed the lawn with the push-mower only at noon on days when the Cardinals were playing home night games at Sportsman's Park. Stan was usually home. It was always hot and muggy. Lil took pity on the yard boy and invited me for lunch, a baloney sandwich. Stan would join us. Over time I probably had a dozen baloney sandwiches with Stan. He gave me a signed baseball with autographs of the entire 1946 World Series champions St. Louis Cardinals team.

Southwest High School

At Southwest High School I was an average student. I realized that there were teachers who could ignite a fire in me. The best was Benjamin Charles Rush III. An ancestor with his name had signed the Declaration of Independence. Mr. Rush was my homeroom teacher and taught history as though he had actually been there. He stood on his desk to issue great speeches from the floor of that hall in Philadelphia. He conveyed the courage and risk those men took on our behalf and the brilliance of their vision of democracy.

I was totally humiliated in my chemistry class. I could not get the concept of a valance. It made no sense to me. I stood by Mr. Cervenka's desk after class. He drew images. I could not get it. No personal future in chemistry. He was characteristically late to lab on Wednesdays. I sat next to Bob. We both watched the TV shows *Your Show of Shows Starring Sid Caesar and Imogene Coca* and *The Texaco Star Theater with Milton Berle* the night before. We memorized them. We reenacted many of the skits and got pretty good at delivering good punch lines for our class.

My dad, employed by the St. Louis Board of Education, had been the first physical education teacher assigned to my high school when it was founded in the late 1930s. He coached gymnastics, football, and track. He became director of physical education for the St. Louis Public School system in the late forties. I felt I was a legacy in sports there but with limited talent. I was small and didn't really grow until I was in college. In high school I went out for football, and it was not a good match. I ran track, enjoying most long-distance running. We didn't have cross country teams in those years but that would have been my best sport. I also ran on the four-by-one-mile relay team. Again, it was clear there would be no scholarships to play intercollegiate sports. But I did enjoy running.

Pots and Pans

A summer camp job provided an experience that helped me identify an ability that was to be treasured and nurtured. As volunteer on the work staff at the American Youth Foundation Camp Miniwanca, in Shelby, Michigan, I got free room and meals. Spending a couple weeks there at the end of summer before heading back to college was a great and cheap break. The kitchen staff where I was assigned had various jobs for meal preparation, serving, setting tables, and cleanup after meals. The worst job was washing pots and pans. Very large, deep pots and vast pans usually had burned food laminated to the bottom.

Scrubbing and scraping went on and on over in the corner where the big wash sinks were. All the workers rotated around among the various jobs, hating most the P&P duty. To compensate, the P&P workers were able to head out to the beach on Lake Michigan or the sail boats on the inland lake as soon as their job was done, usually at least an hour before everyone else.

I saw an opportunity. I negotiated with the kitchen boss that I would recruit a crew to do P&P every meal and that we would get very good at it. And we'd love the usual extra hours of freedom. I proposed to five other boys and girls that I enjoyed that they join me as permanent P&P crew and all agreed. We had the most fun singing camp and work songs, using the pots as drums, making noise, feeling connected to a crew within the larger, unorganized group of volunteers. And we did a spectacular job with the cookware. I liked the feeling of seeing the opportunity, negotiating an arrangement, recruiting to the crew the people I most wanted to spend time with, and doing our job. That's my earliest experience I can recall of functioning as an organizer.

The world I grew up in was all white. The only exception was Arcelia, the woman my parents hired for help in housekeeping and laundry a couple times a week. Arcelia was Black and powerfully deferential. Her husband sat in their car in front of our house the whole time Arcelia worked. He wore a coat and tie and looked straight forward. A couple times I tried to greet him. He seemed not to hear me. This was my only experience of racial diversity until I was in college. The St. Louis public schools were segregated.

Christmas Postal Worker Walks through Poverty

In 1953, on a Christmas break at home from my studies at the University of Missouri, I got a job working as a short-term temporary worker for the US Postal Service. Mail delivery reached its peak during the Christmas season and extra workers were needed. I was assigned to the post office that served the Pruitt–Igoe housing towers and areas nearby. It was the post office that served the most segregated and poverty-stricken postal zone. Twice a day I delivered the same route for two weeks.

The exposed stairs and hallways were wooden and on the outside of the three-story brick buildings. There were no interior hallway and no elevators.

I showed up at 6:30 a.m. at the post office, filled my bag with the deliveries for each trip, and hiked six blocks to the start of the route. At the end of the first round, I stopped at the auxiliary mailbox to which the mail for my second round had been delivered. I was given a special key to open the box. I was a federal employee, an agent of the United States government. I wore a mailman's cap but my own coat, gloves, scarf, and boots.

So, I walked those exposed stairs and hallways and experienced a lot of silence from residents who saw me. I was the stranger, the outsider. This was a very Black area. I did not have a clue what to expect or prepare for. I was not sure what was happening as I made my rounds. People either stared at me in silence or looked away. It was easy to see the terrible conditions of poverty. This look into the lives of people experiencing poverty created a scar on my soul.

The one tavern on the route was open and noisy. Silence fell when I entered. Everything came to a halt, all eyes trained on the white kid with the mailbag over his shoulder. I dropped the tavern mail on the bar where the bartender pointed, then departed. The noise restarted immediately. By my second day I realized that the noise was loud, rhythmic music playing on the jukebox, playing tunes I did not know. And the noise was also boisterous laughter and loud banter. They were, as far as I could tell, all men, all Black. The third day in the quiet when I put the mail down, I said to the bartender, "Merry Christmas."

The fourth day he said "Merry Christmas" back to me. The fifth day the noise did not stop when I entered. Only me, I was no longer the threat. Only the bartender could hear the exchange of Christmas greetings. I was no longer the full outsider. I was no longer worth stopping the party for. Two men waved as I left the final delivery.

I have reflected a lot on that experience. I treasure it. I remain curious about the big sounds of laughter and fun that I heard. It was not like anything I have ever heard at a bar full of white people. I remain convinced that there was a lot of good stuff going on out there, stuff I would probably not be permitted to experience with them. My whiteness was a barrier. I was curious about the life lived in those apartments where I delivered mail. There was life there too, but I was an outsider to it. I felt something had broken open in me, an awareness that has been part of me since.

I have debriefed that experience with African American friends through the years. Why were these men in the bar during the day? No jobs. They wanted jobs. When they got a job, they were not in the bar. They came together to keep their spirits up. They shared their pain and sense of uselessness. That's most of what I was told.

I learned that immersion in new experience was a faster, more powerful way to learn than reading books. And I promised myself I would always remember this experience and use this memory to keep myself engaged in working for justice.

The University of Missouri 1952–1956

I had two options for college: live at home and go to Washington University or enroll at the University of Missouri in Columbia. I was eager to get out on my own. It was an easy choice.

My dad loaded up the Chevy to drive me 125 miles due west to Columbia, Missouri, and helped me move into Defoe Hall, a dorm for independent (non-Greek) men. He told me many years later that he was never prouder than he felt as he drove back to St. Louis realizing that he had a son in college. His father had a degree from the Teachers College at Indiana University. And Dad had the same degree and years later spent two summers in Bloomington, earning a master's degree.

Dad showed great forbearance in helping me move up four flights of stairs in Defoe Hall. My stuff included my new full set of drums. My high school friend, Jack, had taken me on to teach me to experience the joy of jazz. Then he invited me to form a band with him. He was a good trombone player. He knew I had had piano lessons and hoped I could play in his band. Playing in a band seemed like an exciting prospect to me. But I could not, because I don't have the ear to know what key the band is playing in. So, he suggested, I could play drums in the band without having to worry about what key the tune was in. I bought a used set, base, snare, tom-tom, high hat, and two large cymbals plus sticks and brushes. I would learn on the job. At college Jack quickly formed a band and got a job for us playing for a sorority dance in the field house. Late in the evening there were shouts for a drum solo. I was not ready. Nowhere near ready. Plus, I had a natural tendency to speed up the tempo. With my drums setting the rhythm I pushed the band at an ever-increasing tempo. I did not realize that was happening. Jack would turn around and yell at me, "Slower! Slower!" I sold the drum kit and bought my first suit.

I often wonder how speeding things up gave me a clue for a vocation. Seems like in every job I ever had, I constantly wanted to speed things up. I've begun to note there is an entrepreneurial heart beating in my chest. I want to build, expand, speed up, deepen the work I take on. This is the earliest evidence I see of this.

I moved into a dorm for non-Greek students because I knew nothing of Greek life or its importance, if any. I figured I would check it out after I entered life as an undergraduate student. In my second year, the dean of students hired a dean for independent students with the task of bringing resources and a semblance of self-governance and structure to the life of independent students. The new dean began a talent search looking for leadership potential among the residents of those four dorms on the hill—a classic move for community organizers.

Given that I had been voted Knight Owl, I was at that moment in an obvious position to help do this organizing. I had received some real status on the campus.

Knight Owl

Jerry, from down the hall, came into my room one afternoon in January of my second year and asked if he could propose something. I invited him in. We had chatted a few times. I didn't know him well. He said he and several others wanted to know if I would be interested in running as the first independent man as candidate for Knight Owl that spring. I wasn't sure what he was talking about. He spelled it out. The sorority council on campus organized two big formal dances a year, one in the fall and one in the spring. At the spring dance the sorority members attending voted for their favorite candidate to be Knight Owl for that year.

These dances were fancy. They were called balls. Women worn gowns. Men brought their dates corsages and wore their best suits. Up until Jerry's proposal to me, the candidates who competed for Knight Owl for decades were fraternity men. It was a Greek affair. Jerry was suggesting that an independent enter the competition. Never happened before. Way out of the box thinking. The new dean was encouraging this move.

Fraternities applied on invitation from the Sorority Council to run their candidate for Knight Owl The council picked a final six to compete. The "campaign" was restricted to fifteen-minute presentations at the series of sorority houses by the candidates. Each put on a little talent show given over several nights at the sorority houses. These were usually skits, songs, or advocacy speeches. My favorite that year, other than my group, was a close-harmony, highly sophisticated singing of "Get Your Kicks on Route 66" by a quartet of Betas.

Jerry was a skilled organizer and put together a campaign that swept me to victory. He found among the men living in the four independent dorms the personnel for a great Dixieland band. They could play a down and dirty rendition of "Night Train" with a notable tenor saxophone soloist. And they played "When the Saints Go Marching In."

It became clear that having an independent in the mix brought a novelty to the proceedings, a little uncertainty to the party. Just that that bunch of men up on the hill living in those dorms could put together this effort to break through the restrictions of tradition created excitement. Our band entered the sorority houses one after another over three nights, with a piano player, a crew carrying in a full drum set for our spectacular drummer, and a shiny brass trumpet, trombone, saxophone, and bass. The glorious loud noises they played and the rhythms rocked those houses with explosive energy. We became a most-anticipated event on the circuit. My job as candidate was to say a little as possible, look as sophisticated as I could fake it, and let the band roar. I introduced the band members, thanked women for their hospitality, said a little about jazz history (it was born in New Orleans and traveled up the Mississippi . . .) and urged their support for the first independent to run for Knight Owl. The campaign had a kind of movement feel; we were giving them the opportunity to break new ground, to release new energy, and to bring in a little wildness.

The night of the dance, when the ballots were counted, the independent won by overwhelming margin. Applause rang out in the field house. I was invited to the stage to be adulated by all the beautiful women, to be properly dubbed Knight Owl and to receive the trophy that was mine to keep for a year: a stuffed owl mounted on a wooden board with a brass plaque attached. My name was engraved as 1953 Knight Owl I was also the first sophomore to have won.

I was astonished and overwhelmed by it all. I enjoyed the excitement and the attention of course, but it was way out of character for me as I had understood myself. I was a great number two helper for other leaders. I was normally support for the leader. That's who I was comfortable being. Here I was number one in the eyes of the sorority women at the University of Missouri. I collected hundreds of hellos and smiles for about a month. By then I was, as we say, "so yesterday."

Notably, my dating for a while was no longer limited to women who lived in the independent women's dorms. Sorority women expressed interest. I even had one date with a student at nearby exclusive Stephen's College, a woman named Betty Birdseye of the frozen food family. But that was not my crowd.

Student Government Association (SGA) Thinking Politically

The more liberal campus political party immediately asked me to run for student body president. They coveted those votes up in those dorms on the hill. It was a long tradition in the state that men joined one or the other of the two parties competing year after year for the Student Government Association (SGA) positions. Then as they entered law school, moved on to the Republican or Democratic State parties, and joined politically active law firms, they eventually ran for state or federal offices. That focus was evident among friends in student government. Decisions now could have implications down the road in their careers. Friends and enemies made now could be forever. Cleverness now, keen strategic thinking now, good speech making now, and good analysis now could determine a lot about one's future.

One friend from that time served on the Missouri State Supreme Court, another served as governor, and one a US Senator. One ambitious guy served as the spokesperson for the US Department of Defense during the war in Vietnam. As slick as he was, he did not sell the war to us.

I soaked up a lot about thinking politically during a couple years in student government.

Decision making was partly about what was right or wrong but also about how decisions would play politically. How would decisions affect groups of people? Would they strengthen our alliances or weaken them? How would they factor in when election time rolled around?

One clear memory of these years was sitting in the student union watching on TV the Army–McCarthy hearings. It was an extraordinary moment of political accountability. Public life had its attractions such as I was seeing in that Senate Committee Room.

Two other experiences helped give shape to my understandings of myself. On the first of December 1955, my junior year at the university, the news of Rosa Parks's refusal to move to the back of the bus broke open realities few white Americans had in our understanding of how the world worked. It did not work for everyone the way it worked for us. It was time to lift to brighter light America's original sin of slavery, to move the country toward a wider conflict over race in America. The civil rights movement grabbed national headlines.

The Supreme Court had issued the Brown v. Board of Education decision in May 1954. The struggle to integrate the Central High School in Littlerock, Arkansas, in September 1954 and the Montgomery Bus Boycott in 1955 were being reported in the local newspapers. These developments put me in touch with my experience as a temporary mail delivery person a few Christmases earlier. They reminded me of the challenges I felt about race, about so much that I became aware of but did not understand.

Integrating Movie Theaters in Little Dixie

While sitting in the SGA office in the Student Union I asked if there might be interest in looking at the segregation in the two movie theaters in town. After a brief discussion I agreed to go to the theater managers to explore what their policies were on allowing a racially mixed audience. The big movie theater downtown was part of a chain which had a whites-only policy. The smaller theater was locally owned and had a balcony where Black people were accepted.

Several days after my conversation with the manager of the smaller theater, word got back to the campus through a statewide law firm that the SGA was way out of bounds going off campus and raising questions about how local citizens ran their businesses. I could not generate a commitment to a movie theater boycott because the owner was a big donor to the Republican Party. Neither the university administration nor the students with eyes on a future in state politics thought we should be taking my suggestion. So, we developed a program for increasing enrollment of Black students at the university.

I did learn a little history. The greatest resistance in Missouri to ending slavery was in the central part of the state known as Little Dixie. Located in that area were both Columbia, where the state university is located, and Jefferson City, where the state capital is located. Folks were proud to live in Little Dixie.

It was not easy for me to walk solo into those movie houses to raise questions about their racial segregation practices. I had not seen that sort of thing done. I had no role models to follow. I worked out in my mind some clarity that in society sometimes raising questions of moral importance was critically required and I was beginning to see what kind of world I had grown up in. I began to feel an energy to see change come to some of it. This I wanted to nurture.

FM Radio Jazz Disc Jockey

A technical wizard friend built a ten-watt radio station in his dorm room across the hall. He said the range of the signal from his little radio was strong enough to reach all the men's and women's dorms on the hill. Now, what to do with this capability? He connected my LP turntable to the equipment, and I played disc jockey for an hour a day for several weeks.

When a new commercial FM radio station was licensed and started broadcasting from a small building on the north edge of town, they advertised for ideas about programming. I picked up several of my jazz albums one day, drove out to the station, and chatted with the manager. I told him that I would personally provide two hours of programming on Saturday mornings, playing and chatting about jazz. I said I would provide all the recordings and would not need any payment. It would be free to him. He agreed on the spot.

So, the next Saturday I showed up with records under my arm and some thoughts about the program I was going to do that morning. There was one staff member at the station. He was playing records and making community interest announcements. Also, he served as the engineer. I told him I had the 9:00 a.m. to 11:00 a.m. time. He had not been informed but took my word for it. I came across as authorized and competent, I guess. He showed me the slide on the console that I should use to turn the microphone on and off and the one for turning on and off the music from the turntable. He left and, at nine, I started playing my theme music, "Concerto to End All Concertos," by Stan Kenton and his band. I chatted away and played music I liked, more Kenton, the new guy Dave Brubeck, and Stan Goetz, Miles Davis, Ella Fitzgerald, and others. I wished all the coeds a great morning and a good date that night. I talked a little about things I thought were interesting on the campus.

At eleven the staff guy showed up, and I signed off. He said I did a good show. Episode one of *Seminar in Jazz with Paul Kittlaus on Radio Station KBIA: SIJ with PK on KBIA*. This lasted six weeks. I was very close to graduating and resigned. The manager told me that I had developed a good following and he was hoping to get some advertisers for my show. KBIA is now owned by the University of Missouri and is the NPR outlet for that area.

I discovered that what interested me would interest others. That I could put things across and hold people's attention. And I had found the chutzpah to talk myself into a job sharing my musical interests by radio over a regional broadcast.

Teachers

I searched the course catalog looking for professors who ignited my brain, who challenged me and held me accountable, who offered friendship and affirmation and interest in me. I took a class in Medieval Intellectual History because it was taught by Professor Lewis Spitz. In Psychology a couple teachers engaged my interest.

I took several courses in the highly rated Speech Department. Professor Bower Ailey, the author of a widely used textbook slammed his notebook closed at around the third sentence of a speech I was making in the class. I had not prepared, and he saw I was faking it. After a moment of silence following the loud slam of his notebook he said, "Don't waste my time." I was humiliated but on reflection respected that and learned from it. I have been reminded of Ailey's confrontation when I have heard that it is better to stay quiet and let people assume you have nothing to say, than to speak and prove it.

Another speech professor gave me an amazing gift in the form of critique after an expository speech in front of an audience in the auditorium. He said that the way I walked up to the podium and prepared to begin my remarks had the effect of generating confidence and eagerness to hear what I was to share.

Just those two experiences, the hard wall of accountability and the words of encouragement both were significant lessons.

Unitarians: Open Dissent in Church Welcome?

The clue that set the direction came when I joined our next-door neighbors to attend the Sunday morning service at First Unitarian Church of St. Louis. I was on Thanksgiving break from the university. The associate pastor gave the sermon. He argued that the senior minister had been wrong in the previous two sermons. The coffee hour after the service was loud with debate among the people. I came to see that Unitarian worship was about challenging ideas that inform life. The notion that orthodoxy was constantly challenged, fresh thinking and advocacy for one's thinking was appreciated, and conflict was welcomed on the path to truth was refreshing and new to me. I loved that environment.

I went back to the university and organized two conversation groups seeking to recreate the intensity of conversation I heard in the coffee hour. I invited friends to share what they believed about religion. These sessions completely absorbed me. I loved those sessions and others did also.

All that led to a formulation of questions that I needed to think through. The search for the direction my life should be informed by some understanding of what purpose human existence was formed to serve. This was a classic college level intellectual activity, but it offered a path to a decision about what I would become and what further education I might need.

I spent the next several Sunday mornings visiting churches around Columbia, Missouri: Presbyterian, Methodist, Congregational, Lutheran. None of them was a bit helpful for the question I was asking. Next semester I enrolled in two philosophy courses. No help there.

My question about life's purpose seemed most likely to be answered in the field of religion if I could find a seminary that was not bound up in pitching orthodoxy and dogma.

I applied to both the Meadville Unitarian Seminary and the congregational seminary affiliated with the Divinity School at the University of Chicago. The Chicago Theological Seminary (CTS) responded first with acceptance. I began my study in the fall of 1956 and graduated in 1959.

Genie Holmes and I were married in August 1956 and headed off to Chicago together.

My Career in the US Air Force

I was in a hurry to be accepted at a seminary because I was seeking to change my status with the US Air Force from pilot trainee to chaplain trainee. As a freshman at a land grant university, I was required to take two years of Reserve Officers' Training Program (ROTC). When I became a junior, I had the opportunity to enroll in Advanced ROTC program which would provide scholarship support and would oblige me to three years of military service as a pilot starting as a second lieutenant. At the time I had to make the decision, I was unable to see another next step for me. So, I enrolled for two more years of ROTC. By the time I graduated I saw that my decision was the wrong one. I was told that I could switch from pilot training to chaplain training and be allowed to attend seminary and then serve my three years as chaplain. I was required to show that I was registered in a seminary, thus the importance of a fast response, which I got from CTS.

Just to complete this episode with the Air Force, when I completed seminary and was ordained, instead of communicating with the Air Force indicting my readiness to serve my three years as chaplain, I accepted the call to the church in San Diego and wrote a letter of resignation from the Air Force. We moved to San Diego, and I began work in my first church. A couple months later I received a certificate of honorable discharge from the US Air Force. Looking back, I am astounded at my naivete, audacity, and extraordinary good luck. Korea was in the past. Vietnam was in the future. My story was in the few months of military quiet in between.

Chicago Theological Seminary 1956–1959

I did not enroll in seminary to be trained as a scholar in a field of religion nor a local pastor. I was on a personal search.

We were given access to the best of Old and New Testament scholarship and research. Same for church history, theology, and ethics. We had opportunity to meet with the men serving the big churches and who were thus understood to be successful. I missed, thankfully, the session when one of these successful tall steeple ministers told us how he organized his desk.

I was interested in the meeting place between theology and psychology and selected as my field of study religion and personality. Within this field were education and counseling. I was drawn to the teaching of Ross Snyder whose work was primarily in theories of education. He required us to be working with a youth group and to train ourselves to listen and seek to understand the dynamics in the lives of youth in that point in time. We wrote verbatim conversations and looked for how insight was revealed, how types of questions opened or closed off deeper exploration.

The decision to study at the Chicago seminaries was perfect. Grades were generally awarded by how well you used the resources of the various fields of study to make your case rather than that you had arrived at the same conclusion as the professor. Probing curiosity, applications of doubt, and respect for scholarship were important disciplines.

My seminary education and call to ministry settled one major part of what was to become of me. Whatever my specific work was to be, it would arise and be expressed from within the life and work of the progressive United Church of Christ.[1]

1. The United Church of Christ was founded in 1957 bringing together the Congregational Christian Churches and the Evangelical and Reformed Church.

Chapter 3

Moving into Justice Work 1959–1964

IT IS HELPFUL TO remember that Dwight David Eisenhower was president when I received my seminary degree and, a few months after, was ordained to the ministry of Jesus Christ in 1959.

Colleague the Rev. Jim Johnson suggested that our seminary education was classic 1950s. By this he meant that we were being prepared to serve a church and society that were basically stable and faced only evolving change if there was going to be any perceptible change at all. It was at the end of the Eisenhower era.

I heard the comedian Mort Saul explain the difference between the old Republicans at that time and the new Republicans, the ones who followed President Eisenhower: "Old Republicans don't believe in doing anything for the first time. The new Eisenhower Republicans do believe in doing things for the first time, but not now."

In post–World War II America as the GIs came home, public policy and private real estate development was shaped to create vast affordable, suburban enclaves of middle-income housing, particularly for white veterans. The new social science of city planning was guiding development. Real estate was designated for shopping malls, schools, and churches. Rich with church extension funds, church leaders entered polity discussion among Methodists, Presbyterians, Lutherans, and Congregationalists to determine who would develop new congregations on which available street corners. It was called church planting.

The church functioned as a mediating institution in society. It connected people to one another; it gave them identity and purpose. It provided the glue that held the pieces together. It was one among many institutions that mediated the space between an individual person and the larger national

18

identity. The city planners knew that to create a new, desirable community, there had to be a church in the mix.

The late forties and the fifties were a time that fit the notion that churches built would be churches filled. The engine of evangelism was built into the assumptions about what makes "the good life." Families moved to a new home in the suburbs and went to church on Sunday to get to know the neighbors. Those communities and congregations served a carefully defined cohort of society: white and middle class. Men were in charge. Women were housewives. Homosexuality did not exist, and everyone was patriotic. I bought into all that.

I went to a concert by the folk singer and activist Pete Seeger in Mandel Hall at the University of Chicago. Pete introduced me through folk songs and story to a whole rich history that I had not been taught in school. I heard and sang about labor unions; the dust bowl; Okies riding the rails west searching for jobs; the deportees; and men working in coal mines, serving time in prison, and refusing to cooperate with congressional committees searching out communists. Something in me shifted during that concert, something about things going on out of my sight, an energy running through society breaking things, a rebellion seeking to build a different kind of society that was fair for all people. Those stories and images found a place in me. I was reminded of days delivering Christmas mail in the ghetto in St. Louis. It reminded me of the feeling that grew in me as I moved door-to-door that it was not fair that people should live in such poverty.

I preached to a congregation only once during my time as seminary student intern in a church. This was in my senior year, 1959. I remember the title of that sermon, "No Flags to Fly." I do not remember the particulars nor the text of that sermon, but it was clearly about something in the culture that I felt was missing for me, something absent from that moment in history, some cause that would take hold of us and help us engage in reform, rebellion, revolution, tearing down, and building up. I do not know where all that came from in me.

It may have been as simple as my wanting to find out more about myself by going against what was going on, by standing over against things. Another source of my struggle was the exposure to deep poverty. I believe it also had to do with wanting to part of movements for change. I knew nothing about where they could be found but I began looking for them.

While in seminary, through the local news, I was aware of the work of Saul Alinsky then organizing The Woodlawn Organization, a few miles north of Hyde Park in Chicago. His work in the forties in the Back of the Yards community was the model of community organizing. It interested me.

Another powerful influence on me was that I had Tom Lasswell as a friend. We met in seminary and bonded carrying refrigerators up and down stairs as classmates moved in and out of seminary housing. He came from a family that argued constantly and enjoyed the disagreements. I grew up in a family that was peaceful . . . appearing. I drew a sense of freedom from Tom. He drew me out, he challenged me to argue, to be critical of stuff. His father was a chicken farmer north of San Diego and a staunch Democrat. Tom's father's first name was Truman. Tom soaked it up. I grew up in the city, St. Louis, Missouri, and we voted for the "best man for the job" regardless of party. We avoided loud voices. Tom was most alive when the decibels went up. There was a hierarchy in my family. In Tom's there was free-for-all. Loud voices!

Tom called out a new kind of courage from me. I was much more willing to make a fool of myself in front of a youth group after meeting Tom. I was less buttoned down after Tom. I was also bolder to challenge people when I did not agree with them.

Upon graduation, Tom secured a position in youth ministry at a UCC church in Lemon Grove, near San Diego. And through him I was interviewed for a similar position at the Kensington Community Church in San Diego. I was called to that position. The assumption in each of our churches was that their future was in those youth groups and the journey from here to there was going to be smooth.

I had learned during my seminary internships and study of developmental psychology to value the rebellion that arose in teenagers. Adolescence was a time of shaping purpose, personality, and value. I also learned that parents were not pleased with youth ministers who befriended and encouraged that rebellion.

After three years of graduate study, I was awarded a master of divinity[1] from the Divinity School of the University of Chicago and from Chicago Theological Seminary on the south side of Chicago. I was ordained as pastor and teacher in the United Church of Christ at the Kensington Community Church in San Diego in October 1959. The assumption was that one's career followed this path: minister for youth and education, then associate minister, then solo pastor in a small church, and finally senior minister of a multi-staff congregation.

Tom and I drove to Los Angeles on July 15, 1960, to attend the final event of the Democratic Convention which had nominated John F. Kennedy as its presidential candidate to run against Richard Nixon. We wanted to be present to hear his acceptance speech. It was his New Frontier speech.

---

1. Then called a bachelor of divinity.

A friend and I watched that speech recently and she said, "He pretty well describes what happened to you in those years." He said the sixties would bring us "unknown opportunities and unknown peril."

Kennedy was inaugurated on January 20, 1961. I cannot fully express the thrill I felt, the sense that a whole new world was opening, as I listened to Kennedy's inaugural speech. He spoke of "a new generation of leaders," and he instructed me and my generation to "ask not what your country can do for you. Ask what you can do for your country."[2] Change was being invited, change was being announced, declared, proclaimed.

I was experiencing cracks in the structure of my understandings of the way life was. I grew up and was educated in the Roosevelt, Truman, and Eisenhower worlds but went to work in Kennedy's world.

My first two ministries ended badly. The third ended when I decided to take a whole new direction for my life and work.

The three together yielded very important hard lessons about skills and experience I could develop, ones I did not have. The challenges taught me what roles I could play with joy and skill and helped me find the places that matched my passion. Frederick Buechner wrote, "The place God calls you to is the place where your deep gladness and the world's deep hunger meet."[3] I was working my way toward finding my deep gladness in the vocational sense that Buechner talked about that met a deep need in the world. It was a stumbling, wandering process. Halfway through my first year in my first church, I heard a sermon by the Rev. Dr. Robert Spike, a national church staff member, who already had the reputation as a radical. He worked on civil rights issues. His sermon title was "Even Waiting Is from God."[4] He, too, felt that something vital was missing from our collective lives.

San Diego Kensington Community Church 1959 to 1961

We moved from Chicago to San Diego in July of 1959. Genie flew from Chicago with our new son Mark to stay in St. Louis with my parents while I closed the rental house in Rolling Meadows and drove to San Diego. I got my kicks on Route 66 which ran from Chicago to Los Angeles. It was established in 1926 and was the route used by those fleeing west from the dust bowl in the 1930s. Most of it in 1959 was two lanes or three lanes, the center lane for passing used in both directions. Route 66 passed through

2. Kennedy, "Ask Not What Your Country," para. 25.

3. Buechner, *Wishful Thinking*, 95.

4. Robert Spike, sermon given at UCC Clergy Post-Easter Retreat, Avalon on Cantina Island, April 19, 1960.

many small towns along the way. My migration west was well before air conditioning was common in vehicles. General practice was to have a canvas bag filled with water hanging on the grill work in front of the car to be used to refill the radiator when the engine cooling water in the radiator boiled away in the heat. Long distance truck drivers and some wise motorists drove across the desert at night.

At Phoenix, I left Route 66 and cut south to Tucson where I took Route 80 west along the Mexican border to San Diego. After every range of hills and mountains I crossed once I had entered California, I was sure I'd see the Pacific Ocean. I arrived in Kensington without ever seeing the Pacific. I soon learned from the youth that the ocean was not that far away.

I could not believe the mountains, the arroyos, the smell of the ocean and the eucalyptus trees, and the twenty-minute drive to the beach from Kensington. It was a pleasure beyond imagining going with Tom to the La Jolla caves and donning diving gear, then easing ourselves into the ocean timing our entry to the rhythm of the surf washing over the rock that was our entry and exit point. I swam around looking down, breathing through the tube, looking at the sun-brightened shallow bottom of the ocean. So many kinds of fish, rocks, and kelp! He showed me how to take a deep breath and dive, to locate and pry abalone off rocks with my ab knife. We took them back to Tom's home where he deep fat fried the meat of the abalone. We ate them with accompanying beer and storytelling of our adventures in the ocean. St. Louis, my hometown, seemed far away and that was okay with me. I loved the smells and colors of my future in California, especially the menthol smell of the gorgeous eucalyptus and the magenta of the bougainvillea.

My mother was eager to skin dive when she came out for my ordination. When she was climbing out on the big entry rock, her timing was off and a big wave dragged her over the surface of the rock. She received a bloody but shallow scrape wound on her forearm. She worked hard to keep the injury from healing so she could go home and tell her friends that she got it skin diving in the Pacific Ocean.

My ordination service included several Chicago Theological Seminary graduates: the Revs. Tom Lasswell, Chuck Burns, Curtis Claire, and Clyde Dodder. My primary task, I was told by the Rev. Lester Bond, the senior minister, was to build a youth program for the new youth center they had just built.

I quickly gathered a high school youth group of about forty-five. The church was tucked in an established neighborhood of families of various ages. I was good at asking questions and listening. Kids came by the youth center to talk on their way home from Hoover High School. We did a lot of that, and the circle grew bigger. I was eager to learn who they were and what was going on with them. The church provided a ping-pong table and eventually a pool table. Ping-pong became the scene of some fierce challenges. Those helped. The musical, *The Music Man* by Burgess Meredith, became popular. It drew attention to the association of pool tables with skipping school, cursing, smoking, and gambling. Not good for a church to encourage all this. Even though it had been the senior minister's idea to bring an unused pool table from the Copley YMCA to the youth center, since it was a bad thing, I was blamed.

The kids chose to name the quiet, meditative space in the building "Prayersville." It was a takeoff on the popular TV show, *77 Sunset Strip*. It was cool for the kids and drew them closer to the church. But some of their families began to express that this part of my plan undermined family. My politics and views of ministry and culture were not matching well for the senior minister and leaders of the church.

Tom had taught me three chords on an old guitar, and I figured out that I could accompany myself with any camp song I ever knew. Plus, I practiced so I could play and lead the singing of many of the Seeger folk songs. The kids loved that activity and soon, as a birthday gift, bought me a used banjo at a pawn shop at the Navy pier. I switched to that easily. There was a lot of rebellion in those folk songs.

The worst act I was accused of, in the spring of 1960, was to take the youth group to hear a concert by Pete Seeger. For several days before the concert, it was made clear to the citizens who read the *San Diego Union*, a conservative Copley newspaper, that Seeger had refused to sign the loyalty oath and was thus a communist.[5] That was more than parents could tolerate.

I can still remember the conversation on the sidewalk in front of our home. Senior Minister Bond said I had two choices. I could go back to school or move to another church. He gave me three months to move on.

I had succeeded and failed at the same time. In my view I did what I was charged to do but in ways the church leadership and many parents did not approve. I remember the realization coming to me during the devastation I was feeling. I would likely cause conflict wherever I would be in ministry. Simply put, I was interested in change and most churches and senior ministers were not. Some conflicts would be intentional and some unintentional. So, I had better expect it and choose my battles carefully. Conflict was not necessarily a sign of failure. It seemed clear that I was part of a new generation of clergy with ideas and energy for creating a renewed church. Most in the church seemed to like it as it was.

5. Davis, "Folk Singer."

I know how arrogant this sounds. I felt deep assurance even though I seemed to be messing up the work given to me. Maybe I was doing it right, but others were too tied to the past. I've occasionally wondered about that deep confidence at times when there was little evidence to justify it and have wondered where my deep confidence came from. Perhaps from my mother. She was so uncertain about herself. Yet she made a great life for herself without the nurture and encouragement of her own mother who died when Mom was eight years old. I believe she had deep confidence and, like me, a vast curiosity.

Adam was born at Sharp Hospital. I was called home from a youth retreat at an abandoned hotel on the Ridge Route north of Los Angeles. One carload of kids had to come home with me. They were excited about this birth and eager to be with me. We drove through the dawn hours on the 101 in Los Angeles heading south. When we got within radio range of San Diego, we tuned into a station sharing religious news of the week. I had recorded the program the previous Friday before we drove north. Truly weird. Lots of cheers by teenage campers who had gotten up in the middle of the night. Happy father.

One final observation about my work at Kensington. Through the sixty years since I was fired, I have been surprised to receive letters, emails, and phone calls from people scattered around the country who had been members of that youth group. Two of them were clearly making amends, step eight in the twelve-step program of AA. In neither case did I remember any incidents that required amends, but I was delighted to hear from them. Wally just wanted me to know that I had taught him three chords on a guitar, and he had built a very successful career in the music business as a mandolin performer and recording artist. He was a music store owner in San Diego. He sent me one of his recordings. Another recently found me on Facebook and wrote because he was remembering Prayersville, folk singing, and playing pool. Bill let me know that he owns a fishing and outdoor adventure company in Oregon serving as a river guide.

Los Angeles Northridge Congregational Church UCC 1961–1962

Chuck Burns, learning of my need for employment, asked me to come to Northridge in the San Fernando Valley of Los Angeles to serve as copastor with him.

Chuck, the founding pastor of the church, was reaching out to help me since I had been essentially fired from my first church employment in

San Diego. The Northridge Church was completing the building of their new sanctuary. Chuck took a gamble that this striking new building would create a surge of new members, a surge in budget and need for program development. It turned out that the growth in membership at the Northridge Congregational Church was steady but not fast enough to support two full-time ministers.

Some good stuff happened in my brief time in Northridge. I was a beginner and naive. My first day at Northridge I sat at my desk wondering where to begin and what exactly beginning would look like. I noticed I had a phone that had blinking lights and push buttons on it. That was a first. I found the intercom button and asked the secretary assigned to be my helper to come to my office. I did not know who she was or what I wanted from her. I heard her high-heals clicking across the polished concrete floor and up the wooden stairs, coming closer all the time. I was stressing out. She walked in the door with four sharpened lead pencils and a dictation pad. I have no memory what happened next, but we became friends and good work partners. Funny the things one remembers of the big crisis points in life.

I recruited several artists to help me organize what became an impressively successful monthlong art show at the Northridge church. We reached out to entertainment and show business talent in the area. Most of them were "between projects" and thus available to invest their many talents in this art show project. We had wall-hung art, sculpture, music and dance performances, lectures, and stimulating conversations between artists and religious leaders. The Rev. Jack Matlaga, who was serving as pastor to the arts community in North Beach in San Francisco, was our guest for a weekend. He stimulated conversations with artists and deepened our understanding of the similarities of life in the spirit as understood by both those in the Christian faith and artists. He preached but I missed the sermon because I had taken Genie to the hospital to deliver child number three, Ann.

The gamble to employ two pastors did not work out. The second person of the copastorate had to begin again an urgent search for employment. So again, in 1962, I began to search for a new position in ministry. My confidence was shaken. I was concerned to be facing a search again on little notice. I was then father of three children and not sure how I was going to feed them.

Los Angeles Congregational Church of the
Chimes in Van Nuys 1962–1964

The Congregational Church of the Chimes in Van Nuys, also in the Valley just a few miles south, was looking for an interim minister of Christian Education and Youth. That opportunity fit perfectly as a solution to my dilemma: I could start immediately, it was ministry in which I felt experienced and confident, the location did not require a major move, and it was temporary so I could work to clarify what my particular gifts and passions might be and how I might seek positions to use them.

Our family moved to Studio City in the southern part of the San Fernando Valley. I began work in a very successful 1950s church. It was the envy of many post–World War II new church starts.

The Church of the Chimes in 1963 had 1,500 members, a beautiful sanctuary that seated 800, a chapel for 200, and education buildings on the rear of the property. There were twenty well-furnished large classrooms, several comfortable fellowship rooms and patios, and a large auditorium. At the center of the campus was a two-story elegant mansion suitable for offices, clergy studies, and reception space. This congregation was a grand success of the suburban ministry.

They knew they were a success and felt pride in how much they had accomplished in a short time. The senior minister was handsome, smooth talking, with a countenance that conveyed the model of success that drew people to him. They would be safe with him.

On the staff we had a part-time minister of visitation. He was a semi-retired pastor who could make eight to ten pastoral calls in an afternoon. He did it six days a week. His annual reports were statistically amazing. I learned his secret. He rang the doorbell and stood too close to the screen door for the occupant to open it. The visits all happened through the screen door. Most woman did not work outside their homes and thus were home when he called.

I had seminary training in pastoral counseling. My calls on people took place in their living rooms and lasted way too long. I was waiting for the big personal issues to arise so that I could exercise my counseling skill. They seldom arose. People liked a visit from a minister but preferred it through the screen door.

We had one thousand children and youth enrolled in Sunday School. Nobody ever missed a Sunday. There were forty-five teachers organized like a small college: departments with deans, specialists in art and music. They told me that teaching in that Sunday school was the high point of the week. It required that they leave home and engage in interesting volunteer work. They requested religious enrichment to help them be better teachers in all facets of religious education including Bible study and theology. These teachers were my focus. They helped me organize two major classes.

The Bible study met 10 a.m. to noon Tuesday and the theology class met same hours on Thursday. These women all called themselves house-wives. They had schedules that could accommodate these classes.

The Bible study was lectionary based. Every week we looked at the four texts assigned to the following Sunday, fifteen minutes to each text. Each was presented by a class member who had read *The Interpreters Bible* in the church library and provided some exegetical insights and then told us how that text might have something to say about their own lives. There was a lot of intellectual and personal information shared on those days. They loved the research assignments and making their reports.

One told us that her husband had called, wanted her to run an errand for him. She told him she was busy. "I'm doing my exegesis!" Hubby didn't know what to do with that. That story stood that morning as a watershed moment for everyone in that room. We were imagining the possibilities of a housewife having something more important now than running an errand for her husband. We felt the earth move. The possibilities seemed immense.

The theology class did not start with reading *The Feminine Mystique* by Betty Friedan. But when we got to that book, it transported the class to a new powerful emotional space. They expressed shock that here were clear images of how women were programmed into a life that had responsibilities and security but a very claustrophobic existence. They experienced limited engagement in the adult world around them. All this was immediately obvi-ous. The women only needed Friedan and the experience of doing exegesis to open new questions about their lives.

This seemed to explain so much about the restlessness they were feeling. It set off new energy that required the challenging and resetting of some very important and old traditions and sex roles. They concluded that what they were experiencing in this class, if pursued, would take courage, confrontation, and determination. Not all saw this but for several there no turning back.

I played tennis on Saturdays with men in the church. Several of them were husbands of the Sunday School teachers. After tennis we got root beer floats nearby and talked. The husbands wanted me to explain what I was doing to their marriages.

Several seemed to get it that it was not in their long-term best interest to be a brick wall as their wives began to explore new possibilities. I shared with the men that in the forties and fifties, I was taught how husbands and wives had specific rolls to play, a one-size-fits-all model. And I shared my thought that it was best to get out of the way as this new energy flowed. It was helpful for the men to share what impact on their lives these changes had. Things were changing on both sides of these relationships. To my knowledge most of the marriages survived this renegotiation.

I have been asked forty-five years later in my own retirement to speak at memorial services for two of these women. I was deeply moved in both instances listening to the daughters of these women who said things like, "Thank God you helped my mom be free to search for herself." They helped me travel the same territory, to rethink my own understandings of these relationships. They had bought into the cultural role in the 1950s of being housewives. That's what they called themselves. But around those study tables they experienced doors opening in their minds and energies they were delighted to explore. My job was to provide a research library and a safe space for conversation.

One other thing to mention about this brief time. President Kennedy was assassinated in Dallas on November 22, 1963. I was scheduled to preach the following Sunday, one of the two times I was invited into the pulpit during my time there. The senior minister did not try to preempt me as I expected he would. He was not sure what to say. I wish I could remember what I said. We heard during the time between services that Lee Harvey Oswald had been killed in a Dallas police station. Shock and confusion are what I remember feeling. These things don't happen in America.

Oliver Wendell Holmes Jr. Gives Order to My Thinking

A life-shaping event occurred on a January 1964 morning. I was still uncertain how to direct my ministry. At my desk at the church, I came across a line from Justice Oliver Wendell Holmes Jr. from an 1884 Memorial Day speech in Keene, New Hampshire. He was reflecting on the generation that had fought the Civil War twenty years earlier. Some men had volunteered and some not. He said to them,

> I think that, as life is action and passion, it is required of [us] that [we] should share the passion and action of our time at peril of being judged not to have lived.[6]

That rumbled around in my head a while and ended up requiring me to ask myself, "What are the actions and passions of my time and how do I share in them?"

6. Holmes, *Speeches*, 3.

Answering these questions set the agenda for the rest of my life. My task as a human being and a Christian was to share in the action and passion of my time. I was not to be a spectator for my time in history. I was not to be the object of history but a shaper of it. My vision of being a pastoral counselor sitting in my study doing one-on-one healing work was gone. My new mission was to locate the action and passion and to find my way in.

In 1964 I identified these five as my list of "action and passion" in my time. What I could see were the big, hard, open questions before the society and were questions that the church had resources to bring to the work. The issues were the following:

- War and Peace
- Poverty
- Population Control
- Civil Rights
- Civil Liberties

Of course, looking back, I missed the abortion issue, the women's movement, gay rights, and the environment among others. Population control became a concern for world hunger. I must have prepared this list prior to my theology classes with teachers, or I would not have missed the women's movement. To get grounded on these issues I began a search for people and organizations that were already deeply engaged in these issues.

For example, the UCC was committed to renewing a church in Watts. This was before the 1965 Watts rebellion. The UCC Board for Homeland Ministries (BHM) made a grant and two men, the Rev. George Killingsworth and the Rev. Speed Leas, both with urban ministries experience, were brought into the Immanuel UCC. I engaged with them as much as I could to learn what the issues looked like from within the ghetto. Of course, these were white guys, but I was still ready to rely on experts and helpers rather than on those who were poor and Black. I watched Speed and George and learned a lot as they worked as community organizers and as they worked alongside people in the community to develop a program.

Speed was an excellent grant writer and fundraiser. George saw possibilities among artists and musicians who were quick to join in the programming. When the Watts rebellion did happen, I was part of efforts to run food and medical supplies into Watts. The stores were burned down, and the police and National Guard occupied the streets like the Romans shut down Jerusalem during Jesus's life.

I found others to help me learn about work in the other areas on my list.

I was deeply influenced by the work of Gibson Winter in his research published as *The Suburban Captivity of the Churches* (1961). His major insight was that as the post-war metropolis expanded, it separated the world of work, the center city where business, industry, and government were located, from the surrounding suburbs where home and family life were located. The churches spent millions of dollars starting new churches in the suburbs and consequently focused the work of the church on families, nurture, and Christian education. It abandoned any responsibility for business, industry, and government. There was no place for thinking about housing for people who are poor, for justice for farm workers, for questions of civil rights. The pastoral took the lead and the prophetic ministry receded. Winter developed several ideas about how this could be addressed.[7] His problem statement about the separation of city life into distinct separate categories made my discomfort at the Church of the Chimes much clearer. I found myself wanting to find ways to resist giving in to this separation, to find a way in ministry to find a place where both pastoral and prophetic ministry could be together.

At the same time, I worked on gathering a group of young clergy colleagues who fit the criteria of activists who seemed to have energy for helping and dragging the church into engagement with history. I tell that story next. Then I tell the story about our move into Pacoima to begin my first solo ministry, one that turned its eyes on the surrounding community.

7. Winter, *Suburban Captivity of the Churches*, 127.

Chapter 4

Building a Justice Team, Taking Risks, and Involving Our Families

As I followed my call to seek justice work in my ministry, I knew I was taking several big risks. Beginning with the Pacoima call, my work was experimental and improvisational. There were few helpful models. There were lots of ways to fail. Funding was insecure. It was not clear what success looked like.

I needed a team of friends who were also taking similar risks, who would listen to my struggle, affirm my efforts, and confront my illusions; who would honestly share their stories; who would plot strategies that would challenge old ways of doing things; and who were not afraid of conflict. I sought out campus ministers, other urban church leadership, and those clergy who had gone to the Freedom Summer Voter Registration Drive in Mississippi the summer of 1964. I was searching for clergy colleagues who were relatively the same age, same status, and of similar interests. These fellow clergy would become dear colleagues who made, I believe, good trouble in the Southern California Conference of the United Church of Christ in the sixties and early seventies. In retrospect our work is regarded with respect. At the time our disruptive activity calling for more resources for anti-racism and anti-war work and bolder public statements by the church was painful to the people who feared conflict and change.

Born in a Bar in Beaumont

Tom Lasswell and I had easily made common cause. We had been seminary classmates and were seeing a church that was having a hard time holding on to its role in a fast-changing society. Generally, the church is a conservative, values-sustaining, steady force in society. We had read the prophets who spoke truth to power. We were clear that Christianity had important words and actions to offer. We acted as though we knew where God was trying to move the people. We wanted to see the church in that role now.

We went looking for allies among the other clergy in our conference. Tom and I found colleagues with similar perspectives, we formed coalitions with other groups in the battles, and we stood by ourselves when necessary. In the 1960s some of us saw the church as a potential leader in the public turmoil about the Vietnam War, civil rights, human rights, the environment, and poverty. We wanted to spend the churches' prestige on the side of change. We tried to speak prophetic words out of the traditions of the faith. We had heard Saul Alinsky who reported that power in the society came from two sources, piles of money and piles of people. Perhaps we would activate enough people in the church to make its power felt. So, we found each other.

The UCC conference minister, the Rev. Clarence McCall, named us the "Young Turks." We did not choose that name but were happy to go with it once it got into circulation. McCall died suddenly shortly after becoming our conference minister. He was one I thought we could work with, who would partner with us in many of our efforts. We mourned his death. We were eager for new leadership in the position of conference minister.

In 1963 came the triggering event that stimulated us to form our group. It occurred at Camp Pilgrim Pines, the beautiful, all-weather, UCC-owned camp in the San Bernardino Mountains at five thousand feet elevation. At the post-Easter minister's retreat, the newly elected conference minister Howard Stone Anderson, who had been serving First Congregational Church UCC in Washington, DC, introduced himself to us in two lectures. Anderson's lectures consisted of a pile of his old sermons. He read them one-by-one telling us the text, the opening joke, the three points, and the punch line. He had been introduced as "the Bob Hope of the church." He got through about thirty sermons in an hour.

This was not the future of the church! The streets and the campuses required the presence of a voice for the faith, a prophetic word that could mobilize hope or push us, as Al Cohen (one of the Young Turks) often said, "to work for the kingdom." It was time to sing a new song for the Lord.

Anderson had been selected for us by the old boys' network in the UCC. Despite our congregational polity, our conference accepted who was offered. Big mistake. Great way to alienate your young corps of ministers. We were deeply disappointed and let down by the prospect of Anderson as our leader in the conference.

Tom said we needed to drink some beer and talk. I proposed we pile in Speed Leas's VW bus and look for a bar down the hill in Beaumont. Going out to look for a bar was not in the range of things expected of young clergy in those days. But we needed to talk. This was the birth of a bond and covenant among us. I don't know the name of the bar, but I remember that the beer was good and served cold in pitchers and that cowboy music played on the jukebox. We let off a lot of steam. What we experienced up on the mountain was not the church we sought to bring into being for this new day.

I asked if we were serious enough to meet again in the next few weeks and talk together about how we might resist Anderson's vision and present proposals for the future of the conference. We agreed.

The drive back up the mountain that night was considerably slower. The little air-cooled engine in Speed's bus was not able to generate much momentum. Plus, we had to stop several times in the woods to water the trees.

A week later I sent a letter suggesting date options for us to reconvene.

This is my version of the creation story of the Young Turks. Born in a bar in Beaumont. I'm pretty sure Elijah gathered his people this way.

Our second gathering occurred in George Killingsworth's garage in Watts. In another radical and enlightened move, we invited our spouses to join us. They ought to get to know one another, we thought. And that made it possible to plan the meeting as a potluck supper. We gathered, many of us driving an hour or more to the inner city of Los Angeles. As we ate, we introduced ourselves around the circle. There were seven ministers and six spouses. The time came when it made sense that the gathering moved from food and fellowship to plotting. I invited the men to move from the house to the garage that George had set up for plotting. I pictured, I'm sure in company with all the men, that the wives would clean up and do the dishes and wait for us to finish our business. We had no way to anticipate that, on that very night, the new creation was about to show itself to us.

We men started energetically to discuss how we would disrupt the next Conference Annual Meeting to make our demands known. After about fifteen minutes, the door between the house and the garage was flung open. Our wives marched in and announced that "this is our group too, so we are here for this discussion." That was something new in our lives. In retrospect it was about time we heard stuff our old ears had been missing. But at that moment it just seemed astounding, that demand for a voice. Too chicken to express my actual feelings, I welcomed them, and we made room around the circle.

I explained that we were talking about doing a sit-in or taking over the microphone at the annual meeting and presenting our demands to delegates. Like the model of Black Power groups, we would not let anyone out of the room until our demands were met.

Noralyn Johnson held up her hand. I nodded to her. She asked, "What are our demands?"

Well, we hadn't gotten around to that yet. We were mobilizing our testosterone first. We were testing each other's resolve, trying to see how far we were willing to go or how much of this was hot air. We did develop demands in short order.

Among them was a response in opposition to a proposed reconfiguration of the boundaries of the associations of the conference. The proposal completely separated the inner-city from the suburbs. Our position was that the boundaries should be more pie-shaped so that they included both inner-city and suburban congregations together. A reply from the chair of the board of directors dated April 7, 1965, was addressed to "Rev. and Mrs." This means we had sent our letter with these demands and signed it as couples where that was appropriate.

The turmoil in the society required a shift from reform of the conference to a much more significant issue: getting it to adopt a strong anti-war statement. From 1964 to 1968, we sponsored and argued for anti-war resolutions at the Conference Annual Meetings. We intended that the debate would be an educational occasion for the delegates.

Each year for three years our resolutions were defeated but each year we were winning a larger percentage of votes. Finally, in 1968, we gained a majority. After we lost the first time, a group of the people from the Pacoima church put on sack cloth and ashes and held an all-night sit-in in the chancel of the Pasadena Church. I persuaded them to vacate the chancel in the morning promising that we'd keep coming back year after year until we won the vote. The anti-war agenda was our major focus with the conference during this period. We had other minor agendas like getting more funds for inner-city and campus ministries.

In 1989, twenty years later, I was elected to serve as moderator of the Southern California Nevada Conference of the UCC. I was senior minister at the First Congregational Church UCC in Santa Barbara at that time. Being moderator included attending the conference board of director's meetings. At my first meeting, the twenty or so members introduced ourselves. The chair of the board took a few minutes, after introducing himself, to report that he vividly remembered me. I was his primary opponent in the

Vietnam debates at the annual meetings back in the sixties. I immediately recognized Charlie Zaca of the Woodland Hills church. We did go head-to-head in hours of floor debate. He was still the general manager of one of the largest department store chains in the state. He told the story that after the anti-war side finally got its majority, he received a phone call from me saying that I had been on the losing side of so many votes that I knew something of how he felt having lost that vote. I wished him well. Charlie said he had always felt grateful for that call and that, over time, he was sure we both mellowed a lot.

I tell this story because Charlie loved the UCC and was as committed as I was to have had this public argument, to air out all the ways of thinking about these nettled issues, about what the gospel called for, and to find the place we wanted to stand and where we hoped people would join us. Many church members were afraid of conflict and would do whatever they could to avoid it. I loved Charlie for his courage. His courage called out mine.

The Turks' focus expanded from conference issues to conflicts in our own settings, on campuses and in inner-city congregations and communities.

The Core Group

All ten of us in the core group of the Turks had graduated from seminary and were ordained in the late 1950s and early 1960s. We were educated at Union Seminary in New York, Yale Divinity School, Eden Seminary in St. Louis, Chicago Theological Seminary and University of Chicago Divinity School, and Pacific School of Religion in Berkeley. We set out for Southern California to begin our work as pastors. Unique to this set of young ministers was that we were called into two unusual roles: campus pastors and pastors of urban churches. Working in these settings exposed us to parts of the society where the stance of the church had to be both pastoral, caring for the broken and wounded, and prophetic, exposing the brokenness and lack of justice in the society and the economy.

Below are names, the ministries served, and the spouses of the people in that period who were part of the Young Turks. We worked together for the period of 1963 to 1970.

1. George Killingsworth was copastor at the Immanuel United Church of Christ in Watts.

2. Speed Leas served the Immanuel UCC with George. He became director of the Center on Metropolitan Mission In-Service Training

(COMMIT), an ecumenical urban training center. Connie joined the staff at COMMIT as a trainer.

3. Bill Moremen served the Western Knoll UCC, an urban church in Los Angeles. Grace was an author and teacher.

4. Jim Johnson served Morningside UCC in Inglewood, part of greater Los Angeles urban sprawl. Noralyn was a teacher and homemaker.

5. Tom Lasswell served as campus pastor at California State University Northridge (then called San Fernando Valley State College), where he worked with radical student anti-war groups. Mary was a teacher.

6. John Colburn served Colonial UCC in West Los Angeles and later the Church of Christian Fellowship. Carol was a campus minister at Los Angeles City College.

7. Al Cohen served as campus pastor at California State University at Fullerton, then at California State University Los Angeles. Ann was a ceramicist and anti-war worker.

8. Lynn Jondahl was campus minister at California State University Los Angeles.

9. Jay Lintner was staff on the Los Angeles County Human Relations Commission. Joanna was a social worker.

10. I served an urban church in Pacoima in the San Fernando Valley of Los Angeles. Then I was director of theological training at COMMIT. Genie was a public school teacher.

At various protests there were many more who claimed belonging to the Turks or following the Turks' lead. And now fifty years later, I still meet people whom I knew at that time who either remember the Turks fondly or who consider themselves as part of the group.

Working Together and Empowering Each Other

There were three ways we functioned together.

One was the action in the context of the Southern California Conference of the UCC. These were the efforts to persuade the conference (a) to fall in love with the city for God's work and to provide financial support for urban ministry, not just the suburbs, and (b) to speak out corporately against the Vietnam War.

We analyzed the situation we were facing and clarified our objectives. We called other friends for their take on things we were interested in. We did the political work of telephoning delegates to the annual meetings to seek their support and suggest roles they might play in the debate. We drafted resolutions. At the annual meetings we had after-hour debriefing sessions. As delegates arrived at several of these meetings, they sought us out to ask, "What are we working on this time?"

The second collaboration was to rally in support of some larger action. We participated together in public actions. Peace groups were making plans for an anti-war event at the Federal Building in downtown Los Angeles. Several of us were involved in the planning. The purpose was to counsel and assist men who had decided to turn in their draft cards. A new federal law made it a felony to advise draft-age men to burn or turn in their draft cards.

A liturgy had been worked out for all the clergy to read together urging the young men to commit a felony and give us their cards. We were to take the draft cards into the Federal Building and put them on a counter or give them to somebody, also against the law. The media was alerted.

The Turks decided to encourage each other, if available, to share in this experience. For many this was a first time for committing civil disobedience. We anticipated that we would immediately be subjected to arrest and be taken to the jail.

We had a gathering at our home in Pacoima to think through what this might mean. We wanted legal help alerted and available. If we drove down, we needed someone to take our cars back home. We hoped to locate someone who would arrange bail money. In another room the women were discussing how to live cooperatively if their husbands were in prison. Several made plans to move in together and join families.

A few days before the event, the UCC clergy attended their annual retreat at Pilgrim Pines. I asked the retreat planners to allow a group of us to address the group, maybe fifty or so clergy. On the first evening four of us sat on the stage and told everyone that we planned to be handing in draft cards and submitting to arrest. We said we were aware that there might be a reaction in their congregations that a group of UCC clergy were involved and would perhaps be jailed. We wanted them alerted and prepared. We shared our rationale and responded at length to their questions. To my surprise none of the clergy criticized us for taking this step. I had expected that we'd hear resistance. I guess the war had been going on long enough that this kind of resistance seemed okay. We were thanked not only for the heads-up but for doing the act of resistance.

We did what we planned. Police were present and outfitted for World War III. When we had the cards in hand, three of us walked to the door of the Federal Building and found it locked with armed guards inside and out. We left the cards in a pile by the door. Too boring for the media. No arrests or floggings. Nonetheless, the young men had given up their draft cards and likely faced legal proceedings and prison time. The rest of us went home both happy and disappointed. We were looking for a big show of resistance and were prepared to sacrifice for it. It was not to be. The government had learned a few things about handling protesters such as us, letting the gathering happen and letting the speeches be made, absorbing the event as just so much hot air.

This kind of experience led to talk of escalation of our protests, including blowing up buildings and parking dump trucks on the roads through LAX with the effect of clogging traffic. Stuff like that. Once our efforts failed to stop the war, we became more radical. I had some of these conversations but never acted on them.

A year earlier, I was in the most serious of these conversations. It happened after an evening meeting in the days after the first Watts rebellion. Chris Hartmire and I felt that something serious had to be done to get the Los Angeles Police Department and National Guard out of their occupation of Watts. There was so much suffering with people unable to buy food, get to their jobs, or go to a hospital. We stopped at Canter's Delicatessen on Fairfax to talk. Canter's, open 24/7 all year, was a favorite late-night stop. We talked of doing some scary things like considering acts of violence. I frightened myself out of moving on these ideas fueled by passion and anger.

The third way we functioned together was a form of remote support. A Turk worked on a project and, in some cases, took great risks without direct support from any of the rest of us. When I later learned of these efforts, I always felt some private sense of ownership. I felt fueled by the sense that a victory or a defeat or a major effort with result unknown was in some measure a result of our expectations on one another. I deeply felt that being a Turk meant working boldly for peace and justice and the environment.

Al Cohen told me this story in an interview in 2009.

> John Moyers was my successor at Cal State Fullerton. The skillful and articulate Black organizer in Chicago, Fred Hampton, had been shot in his bed in Chicago on December 10, 1969. John is the only self-proclaimed communist living in Newport Beach at the time. So, Ann and I went down to spend an evening with John and his wife in Newport Beach.
>
> It was raining, it was cold, it was miserable. There was a fire in the fireplace. And we sat around trying to figure out, in response to Fred Hampton's death, what was the most vulnerable white icon that we could attack in some way. And we decided that the Rose Parade was the obvious symbol of white America. At that point in time the Rose Queen and every member of the

court were bobby-socks blonds with blue eyes—right off the silver screen. I think there was only one Black person in the entire
structure—hundreds of people—of the Tournament of Roses.
That person was Dan Towler, a professional football player with
the Rams, who was a pioneer in breaking through some of these
things.

We decided to appear on the lawn of the Wrigley Mansion
in Pasadena, the headquarters for the Tournament of Roses, on
Orange Grove. You joined us.

This is where the parade assembles the night before the parade. Right after Christmas, we intended to challenge the Tournament of Roses on the racist image that they portrayed. And
our idea was that the Southern Christian Leadership Conference wagon train should be included as an entrant in the Rose
Parade. That certainly would be a symbol.

Well, these poor people in the mansion should have ignored
us. But no, they decided to debate us—separately. The news
people, including TV, would go inside and interview them and
then they came out on the lawn and interview us. These would
be side by side on the six o'clock news. Well, it sort of ended in a
stalemate at the time.

Somebody threatened to burn our house down. My kids
took the call here at the house. So, they were here huddled together holding each other up when we got home from wherever
we were right after this happened. But what was the outcome?
The outcome was that the next year they had Billy Graham as
the grand marshal of the parade, which I thought was a kind
of Elijah on Mount Carmel experience. Who's got more power
here, Billy Graham, or these ragtag ministers? But. But, every
year since then the court has been racially integrated.[1]

In that same interview Al shared his account of his transition from being a Naval Academy graduate to being a campus pastor working for peace
and justice. He told me that "you and Tom stayed on my case and kept me
from sliding back." This is one example of how we influenced and shaped
each other.

When we met to plot our challenges to the church, we were not easy
on each other. Some of it was competition for leadership, for the best plan,
for the most risk-filled proposal. Some of it was the enjoyment of the best
put-down. It was not easy to be a Turk, including when it was just us. The
ironic sense of humor (saying the opposite of what you wanted to convey),

1. Rev. Al Cohen (campus minister at California State University, Los Angeles),
from author's interview, July 25, 2009.

the clever put-down, the sarcasm, the heavy criticism of ideas was common and was sometimes painful. I experienced it as a challenge. If I thought I had a good idea, I put it forward even though I was sure I was not going to be celebrated or even respected for it. And I decided to hang in the conversation advocating for what I thought was the way to go. Several of us who had played on athletic teams knew the purpose of toughening harassment. Tom's experience in the Marines told similar stories.

I always was eager for social interaction and plotting strategy conversations because I grew up in a family where sarcasm was rampant. To survive and enjoy this form of connecting I learned how to enjoy the cleverness of a remark and learned how quickly to put out an even more cutting remark. The Turks had some graduate school sarcasm artists. I was ready to match wits. But those who were not used to this kind of play were put off, wounded, or felt devalued by it.

In one long conversation a proposal was put forward that we needed to acknowledge the pain we were inflicting on each other and that we should set aside a Saturday to put ourselves in the hands of a group counselor to help make our life together more respectful, to reduce the painful put-downs. But a few won the day by making it clear that "we don't have time for that."

Several signed up to participate in a training program at the Urban Training Center for Christian Mission for the month of October 1968. This team included Al, Tom, Speed, and me.

Another group went to Selma at Dr. King's call. These included Lynn, George, Al, and me.

Another part of the group was active in forming the "Corridor Ministry" in central Los Angeles. This included Bill, Jim, John, and Speed. The ministry was an initiative of the Ecumenical Institute (EI) that provided leadership. "The corridor" was the territory that fell under landing path for planes flying into Los Angeles International Airport. EI had a formula for this type of community organizing, working with leadership of congregations in the area to analyze and plan social change projects.

Most of us were active participants in the Greater Los Angeles Goals Project, a cooperative venture of the Los Angeles City Urban Planning Department with the World and National Councils of Churches. Urban planning is always under heavy pressure from developers, real estate interests, and others who seek to make a fortune by influencing planning decisions. The Goals Project was an effort to create another pressure group, citizen power, to push the Planning Department to make decisions that support a different vision of what the city could become. The visionary Los Angeles director of City Planning was Calvin Hamilton, an active Presbyterian, who saw the network of churches spread around the city as a possible source of counterweight to the developers. He had experience with the World Council of Churches and worked out a cooperative plan for developing neighborhood conversations about how regions should be zoned for best use for citizens. For a year or so, some interesting community celebrations were organized and some good conversations about what would improve our community were convened. But the project was not sustainable because it lacked substantial funding for organizers.

There were occasions when I got phone calls from one of the campus pastors asking for help in situations of confrontation between angry students and administration. Tom called from Cal State Northridge when the Black Student Union had occupied the president's office. A negotiator was needed. I suggested we ask the Rev. Dr. James Hargett, minister of the Church of Christian Fellowship in Los Angeles, to join us. Jim had the intelligence and personal authority to talk with the students in a way that he quickly gained their trust. He then did the same thing with the administration. He explained what the students were asking for, much of which turned out to be acceptable. Within hours Jim had the key leaders on both sides working together, writing a press release on how the students and administration had come to a satisfactory agreement.

Gathering Our Families to Play and Plot

One of the ways I drew strength and courage from the Turks was in family social gatherings. The Turks gathered, often carting the whole family across the county, for our times together at each other's homes. We shared potluck meals, told stories about what was happening in our various work settings, our city, and the world. And then we held our strategy sessions. What's next? What's broken that we need to fix and what do we need to break? Each time it seemed something more radical and dangerous was called for.

I vividly remember late one night, driving our VW bus from a Turks gathering, up what we called the San Diego Freeway, now the 405, from south of Long Beach north to Pacoima. It was about an hour and a half drive at midnight. As we were driving under the flight landing path of Los Angeles International Airport, two parallel lines of planes, like strings of pearls, strung up in the east heading into the main runways, flying close over our heads as they approached their landing. We'd had a great time with dear friends. Genie was asleep next to me, and the kids were asleep on the back seat. The little engine of our bus purred along with confidence. I felt wide awake. I had the radio tuned to KBCA, 105.1 on the FM dial, the all-jazz station. They had on the turntable John Coltrane's magical "My Favorite Things." I was overwhelmed by a sense, in that moment, of well-being, of everything at that moment being in its proper place.

An extended family feeling had quickly developed among the Turks. Most of us had not grown up in Southern California and had no traditional family gathering at the holiday times. Twice a year we established annual holiday gatherings as regular events. We had a Memorial Day picnic at our home in Pacoima. All families brought meat for the grill and a salad or dessert to share. I provided the Pepsi and Budweiser in ice-filled washtubs. I set up horseshoe pits and a volleyball court in the back yard for adult competitive appetites. Memorial Day in 1968 was on Thursday, May 30. The California primary election was June 5: Eugene McCarthy vs. Robert Kennedy. Turks were deeply divided on whom to support. There were a couple hours of beer and debate, Bobby or Gene. So, our volleyball game that day was the Go-Bobbys vs the Go-Genes. No record who won. I checked in the archives of the *Los Angeles Times* sports pages—no record. Memories are quickly refreshed by looking at the big group photo Don Rogers took each year. The one on my desk counts twenty-one adults and thirty children and youth.

On New Year's Eve we gathered at Ann and Al's home on South Madison Avenue in Pasadena. Lots of shared food, drink, and conversation. We all brought sleeping bags, adults on the first floor and kids upstairs. Bedtime was sometime after midnight. As usual, the first floor was ready for sleep quite a lot sooner than the second floor. Various fathers took turns trekking up the stairs to give orders to the troops. Our final move was always to send Speed up. It was quiet after that. Never found out his secret.

In the morning, we ate breakfast and walked twenty minutes up Madison Avenue to Colorado Boulevard for the Rose Parade. Getting there at 7:30 a.m. or so allowed for finding a good spot on the sidewalk to settle and wait. In the afternoons we had a touch football game on the Cohens' front lawn.

For several Thanksgivings we packed up tents and camping gear, Coleman stoves, lanterns, and food. We drove south in several vehicles to cross the border at Tijuana, Mexico, and on to Faro Beach near Ensenada for several days of camping, cookouts, swimming, and beach football. Every year we had a rousing father vs. children football game on the beach until the year the kids won. We abandoned that sport.

Some of us participated in an annual late August camping trip at Red Rock Crossing just south of Sedona, Arizona. Four or five families loaded up tents, sleeping bags, cooking gear, and food. In seven hours, we were setting up a small village alongside the creek amid the beautiful red rock formations. Arizona schools started a week earlier than California schools, so we found the usual site clear when we got there.

Al taught me two important lessons that stick with me. If you don't use your Coleman equipment for a long time the cork dries out and you can't pump up the pressure to cause the fuel to draw. So, no lights and no fire on the burners. Where do you find a drop of oil to reactivate the cork in the Coleman pumps when you're in a remote campsite an hour on dirt roads away from any store? You get it from the dipstick in your car engine.

And after a night of heavy rain soaking the landscape, swelling the creek, saturating your tents and equipment, in the morning where do you find dry wood to start the campfire? Up in the trees, Al said. So, you get out your rope and you find a heavy rock, you tie the rock with one end of your rope. You toss the rock over a dead branch and grab the rock and hold the other end of the rope and tug on the rope looped over the branch. You hear a crack and run for it. The branch falls where you were just standing and snaps into many campfire-size pieces and your fire is ready to light. By the way, getting someone who can throw the rock over the limb is not easy. You start with your youngest child and work your way up to the oldest child and you hope it's too tough for even them. So, Hero Dad must finish it off. That often worked.

One of the ways we experienced racism in our daily lives was in our families through interracial adoption, marriage, and living in integrated neighborhoods. Turks embraced those opportunities. While it is common-place now to see multiracial families, it was not commonplace in Southern California in the 1960s.

My family moved into Pacoima, a predominantly African American and Chicano community. Two families entered the process to adopt African American children. Two other Turk families have African American grand-children. One married interracially.

One story illustrates the rampant racism that made some of these decisions heroic.

Ann and Al and their four children lived in Fullerton during the time Al served as campus minister supported by United Ministries in Higher Education (UMHE) at California State University at Fullerton. They decided to add another child, an African American, through adoption. Turns out Fullerton amid Orange County was not ready for this. Opposition in the neighborhood spread. Ann with dark-skinned two-year-old David were shunned in the grocery stores and on the streets. Graffiti on their garage door said "N . . . Lover." The social service agency and Al and Ann, after heartbreaking struggle, concluded that this was not a good neighborhood for David, and he was returned to the care of the county agency.

Al had called the police when the graffiti appeared. An enterprising reporter for *The Orange County Register* read the police reports each day and came to interview the Cohens during which they told the story of David's recovery by the social service agency. This was a great story to show the world the status of race in the US. After appearing in the Orange County newspaper, it was picked up by the wire services and appeared all over the country, the next day in papers in Europe, and even in *Pravda*, the Soviet Union paper.

I learned of David's return to the agency in a local radio news broadcast about threats of violence from the community. I started phoning the Cohens and the line was overloaded. Even though it was a ninety-minute drive from Pacoima, I drove south to their home in Fullerton. The driveway was filled with cars. One I recognized, Lynn Jondahl's old gray Porsche. In the living room I found the president, the media director, and the provost of California State University-Fullerton; several longtime friends of Al's; a staff member of the congressman; and an aide to the mayor of Fullerton. And two Turks.

At issue was how to respond to several interview invitations—*Time-Life, NBC, The New York Times, Los Angeles Times,* and a couple local TV news programs including the *The Louis E. Lomax Television Show* on KTTV in Los Angeles. Lomax was a pioneering African American journalist and was the first to host a network news program. The university worried about how it would be seen, the city about how it would be seen. The reporters were eager to make a splash. The Turks were seeing this as an opportunity to do some big-time racism conversation, and we were worried about Al, Ann, and about their children. How would more exposure affect them? The eventual decision was to decline all the invitations except the Lomax interview. That decision was made on the assumption that Lomax would like to get the story out accurately and would be sympathetic. Al was also eager to give more of the story including more emphasis on the powerful racism involved.[2]

For me the decision to go to Fullerton expressed a strong connection among friends. You're in trouble? I'm there with you.

We were active in support of the United Farm Workers participating in boycotts, marches, and picketing in the fields. We had lots of allies in the UCC and ecumenically. There were similar groups in many denominations.

Scattered around Southern California, the Turks were working boldly for peace and justice like I was trying to do. They gave me a sense of scale, of being part of something bigger than I was but which included me. I felt

2. From author's notes from the 2009 interview.

more powerful because I had friends who were giving themselves to the same hope and vision for the world. Even when I was not there personally, their victories and their defeats also belonged to me. And mine belonged to them. The Turks were a primary group for me. Much of my sense of myself, my identity and my take on my vocation and confidence in what I am capable of was formed or affirmed from 1963 to the early seventies by my experience as a Young Turk.

By the mid-seventies, the Turks had spread out across the country in new positions and new ministries. In my own romantic way, I have felt I have been a Turk in the years since. I have felt accountable to the values, to the boldness, to the courage that I learned and practiced with those people.

Around 1973, the Leas family was on their farm near Flint, Michigan. Connie was eager to plant a grove of peach trees, to have a cow to milk, to stoke a wood burning stove in the kitchen, and to make bread every day. The Lasswells were in Bandon, Oregon, where Tom and his dad built a house in the forest and Tom bought a boat and became a commercial fisherman.

Around Christmas time I set up a conference phone call among all I could locate just to catch up on our various adventures and to keep the connection alive. When we got to the Leases, Speed described his work at the Institute for Advanced Pastoral Studies and Connie described her farming experience. It was winter. Her previous life was lived in Southern California. She asked plaintively, "What do farmers do in winter?"

There was a long pause. We were primarily city people. Mary Lasswell, one of the two people on the call who actually grew up on a farm, said, "In the winter farmers read seed catalogs." Sounded like wisdom to the rest of us. These clergy and their families became my most treasured and dear friends and colleagues during this tumultuous period.

We invented our ministries day-to-day. Seminary had not prepared us for such a time as this. Circumstances grew far worse in the streets and on campuses as the days progressed. Students protested the war, the draft, racism, and speech restrictions on college campuses. Protest included not only peaceful gatherings but actions that were increasingly violent, occupying and destroying, even bombing, property. As the United States Selective Service System drafted more and more young men, their resistance included turning in and burning draft cards and leaving the country. Poverty deepened as the War on Poverty was defunded so the Vietnam War could be funded. Jobs disappeared from the cities. Those who grew our food lived in horrible poverty and worked long hours without safety protections of any kind, such as breaks, water stations, restrooms, or sunshade. The largely white police force increasingly militarized and occupied the city streets like an army.

Being a Turk gave me courage because the others were taking risks in their ministries. Most of us came close to being fired or left employment under that threat.

We stood on picket lines, accepted draft cards being turned in by young men, stood between young people and police lines, and mediated between warring parties. We didn't start our social change work planning to do so but when no other options worked, we committed civil disobedience. We took whatever action we thought was necessary.

I do not have a record of how many times we separately were arrested. I committed acts of civil disobedience a half dozen times, twice in farm-worker actions, twice in draft card turn-ins, twice in Vietnam War protests. I was only arrested and jailed once, in the Capitol rotunda in Washington, DC.

The Turks were interdependent and seeking common outcomes. Sometimes the poverty, the injustice, the anger, and the frustration led us to consider radical actions. Tom said it best: "I'll go to jail with you guys anytime." This expression of trust and willingness to stand in public protest risking arrest and imprisonment was the highest compliment Tom ever offered. We agreed on the analysis of the situation and what justice demanded. We were ready to do what was required, together.

Just writing this story with such militant language will probably sound grandiose to many readers. Looking back, most of what we stood for turns out to be widely held now; civil rights is permanently on the agenda for the country. The Vietnam War was wrong. It must be hard to imagine a time when the vast sea of white people thought that the fuss led by those agitators in the south was unfortunate and that war was supported by 90 percent of Americans. Of course, the violence in our streets persists.

In 2004 nine of us gathered with spouses at our home in Claremont, California, at Pilgrim Place. We took two full days to hear each other's stories. When I was taking Tom to the airport, he commented, "Nobody sold out!" The integrity we fought for back in the day was still intact as Tom summed up what he had heard. I agreed. At this writing almost half have died, unfortunately including a couple of the best storytellers among us.

Deep down I am still a Turk as I write this book.

Chapter 5

Living and Working in the
Ghetto and Barrio 1964–1968

THE UCC BOARD FOR Homeland Ministries initiative that placed urban specialists in ten cities in the US was called the Time Tellers Program. The background for this project was an awareness of a major division growing between rich people and poor people in urban areas.

The sense among Board for Homeland Ministries staff was that the church must anticipate this pressure building in urban centers, seek to find local leadership to give a positive voice to the injustices of race and poverty, and develop some proposals for addressing them. The name of the project reflected the need to find out what time it was regarding lack of resources, police oppression, broken justice systems, lack of jobs, and inadequate schools. These and other factors created the stress and potential violence in the inner cities of America.

My feeling was that this program was the answer to my new clarity about my future. I hoped I could secure one of these Time Teller positions. But they had already been chosen. I read in the *Los Angeles Times* several months later that the Time Teller in Cleveland, the Rev. Bruce Klunder, had joined community residents in trying to stop a major construction project that required tearing down a school. On April 7, 1964, he lay down in front of a bulldozer and was run over. This was very sobering and some of the risk of this work became clear. Yet, I still felt that this was the work that called me.

My opportunity came in a phone call from Chuck Burns, who was then serving as church extension minister on the Southern California UCC Conference staff. He knew of my developing sense of call. He said he was ready to renew a church that was in a community that had undergone white flight, leaving Black and Chicano residents surrounding the church. Pacoima was in the northeastern part of the San Fernando Valley of Los Angeles. He hoped I would be willing to take on this project. He could guarantee my salary and expenses for five years. I had to raise the rest from the members of the church and any other support I could find. I agreed to meet with the search committee.

Thus, I moved from a prominent post–World War II successful church in Van Nuys to a now faltering church. I moved from the familiar perspectives of white people to the unfamiliar ways of seeing the world through African American and Latino stories. I moved professionally and personally from a secure position to a risky one, from being an insider to an outsider. I moved from the best public schools to the worst. And my family came with me. This was one of the least understood decisions of my life. It did not make sense to anyone except me and my wife Genie. We chose these challenges together.

Our most risky decision was that the best place for our children to have a chance to avoid soaking up what we now call white privilege was to be in the Pacoima schools, white among Black and Brown, physically, every day during their grade school years. They would attend Liggett Elementary School. It was not high ranked on any academic achievement score. We felt what they would learn in those classrooms was vitally important for living in the America of the future. What they learned could not be learned in any other way. We also were aware of our responsibility to provide support as parents, to hold up the expectation of learning, reading, math, and other fundamentals, and to keep the promise of a college education on the horizon. And what we were learning ourselves was full of fearful and amazing experience. This was immersion education for all of us. Genie eventually became a teacher at the Pacoima Elementary School.

I was now solo pastor, in a failing[1] church, in a ghetto and barrio, sending our children to inferior schools, and living in a high crime neighborhood. Genie and I had chosen against common sense, against the obvious path set out by our race and class. We decided that racism was the primary issue of our time, and we wanted the lives of our family to focus on that reality.

We had read with interest the stories of the lunch counter sit-ins in Greenville, North Carolina, of the freedom riders on the bus routes through the south. We had watched the 1963 March on Washington and Dr. King's

---

1. Failing in the sense that it was unsustainable beyond a few years. Attrition in membership meant insufficient funds to employ staff and maintain maintenance on the property and buildings.

"I Have a Dream" speech and felt in some deep place that this story was one we wanted to join. I had had that experience delivering Christmas mail in the ghetto in St. Louis and of trying, on behalf of the University of Missouri Student Government Association in 1953, to racially integrate the two movie theaters in Columbia, Missouri.

We felt the place we needed to be at that time was to live in an African American and Latino community. We had so much to learn. We grew up white surrounded by white. Beyond white we were clueless.

We would all experience the troubles and the incredible strength within the families around us, among our friends. We experienced being the outsiders.

The Call to Pacoima

This became the most potent period of my life, a time when I discovered who I was, what gifts of ministry I had been given, where my deepest passions lay, and what risks I was willing to take. And I discovered my limitations, skills I did not have. The four years I served as minister of the Pacoima Congregational Church were 1964–1968. I was age thirty-four to thirty-eight, and it was kind of a petri dish for my life.

I was eager to get out there and be fully responsible for a congregation. I was largely ignorant of what I was getting into but eager for the challenges of urban ministry. Pacoima was where I would be able to drill down and learn about the impact of racism and poverty.

I had no thought of a career path. There was a lot that I didn't know that I didn't know. But that was the purpose of my immersion. I was ready to walk those streets, get my haircuts, and shop for groceries in the neighborhood stores.

Pacoima lies within the boundaries of the City of Los Angeles about forty miles north of LA City Hall and had been generally known as a center of gang activity, poverty, and racial unrest. The most prominent outreach of city services was, in the eyes of the street gangs, the Foothill Division of the Los Angeles Police Department located in Pacoima. It was experienced as an occupying force.

I learned this much before I met the leaders of the church. I did not know what their hopes were. I remember the conversation the evening I met with the search committee of the Pacoima church. They were all white and had refused to flee as increasing numbers of Black and Latinos families moved in. It was chaired by Eleanor, the moderator. The committee pretty much represented the more liberal, younger membership. And they were aware of the conference's hope that the Pacoima church would experiment with ways of serving the local community. The financial support was premised on this experimentation. The committee was looking for someone who would engage the wider community and help the congregation explore and find its mission in a community going through racial, class, and cultural rapid change. I was eager to be that minister.

I would preach every Sunday. That was new. I would help guide the raising of financial support. That was new. Pastoral care in that setting would need to be learned. All of that combined with developing models for urban ministry, to reach beyond those who came to church each week, to those who spoke Spanish and those who didn't have jobs or enough to eat.

Eleanor, in a side conversation with me the evening of my interview, described how she and her husband, John, had spent part of the past weekend in an anti-war demonstration in the upscale mall in Studio City. I was amazed that church folks felt the freedom to express their moral and political views in this bold, public way. It was 1964 and everyone knew the church was patriotic and thus for the war. And she was the moderator of the church! John Buchanan was a speech professor at the nearby community college. He opposed the war in Vietnam and had begun a solo silent vigil during lunchtime at the flagpole at the center of the campus. When we discussed what we might do as a church, they were supportive.

I began work in the summer of 1964. We rented an old three-bedroom house on an acre of undeveloped land in Pacoima. The young Mexican family next door taught us about the various kinds of chili, the degree of heat and taste, and the skills of eating chili. Two years later we bought our first home.

Learning to Be a Solo Pastor

All this forced me to come to terms with myself, to explore what I was willing and not willing to risk, what was fundamentally important to be doing when, it felt, the whole world was in turmoil. Instead of providing stability in our society, the family, the church, the schools, and the colleges, the "civil society" was splintering. In April 1965 the largest anti-war demonstration to date with twenty-five thousand protesters assembled on the mall in Washington. Those seeking change (civil rights, anti-war) and those seeking to keep the old order, the younger generation doing battle with their parents, were staring at each other across a cultural, political, and even psychological divide that neither side could fully understand. I mention all this to illustrate the relative chaos for institutional life including churches. Old leadership patterns were being challenged. New forms of the church needed to be explored. This was the context for the time I served as minister of the Pacoima Congregational Church.

During an October 1964 Sunday afternoon worship service at the church, I was installed as minister and teacher for the Pacoima church. Several of my close colleagues, pastors, and campus ministers, the ones who became the Young Turks, were asked to take part in the service. What struck me was how many of them used "creative" in describing me and my work. One charged me with continuing my creative approach to ministry. It took me a year or two to figure out what this was all about. I did like creativity as part of my life. I have written earlier that I was convinced I would always be controversial and attributed that to my being a new generation of church leadership. I believe that to be true, but the constant use of "creative" to describe me needed more than "new generation" to explain it. I did not grow up in the church, did not attend church as a child or youth. My choice of ministry was not based on experience in the church. And my choice of seminary was the Chicago Theological Seminary, which, in my time, was affiliated with the Divinity School of the University of Chicago. This did not show I was interested in congregational leadership skills but in biblical research and scholarship. I had joined seminary friends in making fun of the "practical" offerings—having ministers of big churches spend an afternoon with soon-to-graduate students to pass on practical skills.

What I quickly became clear about was that much of the time, I did not know how ministers were supposed to do things. I envied other young clergy who knew the rhythms of the job, the workflow, how to answer phone calls at night, etc. I was often considered creative, when in fact, I simply did not know what standard practice entailed.

I was faced with the normal responsibilities of a solo pastor but was eager and open to the new time and situations as they unfolded, to the lives, struggles, and celebrations of the families in my "parish," meaning in the neighborhood around the church.

The Missionary Structure of the Congregation: A New Theology for Organizing the Church

The World Council of Churches published a series of study guides focused on the theme *Faith in Secular Age*.[2] These books provided the theological framework and understandings for my work in that church and community. Simply put, they proclaimed that the church exists, as Jesus did, for the sake

2. Williams, *Faith in a Secular Age*.

of the world, not for the sake of the church. They raised questions about how the church is typically organized and how the members of the church were to understand their relationship to the mission of the church.

I saw the church as having a maintenance function and a mission function. The purpose of the maintenance function was to prepare the members of the church for their work in and for the life of the world. They were no longer only consumers of the ministries of the church but also agents of the church. The mission function was to work beyond the membership, to seek to penetrate and transform the world.

One image that was important for helping people understand what I was trying to describe as our purpose as the church was the image of the theater where, in the usual conception, the audience would be the congregation watching the play, the actor on the stage would be the minister, and the prompter would be God. The new image was that the congregation would be the actor, the minister would be the prompter, and God would be the audience.[3]

The UCC national staff were pioneers in this kind of urban ministry. I called for consultation. They suggested I explore our own version of Time Tellers, the program to sensitize white church members to the conditions in which people live and worked.[4]

Immersion in the Community: Researching the Parish

In the spring of 1965 Carl May walked into the Pacoima Congregational Church and asked if we could talk about the Pacoima gang problems. He was the first community organizer that I met. He had already visited with several community leaders and had talked to several gang members. It was clear he was sizing me up, finding out what my orientation was to street issues, gangs, police, social welfare, and my level of courage to engage in effort to organize action.

I was fascinated by his ideas and questions. Did I have any experience with gang work? Did I have a feel for what drives young men into gangs? Did I have any empathy for their struggle to find meaning, vocation, and status within their community? Did I have any experience with the police? Would I be willing to walk "the Boulevard" with him, stopping at the shops along the way, getting acquainted with the shopkeepers and customers, and especially walking into the corners where gang members hung out, engaging

---

3. Weber, *Salty Christians.*

4. Developed by J. Archie Hargraves, urban specialist at the United Church Board for Homeland Ministries.

them in conversation, seeking to learn their names, and, in the longer run, earning their trust? Van Nuys Boulevard between Laurel Canyon Boulevard and Foothill was the central core of the community. Everyone knew where you were referring to when you said "the Boulevard."

The notion that a man could walk into my office, a total stranger, and test me the way he was doing and that he was drawing me into justice issues in the community where I was serving a church; that he was seeking to create something that did not exist in that community; that he was ready to challenge the status quo, the police, the gangs, the shopkeepers and the social welfare agencies to come together to work out a new set of possibilities for the benefit of those who had turned to gangs; and that he hoped to empower these young men for a new beginning for their lives was instructive to me.

After several weeks of conversation, he suggested that I call a meeting of several people he felt might be the core of a new organization. He had concluded that of the people he had been interviewing I was best suited and situated to give leadership to his project.

Carl was a teacher in the sociology department at California State Northridge and was setting up a project for the fall semester. Shortly before our next meeting his office called to say that Carl had died. He had taught me enough already to give me a plan for my personal immersion into life on the Boulevard in Pacoima. I decided to follow his path, his questions, and his curiosity and see where that took me.

From here on things were different.

The mission question we needed to answer was how our church could bring justice and connection to our parish. What did we need to know and to do to become a justice church?

Parish was not a familiar concept in my experience of American Protestantism. We had our people out there in the community and the Methodists, Presbyterians, etc. had theirs. To think that all who lived in the surrounding community were, in some sense, ours was new. Since that was the assumption we made, we realized we didn't have a clue about most of those folks. So, the church needed some form of engagement with the community.

Most of the members of the church agreed that for the month of April 1965 we would cancel all church activities, meetings, committees, except for Sunday morning worship. Most young clergy bent on renewing the church in that era started by renewing the Sunday worship experience. I saved that for the end of the process. I pushed for change in the established program and structure and kept Sunday morning familiar and traditional. Start at the edges and keep the center stable.

We freed up a lot of time for mission. Leadership and many members of our church signed up for this as did people from the Church of the Chimes. Women from the study groups and their spouses were attracted to the adventure. Some community activists in Pacoima heard of our effort and joined with us.

We reflected a lot on the image of the dividing wall of hostility found in Eph 2:14, where Paul wrote about the wall between Christians and Jews. Our wall ran down Laurel Canyon Boulevard at that time and it was between whites on one side and Brown and Black people on the other. We knew we had to take initiative to break down that wall.

The women agreed to get their hair done at one of the three hairdressers, choosing among the two who served primarily Black women or the one that served Latinas. The men got their haircuts at Super Bob's or at Joe's Barber Shop. On laundry days the families went either to Lila's Laundromat or Henry's Wash and Dry. The point was to meet neighbors, the people on the other side of the dividing wall of race, to ask about their children, their favorite grocery store, their experience with the school, or their biggest worry. And do it in their space where they were at home and we were the outsiders.

Our Pacoima Time Tellers, while bold in buying into the program, were hesitant to get out of the car at Joe's Barber Shop, at Lila's, at the Wash and Dry. I am amazed that so many were able to take those steps, who experienced their own courage in a new way. Some were clear that it was not something they could bring themselves to do.

As the early explorers began to report back, word quickly spread that this exposure yielded many dividends—new friendships, new understandings, confrontation with new realities, and many funny stories. People enjoyed telling stories about themselves standing at their front door with a laundry bag over their shoulders and being unable to find the doorknob to get out. To their surprise, all who tried found hairstylists who knew how to do white people's hair.

We had learned how to ask questions. And there were a hundred new questions to ask when we finished reviewing our period of plunge into Black and Latino Pacoima, on the other side of the wall. Others found in these reports encouragement to launch their own experiences. The courage it took to follow through on these commitments was huge.

Just those simple actions generated so much information, so many questions, and such emotion that we didn't know how to process it all. We had several meetings to share our experience and to try to push what we had learned and what we had experienced into some conclusions that would shape our decision about mission. We gathered in small groups to share what we felt, what we learned, with what and whom we connected. I asked, "What do we now know about our parish?"

The month's immersion and several months of reflection produced action proposals. We brought the list down to two projects that had been clearly identified by the parish, that were perhaps doable with current resources, that would have an impact on lives of people, and that had promising prospects for future fundraising and volunteers. We decided that our church would organize to meet the need for early childhood education, preparation of all the children and especially children from Spanish-speaking families for entry into public school kindergartens. Setting up a preschool program for children of families we met and for others that they recruited was our priority. Our folks figured this out for themselves because of making connections across the dividing wall and listening to the priorities of those they met.

We also committed ourselves to developing a proposal to address the youth gang issues, namely conflict among Latino gangs—including two in San Fernando—and between Latino gangs and a Black gang.

We had no clue where this would end up. A lot could have gone wrong, but this was a path to which we were now committed.

A Nursery School to Prepare Children to Enter Public School

The children who were growing up speaking Spanish at home and living in households with low incomes were entering kindergarten at Pacoima Elementary School already behind the English-speaking children from homes with higher incomes. Something needed to be organized to help break the cycle of poverty by providing these preschool children with a comprehensive program to meet their emotional, social, health, nutritional, and psychological needs. We decided to organize and open a free nursery school for the Pacoima children.

We had a Sunday school building that was perfect for this project including plumbing and bathroom facilities and a fenced play yard in the back. Church member Doris stepped forward to be the director. She was qualified by education and experience. Several others in the church agreed to serve as teachers. Four women from the Church of the Chimes expressed eagerness to help. They recruited friends to gather the equipment and supplies needed. They also took responsibility for raising the necessary funds to realize this vision. Doris took care of the licensing.

When we were ready to start the nursery school, teams of volunteers were organized to go door-to-door with pamphlets describing the school in

English and Spanish and encouraged people to enroll their preschool children. The license allowed a maximum of fifteen children. Within a week we had the fifteen and a waiting list of twenty. I was learning to use the media to gain exposure to our project and the photos in the *Los Angeles Times* made fundraising much easier. TV coverage was easy to get for this kind of work. It took five months to get the preschool up and running. I often sat on the floor with the children playing, singing, and laughing.

Families of the children came to befriend each other. One of our volunteers, fluent in Spanish and a graduate student in education, organized a parent's circle conversation to help them see what the children were experiencing and how they could support this nursery school program at home.

When President Johnson announced the War on Poverty in 1965, he appointed Sargent Shriver to organize the Office for Economic Opportunity (OEO) to run the federal anti-poverty effort. One focus they chose was identical to our childcare project and its goals. Staff from the OEO in Washington analyzed our nursery school and used it both as a national model and as a training site for the Los Angeles area. The Head Start program was one of the most successful elements in the War on Poverty.

Street Scene: A School for the Gang Leaders

The *Los Angeles Times* carried the news of a grant of $242,316 (adjusted for inflation this would be $2 million in 2020) by the US Office of Economic Opportunity to the Pacoima Congregational Church for a demonstration project with thirty unemployable youths from hard-core poverty areas.[5]

This announcement came at the end of a two-year community organizing effort. After the church identified that youth gangs were one of the two focal points for our mission work, my work plan was to walk the Boulevard. Barbershops, beauty parlors, pool halls and bars, small convenience stores and bodegas, and a few social services agencies filled the long corridor. Customers for the shops and stores were primarily African American and Latino folks. Pacoima Elementary School was a little further up the Boulevard. And there was "the projects," a small public housing project.

Various intersections along the Boulevard were the main gathering places for different gang members. So, I walked the Boulevard, up and back, for several weeks. Slowly I was recognized as a mysterious but familiar white face, and I bought soft drinks and candy bars and learned names. I found some of the Black young men approachable after some days. It was going to take a long time to create some level of trust, I concluded.

5. *Los Angeles Times*, "Church Gets Funds."

One breakthrough came on an afternoon when I decided to go into a barbershop where an elderly Black barber held court for a lot of men in the community. I entered and asked if he would cut my hair. He looked at me for a moment and then said, "It's been a while since I cut straight hair but, sure, come on in."

My next walk, a couple days later, I was able to say hello to six men by name. I became eager on my walks to get to Joe's Barbershop and stand in the doorway and take all their jibes and pokes and to feel comfortable in pushing right back at them. You don't smart-mouth me without getting some back. We had a good time and gradually they helped me develop some understanding about gangs. Some of them had been in those gangs and their sons were now in them. The men understood out of their own experience that, for some, gang life was the primary experience of family, of belonging. They worried about their kids, about the increasing aggressiveness of the Los Angeles Police Department. They worried about new weapons getting into the hands of the gangs. Their advice to me was to give gang members something to do. Through these connections I gradually found my way into conversations with some of the young men.

Because of past connections with Black men and women in college, in seminary, and in other communities, I felt some, though very shallow, sense of the struggle that these folks were telling me about. They deepened my understanding of the slave-to-freedom narrative and shared the blatant and subtle signals from the dominant culture that were meant to exclude those with Black skin.

The way into the Latino community for me was much more difficult. That history and culture were new to me, and I was very easily excluded and befuddled in my effort to initiate conversation. Language was a barrier at times.

As my points of contact expanded along the Boulevard, I also came to know the staff of the social agencies along the way. Ernie Dillard ran the Boys Club Program. Al Solomon and Hetty Fullenwider staffed the Los Angeles County job training center. Together we identified several community leaders whom we thought could help us take some steps together to begin a multiagency conversation about what we faced in this community. I proposed including several of the youth gang leaders I had come to know. Gradually we developed a common vision of working together toward something we were not yet able to see.

After several months we formed the Committee of Sixteen. I was elected chair and we met at the church because the gang leaders decided it was a safe and neutral space and they had come to trust me enough. The committee spent several months getting to know one another. Some told stories of other youth gang projects people had been involved with, talking about where the drugs were coming from in the community, about who was taking the most risk, and about who was making the most money. It seemed clear that no useful program could develop without breaking down barriers among gang leaders and among the gangs themselves. They told us that favoring one gang over another would increase unrest, competition, and violence. So, with very little in financial resources and little experience among us for what we set out to do, we decided that our first project was to open a youth center on the Boulevard.

Six months later I remember asking myself, "Why in the world I am standing here at midnight in a parking lot where a gang fight is supposed to happen? Is this risk worth taking?" I remember the answer that came to me: "This is who I am. This is what needs to be done." The answer was an affirmation of identity, an identity that sprang from a new sense of vocation and the courage it was taking to pursue the vocation. It was nearing midnight. John and I had agreed we would stand in this parking lot from 6:00 p.m. to midnight. He worked for the Los Angeles County Commission on Human Relations, and I was pastor at the Pacoima Congregational Church. It was February 1966.

The gang members had agreed to leave their weapons, knives, and guns in their cars as they entered the center. We had hoped the center would serve as a neutral site, a safe, nonviolent space with informal programs of ping-pong, pool, etc. that would encourage the gang members to mingle and get to know one another. Gang members had great difficulty loosening up and checking their surliness at the front door. For them a lot was at stake and an "attitude" was the best form of presentation. Don't give an inch in hostile confrontation. Protect your gang of brothers and its prerogatives, its territory, and its markets for marijuana. Fights were expected.

A fight had broken out in our new youth center that afternoon, words hurled first, then pool balls and cue sticks. Following that skirmish, they shouted that they'd meet that night in the parking lot, and they'd bring heavy hardware. We hoped we could intervene in time. John and I felt that we needed to stand in the parking lot for hours hoping our presence would ward off the battle. Around 10:00 p.m., cars packed with young men began cruising past on Van Nuys Boulevard. We could not identify which gang they were with. After about 11:30 p.m., the cruising up and down the Boulevard ceased. That crisis was averted.

It became clear to us that the youth center initiative was not going to work. Planning assumptions were wrong. Playing pool together was not going to evolve into friendship. It was only going to be another place for the old conflicts to be played out. Something more fundamental had to be a common purpose. Creating friendships was not the path toward our goal. When I had asked directly what these young men wanted, they had all said jobs. After deliberation and exploring what other gang intervention programs were doing, we decided that jobs were a more powerful promise to motivate participation. Our second project was to design a job training program for gang members.

I received a phone call from Dick Saul in Washington, DC. He introduced himself as an attorney with the Office of Economic Opportunity—from President Johnson's War on Poverty, the anti-poverty program. He said his job was to search across the country for promising youth gang programs and to explore how the OEO might partner and help the program succeed. That help included federal financial grants. He asked questions about our work. He suggested that the OEO might be interested in working with us in our gang intervention project.

Our group was just beginning to see what we might do together and what our limits were. We needed help. I invited Dick to meet with us, to continue exploring possibilities. Dick was interested enough to fly out to meet me and some of the Committee of Sixteen members. A week later he spent a full week touring the streets and agencies. He visited the Foothill Division of Los Angeles Police Department and reported "you have no friends there." It was after the first Watts rebellion, so police were extra edgy and aggressive. The police lesson from the Watts event was they had insufficient control of the streets. The Foothill Division's job was to control the streets of Pacoima.

The gang leaders were not sure what to make of meeting with an agent of the federal government. Since the police provided their primary government contact and social workers were next, their expectation was not favorable.

We asked each to recruit other members from their gang to the table. The meeting was at the church. I reminded them to leave their weapons in their cars. I knew there were cars cruising near the church assigned the task of protection for the various gang leaders present. And there were police also cruising. I'm confident that the police had informers in the meeting. It could have been a multi-gang war planning session! Probably was. Everyone was edgy and it would not have taken much to ignite an exchange of gunfire. My job was to be calm and confident that we could pull this off.

In the meeting I welcomed everyone, called by name as many as I could remember, thanked them for leaving weapons behind. Joe, the barber, and some friends sat in the back. In fact, everyone wanted to sit in back. It is always safer with your back to the wall. But we could not accommodate everyone. Not enough wall.

The members of the Committee of Sixteen introduced themselves. I introduced Dick. He gave a good thirty-minute account of how America had neglected the youth who are growing up in the inner city. Then he described how the administration of President Lyndon Johnson was working to make that right. He described what his impressions were from his walk-around and what he heard at the police station. Dick said that the approach his program was taking is that no education will work unless the students are learning what they wanted to know for making their way in the world they knew. He ended by inviting thoughts about what kind of education the youth really wanted and what they wanted to learn.

It was amazing to me that the thirty-five people in that room, many lifelong enemies, would sit in conversation across their own walls of hostility about their future, about what they thought they needed to know to make a different future.

Dick made it clear that they would decide on the curriculum and have a deciding voice in hiring the teachers. He said representatives from the various groups would work together to write a proposal for War on Poverty money. The learners had to be in charge.

So, Dick began flying out every two weeks to sit in on our meetings. He gained trust of both the agency leaders and those from the gangs. Dick was rumpled, with a loose tie and shirt sleeves rolled up, unpretentious. He listened carefully, affirmed gang perspectives on the situation they faced. From time to time, he had suggestions of things we all should consider. He always offered them to committee members who would bring them to the table for discussion if they seemed useful. He reviewed the application form to clarify how to move forward to apply for a grant.

Genie and I offered our dining room table as the venue for grant writing. We hoped it would be a sign of our trust and welcome to our gang leaders. It was impressive to me how that environment seemed to transform the dynamics. I feared violence and so did everyone. Our three children were watching TV in the family room most nights. But for those at the table, there was a task to accomplish. It held promise for everyone. It seemed that the street poses and personas were relaxed, and other dimensions of personality emerged, a little humor, some helpful ideas, some actual conversation.

Our task was to start constructing the program with the key question to the youth gang leaders: "We have a grant for your education. What education do you want?" This was not designed in a social service agency or an academic department, but on the street. I was uncertain what kinds of answers we would get in the conversation. I still wondered, if you're a crook, wouldn't you want to know how to be a better one? The answers were a surprise to me. These were hard-core young men and women, many with prison experience. They wanted to know how to do an interview for a job, how to fill out a job application, and how to prepare for a job.

The group selected James Sherman, the twenty-six-year-old leader of the largest Black gang, as program director. He had an easy, natural leadership and charisma, which carried underneath an easily felt threat if you crossed him. I met with James to plan and evaluate meetings.

As a further move to welcome our personal relationship, I invited James to come to church sometime. I was interested in James knowing I wanted to include him in my other work and life. At that point the fifty or so people who came to church on Sunday mornings were all white except when Jimmy and Marie showed up. Finally, one Sunday morning James did come, all dressed up with an almost zoot-suit-type suit and lots of gold chains. James brought two women dressed in slinky, tight, extra short dresses. They had the effect of embarrassing church members. James introduced the women to me and explained that these were the prostitutes he managed. This is not an exact quote. They were clearly in uncharted territory that morning as were we all. James told me later that they just did not feel welcome and comfortable that morning. I'm sure that was true for all of us, but it was a good immersion for everyone.

James was key in holding the gang leaders together to create this project. The Black gang that he headed was much weaker than the two major Chicano gangs. That made him a good compromise. James was deeply intuitive and very smart but with little formal education. He was tall and good-looking, quiet and inquisitive. He helped us negotiate many jurisdictional struggles, turf issues, and arguments. And he sat at the dinner table at my house along with local community agency staff, the attorney from the OEO in Washington, and a graduate student from UCLA, while we worked out the details of the proposal we were to send to Washington.

I asked James about the Black clergy in Pacoima and wondered whether we should invite them to participate as sponsors of this project. He advised that we not invite them. He explained, "They are hustlers just like me and they earn a good living from their hustle. They're not interested in people like us." He said, "Everybody's got their hustle." I took him to be saying that to survive one had to figure out some way to generate income. Stealing, preaching, drugs, it was all the same. I never thought of my calling to ministry as my "hustle," but maybe that was a useful way of looking at it.

After several months of work on the application, we signed it and Dick carried it back to Washington. We agreed to call the project Street Scene. We followed his advice that the church should be named as the fiscal agent. The grant would be made to the church. We would have to upgrade our financial processes from counting income from Sunday morning offerings to managing a federal grant.

When an anti-poverty grant was approved, it was announced by the Member of Congress whose district was to receive it. We were in the Twenty-Second Congressional District of California and our representative was James Corman. Jim was an ex-Marine and big on military spending. He was a social liberal and interested in efforts such as we were making. Our church had already picketed his field office for his enthusiastic support of the war in Vietnam. I was determined to have a face-to-face conversation about the war several months before the Street Scene project became relevant. I had made an appointment and sat with him in his office. The conversation was an authentic exchange of views. I could tell he had already developed his own questions about the war. And I learned that he and his family were active in the Methodist church, and he had carefully read the evolving views of the Board for Church and Society. We added several lunch conversations when he next came back to the district. When he was notified that the Office of Economic Opportunity was going to make the grant for the Street Scene project, and he saw my name on it, he phoned me. That's how I found out.

On the street, there was a brand-new sense of hope that maybe Street Scene was a door out of poverty for these thirty youth as they anticipated the beginning of the program that they had helped design. If successful, it could be scaled up to involve many more.

In the *Los Angeles Times* article I am quoted at length about details of the program. The article explained that the grant announced by Congressman Corman would first go to Governor Ronald Reagan for approval. I am quoted, "Gov. Reagan can veto the grant, approve it, or if he took no action, at the end of the thirty-day period, the grant would be considered approved." And I say that "the latter action is most likely."[6]

Oh, how stupid and wrong I was.

I was already known publicly as a vocal critic of the war in Vietnam and one who had committed civil disobedience. The notion that the government was going to give a radical minister and church a quarter million dollars to pay gang members was a perfect target for right wing attack. The fact that I told them where to focus their effort, on the Governor who can veto the grant, set them to work.

The governor was swamped with demands that he veto the grant.

And veto it he did.[7]

We were devastated.

6. *Los Angeles Times*, "Church Gets Funds."
7. *Los Angeles Times*, "EYOA Will Seek Change."

One provision in the Office of Economic Opportunity legislation included a last-ditch effort to save the program. It provided that the director of the OEO had the power to override a governor's veto. So, I mounted my first national campaign, an effort to fill the office of Gerson Green, director of OEO in Washington, with encouragement to override Governor Reagan's veto.

I made phone calls to the national social action agency of the United Church of Christ and enlisted their support in generating letters. It was a perfect organizing effort for them. Soon letters from all over the country, from local pastors and congregations, from seminaries and the heads of several denominations, and from the US Catholic Conference and the National Council of Churches, were generated.

To help save the grant, Congressman Corman set up a breakfast for the two of us to meet with Los Angeles Police Chief Tom Redden, a deputy sheriff, two city council members, and heads of several business groups in the San Fernando Valley. He asked their support for the override. I explained how the program was designed to work and I saw it reducing the use of taxpayer money on gang surveillance. They asked good questions and especially Chief Redden wanted to know the names of the participating gang leaders. I gave them only the name of James Sherman.

The *Valley News* ran a story headlined "Anti-Poverty Worker Faces Liquor Store Holdup Charge."[8] James was charged with a theft of $600 from a liquor store. The date of the theft was June 24 according to the *Los Angeles Times*.[9] Several friends scattered around the country reported that this story appeared in their local papers. The fact that other media would carry a story of an inner-city guy accused of stealing $600 was a great sign of our program generating wide interest. It also had the backstory of the government giving money to an outspoken anti-war church and minister.

A few months later I testified at James's trial in downtown Los Angeles. Some of my own interactions with James happened at the time this theft was alleged to have taken place. James and I had been together. We hoped that would help.

At the lunch break from the court proceedings, I was invited to lunch with James's attorney and with James just before I testified. I clumsily knocked a glass of water onto the lap of the attorney. He had a fit at the prospect that he would have to appear before a judge looking like he had wet his pants. I doubt that that clumsy act was germane to the fact that James was convicted, and our program was threatened.

8. *Valley News*, "Anti-Poverty Worker."
9. *Los Angeles Times*, "Robbery Arrest Perils Poverty Unit."

The director of OEO would not override the governor's veto. It was over. Hearts were broken in Pacoima on the Boulevard where most of the street action took place. Hopes were crushed. I was devastated, feeling that I had raised the hope of a promising horizon beginning to take shape among these guys.

Looking back, I'd love to know in subsequent years how much money taxpayers have spent for the police work, costs of trials, and incarceration of those thirty young men. That a quarter of a million dollars spent could have been spent on those same youth for a program they designed that held promise of a way off the street hustle game breaks my heart still. That would be my liberal, soft-on-crime, ever hopeful heart speaking. I feel that the lives of thirty who on the verge of being criminals could be employed taxpayers now. And I regret that the experimental model of education we used did not yield any evaluation for the model of asking the learners what they wanted to learn and making that the focus of the curriculum.

The Committee of Sixteen became a critically important peer group at many levels of the community's life. Had the project been funded and successful, that group would have become an influential force in the community because we embodied so many parts of the community from the street to the merchants on Van Nuys Boulevard, to the churches and civic groups, to the postmaster and the congressman.

For a couple years of development and seeking funding, Street Scene was a bright light in the darkness of ghetto/barrio of Pacoima. But it was crushed out. And I am somewhat at fault for giving our opponents the weapons to defeat us. I gave our right-wing opponents the opportunity to put pressure on the governor. Of course, they may have figured this out themselves. I gave the police chief James Sherman's name, though he could easily have gotten it from his own sources. I demonstrated a certain clumsiness all around.

We did at least kick up enough dust that *The New York Times* ran a story by James Loftus on September 28, 1967, describing the project in some detail and highlighting the risks of working with gang youth. The article did point out that James had a record of fourteen arrests but that the last one was in 1962 for which he drew a two-year suspended sentence.[10]

I shared this story in workshops and talks for several years. I received a letter dated March 2, 1969, from Rev. George R. Tolson, Protestant chaplain at San Quentin State Prison.

10. Loftus, title unavailable.

Dear Paul,

It was good to meet you the other day at the regional meeting of the clinical training group . . .

I was, of course, most interested in Jim Sherman and so called him in for a visit. We had a really good one. He seems to continue with his constructive attitude. He impressed me well and I do hope he will come thru this present experience without too much damage.

I knew you would like to know that my experience with him was consistent with yours. He was much delighted to be remembered by you and spoke most realistically, but appreciatively, of his experience with "Street Scene."

With cordial best wishes,

George R. Tolson, Chaplain

It breaks my heart at what could have been.

The funding concept for Street Scene was unusual. My thinking on the subject was largely formed by an informal debate after midnight at Canter's Delicatessen on Fairfax in Los Angeles. Chris Hartmire, Jack Pratt, and I were debriefing a conversation about how largely white church groups could best support initiatives in poverty communities.

I asked, "How should largely white church organizations with money use that money most productively with people who are poor?"

Jack, legal counsel for the Commission on Race of the National Council of Churches, insisted on a chain of accountability with each step having clear goals and purposes that were measurable. How the money was to be spent by the community people had to be negotiated ahead of time and the plan had to be followed. Jack understood he was accountable up the line for each dollar spent.

Chris, executive director of the National Farm Worker Ministry, insisted that white people sitting at desks in comfortable offices had no clue about what was needed and should not be involved in decisions or evaluation. Only Cesar Chavez knew what was needed in his labor organizing and his organization should be granted the funds and be trusted. Chris had experienced the tough accountability within the farmworker organization and felt his trust was well-founded.

The conversation went on for more than an hour and was fierce. I found myself agreeing with everything each of them said. Street Scene reflected this as it called for the OEO grant to be made to the church in regular payments but the participants in the program made the spending decisions.

The New Celebration: Sunday Night Improvisational Worship

While following my strategy of continuing the Sunday morning service people were used to, I developed ideas about what a new celebration might look like. I wanted one that was focused on biblical texts but lifted the concerns, pain, and reason for joy the worshipers brought in the door each time. I looked for much more participation from all who gathered. I worked with several folks who could be helpful creating a worship that would include some experimental and some traditional expressions. We wanted an experience that felt open to the spirit, that had improvisation in it, to which anyone at any time could contribute an idea, a feeling. And we wanted to keep ourselves grounded in the Christian faith.

The service had four sections: (1) the world, (2) the biblical text, (3) the relevance, and (4) the giving of thanks and commission.

We gathered twice a month on Sunday evenings. I asked the people to reflect prior to arrival on what were they were fearing, hoping for, celebrating, and to find some symbol to illustrate it. We constructed a triptych, three four-by-eight-foot pressed wood panels attached by hinges. We could fold it up and store it and, for the service, open it up like a greeting card with two folds and three panels. Folks were invited to thumb tack or scotch tape to the tryptic what they brought: notes, letters, news clippings, ribbon from the wrapping of a birthday gift, greeting cards, or recipes. Ed, the jazz pianist, played as folks arrived. My role as leader of the service was to carefully observe what people brought in. I would ask for clarification if I couldn't figure out what the words and images meant to convey. My task was to soak up what was on people's hearts and minds that evening. It was doing detective work on the soul, given the evidence before me.

I started off by sharing what I took from what had been put up on the triptych: deep worry about the Vietnam War, about our soldiers, about feelings of depression, about issues in the neighborhood, about families in our nursery school as well as the celebration of a new grandchild's birth. That was the shape of the world for us that evening.

Like in my Bible study at Church of the Chimes, three people took turns reading a text for that day and briefly shared their exegetical work on and their personal connection to the text. We used one Hebrew Bible text, one New Testament Epistle, and one Gospel text.

My task here was to think out loud, to share connections I saw between the world and the biblical text. This was improvisation. People were invited to join in. We'd go on from fifteen to forty-five minutes if there seemed to be the presence of the Spirit in the activity. Sometimes this was thrilling, to have a small congregation in conversation about how the world and the text connected on a particular evening. Sometimes, it fell flat. Sometimes I seemed amazingly well-educated and smart and sometimes dull and dumb. Sometimes the congregation rescued me and sometimes could not get my point. But we all appreciated that exercise together. Whatever emerged, the intellectual and spiritual work of the church was exercised. A colleague who, in seminary, observed me in conversation with a small youth group said my greatest gift was to get them thinking furiously. This was what we were doing. It was living on the edge waiting on the Spirit to enlighten us. Occasionally we found a moment of truth in our work together.

I read somewhere "if you're not living on the edge, you're taking up too much space." We all lived on the edge those evenings. And we praised God, gave thanks for the world, and asked for blessings on the life and work of the following week.

There was jazz piano throughout. Ed made an enormous contribution to our time together. Especially after I had shared what was on the triptych, the things on people's hearts that evening, he played. If you knew anything about jazz standards, you would recognize words and phrases that were in the lyrics. We would burst out laughing when we recognized what he was playing in connection to the issues we were discussing. One evening there were lots of evidence that people were getting excited about Christmas later in the week. Ed played "Santa Claus is Coming to Town" but then slipped in "Lulu's Back in Town." It was all in anticipation of Advent.

NBC sent a camera crew out one Sunday evening and our New Celebration appeared in the Monday evening local news. But of course, they ended a pretty good piece with the image of the offering plate being passed, saying something like, "We guess some things will never change."

The Selma March 1965

We watched the TV news with horror when Sheriff Jim Clark ordered his troops, many mounted, to charge the peaceful (and in his view, unlawful) marchers coming across the Edmund Pettus bridge in Selma, Alabama, on their way to Montgomery, the state capital, to take their grievances directly to Governor George Wallace. My flood of anger on top of years of struggle and frustration led me and thousands of others to feel a resounding "yes!" was the only response to Dr. King's invitation to come join the struggle. I still clearly remember watching that Bloody Sunday and, the next day, watching that invitation and feeling the call to that battle.

Fighting racism can take many forms just as racism takes many forms: feelings, attitudes, behaviors, policies, and practices of corporations and governments. The most helpful definition of systemic racism I learned was anything that works to the advantage of white people and at the same time to the disadvantage of Black people is racism. That is helpful because one can look at any exchange of conversation, any physical move or behavior, any policy or practice of a school, business, or corporation and ask that question and quickly determine if it was racist or not. For example, if the primary school graduates a higher percentage of whites than Blacks, it is a racist system working for the advantage of whites.

Clearly the voting laws among many civic policies in the South and elsewhere easily could be called racist. And voter registration laws were seen by the leadership of the Southern Christian Leadership Conference (SCLC) as an important issue to confront. The Student Nonviolent Coordinating Committee (SNCC) had spent several years developing local leadership for a campaign to register voters. Bob Moses of the SNCC reminded us that community organizing methods are a slow, long-term approach to social change. The SNCC model was grassroots level dominated by young people and many women in contrast to the SCLC model dominated by older men. It was dominated by persons I'd call unexpected actors because they arose from within the community.

They faced massive resistance. After agonizing internal debate, the SNCC leaders decided to invite the SCLC to partner with them in a confrontation focused on Selma, Alabama. The SCLC's goals and strategies were very different, but the size and entrenchment of the enemies was so powerful that combining forces was necessary. The SCLC's model was to mobilize quickly large numbers of people for short term demonstrations, and it relied on creating a crisis that would rally public opinion and force federal intervention. It was a top-down approach focusing on King, the president, and the Supreme Court.

The SNCC was not happy that suddenly the area was flooded with media, and everyone wanted to see Dr. King, not aware of the long-term investment of staff work that preceded King's arrival.

The killing of Jimmy Lee Jackson on February 26, 1965, in Marion, Alabama, led the Rev. James Bevel to propose the march from Selma to Montgomery. Bevel was an SNCC staff person who eventually moved into leadership circles of the SCLC. He was appointed as SCLC director of Direct Action in Selma sharing leadership with Amelia Boynton of Selma.

The agonizing event on the bridge created something that fighting racism seldom creates: a front line in the battle, a time and place for the opposing forces to engage each other face-to-face. It was on one level the question of whether the movement for civil rights would be able to prevail over the long history of slavery, Jim Crow, and deeply rooted, entrenched racism.

At another level it was a test of whether nonviolence could prevail over the rush of unchecked forces of violence. How could I not put my body in the middle of that front line? So, a few days after Bloody Sunday I was on a plane from Los Angeles International Airport to Atlanta and another plane from Atlanta to Montgomery where we were met by other volunteers from the North who had driven to Selma to join the battle. I was traveling with fellow Young Turks Al Cohen, Lynn Jondahl, and George Killingsworth, plus Pete Flint, a member of the Pacoima church. From the Montgomery airport we were driven along Highway 80 (the Jefferson Davis Highway), the route of the march in reverse direction, to Selma. It was pouring rain.

The SCNC staff directed us to homes of Black Selma residents who had invited the visiting folks from around the country to sleep on their couches and floors. Jondahl and I stayed at the home of Mrs. Johnson, sleeping on her sons' beds. She was scared to death of what might happen after we left when the KKK decided to punish those who gave shelter to the visiting protestors. And she was thrilled at the opportunity to share the hospitality of her very modest home with "you clergy from the North who have come to help."

The first event I remember was on the steps of Brown Chapel for the daily morning briefing by the Rev. Andrew Young, an aide to Dr. King. Andy started out saying, "Let me tell you where we are. I don't know." What was happening during the four days I was in Selma was an intense negotiation between the SCLC leadership and the US Department of Justice regarding government protection of the march since Governor Wallace refused to use his law enforcement powers to provide protection.

On a second afternoon and evening we met in front of Brown Chapel for speeches and testimony. It rained steadily throughout. The Rev. Hosea Williams, the Rev. Fred Shuttlesworth, and several SNCC organizers spoke as did some local citizens who has been working for several years on building a voter registration organization. They worked hard at keeping our spirits up while it rained, and we waited for the march to start. We all wanted to get ourselves on Jefferson Davis Highway heading toward Montgomery and the confrontation with Governor George Wallace.

Something had to be done with all this northern crowd who had come to march to Montgomery. Until it was clear that sufficient protection was in place to provide a measure of safety, the march would not start.

So, the SCLC staff not engaged in these negotiations figured out some useful work for those of us who came to Selma in response to Dr. King's call. On the afternoon of March 18, 1965, I was in the back seat of an old sedan driven by the Rev. James Orange, another of SCLC staff, heading to Marion, Alabama. An SCLC staff member named Freddie was in the front passenger seat. Two other clergy, strangers to me, were tight together with me in the back seat. Jimmy Lee Jackson had been working with SNCC organizing and encouraging his neighbors to register to vote. He was unarmed and with his mother. He was shot, I was told, protecting his mother.

So, we were being transported by Orange to one of the most racist and violent communities in Alabama, for the purpose, he said, of "humanizing with the folks." Our job was to walk the town square of Marion, the three of us in our clerical collars, and introduce ourselves to the citizens who were shopping, men going to the barbershop or women going to the beauty parlor, people heading to the five-and-dime. He suggested we tell them our names, where we were from, and why we were in Alabama. Frankly, I did not relish the task, fearing for my life. I could easily fanaticize all kinds of pain that would come our way. It took a good deal of courage to do what Orange was suggesting. But I took comfort somehow in the notion that if my name were added to those who sacrificed their lives in this nonviolent struggle for voting rights in Alabama in 1965, it would be an excellent use of my life. I know how grandiose this now sounds but it is the thought that let me put one foot in front of the other and say, "Hi, I'm Rev. Kittlaus from Los Angeles and I'm here to help Dr. King. Who are you?" The three of us spread out around the square and made somewhat of a scene. I can't say I encountered any threats from people. Some were not interested in shaking hands and chatting but, surprisingly, some were.

That evening we enjoyed a fried chicken dinner at the Baptist church where Jackson had been a deacon. We spoke at the worship service that night in a packed sanctuary. This was my first experience of speaking to a loud, lively, southern Black congregation. I was the first of the three of us to stand and introduce myself and say why I was with them that night. I said my name and said I was from Los Angeles and there were shouts and applause in approval of my being there. I remembered my preaching professor at Chicago Theological Seminary saying that a preacher really has only one sermon and that is his life. The intoxication of those shouts, "Preach, brother!" etc. was hard to resist but more was not necessary. Just being there from so far away was way more than sufficient. It was totally obvious that our presence meant everything to these folks. It gave hope and courage. They didn't know me or anything about me, but I was there. I have learned one thing: showing up is important. The service lasted until 11:00 p.m. Out of curiosity I asked the pastor of the church how long their service normally lasted. He smiled and said, "Until it's over."

Men from the church who stood guard outside the church reported that clusters of white men had formed nearby. There was worry about what might happen during the service with so many people jammed in the old church or when the service concluded. At the end with choruses of "We Shall Overcome" in the air we went out into the night with all the rest, not sure what the night held in store for us.

We found our car and Orange got us to the highway back to Selma. He did suggest we keep our eyes on the two cars behind us following us at every turn through the moonless night. If they began to approach, he said he would stop, and we would surrender ourselves without violence. Sounded noble. And foolish. The cars never approached, and we arrived back in Selma where we could restore our regular breathing.

One footnote to this story is that I asked Orange as we drove toward Selma why we were doing things that seemed to have no political impact. He replied that sometimes we march to change the system and sometimes to keep the system from changing us.

That wisdom has helped me feel comfortable in other protest situations. In 2003 seeking to protest the invasion of Iraq a few of us at Pilgrim Place decided to stand in silent vigil at the flagpole on our campus. There was no political point to be made in that politically remote act, but I kept clear in my head that the point was to keep me from submitting to my sense of powerlessness in the face of these great evils in the world. Standing at the flagpole was an act of protest and I did it because, at that moment, I could not figure out what else to do except express my powerlessness.

In Selma, Al and I decided, since negotiations were ongoing between the SCLC and the federal government regarding federal protection and no one knew when the march would begin, that we would fly to Washington, DC, and visit our congressmen. We needed to take some action while the negotiation went on.

Al and I visited the congressmen from our two home districts and from his campus and my church districts. We were unshaven, unkempt, and probably smelly but we still had our clerical collars on and made, I believe, an impression on the members of Congress. They all were interested in hearing our on-the-ground experience since they only knew what was reported on TV news. We reported messages of hope for justice, of the suffering of the people in great poverty, of the generations of exclusion from the democratic process by not being allowed to participate in the electoral process, and of the work the civil rights workers had done to build leadership and community and to create hope among the people. And we said it was now up to the congress to pass the Voting Rights Bill of 1965 to lead the way to the fulfillment of hope.

When we were having our official photo taken with my congressmen, Rep Edwin Reinecke, who had been elected the whip of the Republican freshmen class, Al asked that the symbolic but real coiled whip be taken off the wall behind us. He said to the congressman, "We just come from an area of the country where whips are used on people." It was immediately removed. Walking down the hall afterwards, he said, "He'll look at the whip differently from now on. That's what you call an 'action oracle.'" Al and I were home safely the next day.

We listened at home to Dr. King's speech at the end of the march. There were thousands gathered at the State Capitol in Montgomery that afternoon. Many had marched the whole march, thousands more had come directly to Montgomery to join in the great victory of the completion of the march without violence. One of the volunteers, Viola Liuzzo, mother of five, age thirty-nine from Michigan, was driving a car, shuttling marchers from Montgomery back to Selma. She was shot and killed by a member of the Ku Klux Klan. She was shot from a car which included an FBI informant Gary Rowe who testified against the shooter and entered the federal protection program. So, a triumphant day ended badly. Her name is inscribed on the Civil Rights Memorial created by Maya Lin in Montgomery, Alabama. Murder trials for the four Klan members ended in hung juries and acquittals.

I'm grateful I was there in Selma during those rainy days in March 1965. I had a conversation with a priest from Detroit about confirmation as we waited for the next speaker in front of Brown Chapel. We confessed to each other that we were often baffled by the energy shifts and the sense of rebellion among the kids in our classes. I remember the lined, troubled face and words of thanks from Mrs. Johnson. She was so grateful herself for the fact of our caring and our coming to be with her in this time of trouble. I remember the boost we seemed to give to the young men Mrs. Johnson introduced to us. They were so eager to be photographed with us. I remember James Orange in the front seat of the car, as we drove through the dark night with the headlights of the car following us, feeling that we were in danger from those in that car. I can still see the faces, the tears, and the singing of the people of the Marion, Alabama, Baptist church. I remember how doubtful I was that I could summon the courage to walk that sidewalk of the town square in Marion.

I remember the folks back home at the Pacoima Congregational Church UCC who helped provide financial support for the journey and how eager they were to get my stories when I returned. When I told the church that I was going to Selma, I said I only had enough money to get there but not enough to get home. I said the rest was on them. They provided the additional support. And the welcome home was terrific.

Immaculate Heart of Mary Sisters and Mary's Day

In 1965, at the invitation of friends, our family joined the happy crowd at Immaculate Heart of Mary College in Hollywood (IHM) for their annual Mary's Day Festival. The art department, including Sister Mary Corita, hosted a wonderful, bright, creative, colorful experience. The IHM sisters wore their habits, and they brought us into very joyful space full of dance, visually stunning art and decoration, and lots of folk music. One of the sisters took Genie and me downstairs to their collection of folk art. These were signs you would find in a circus or handmade, moveable instruments or games. Many would call it junk but some of the art department found it engaging, much like Sister Corita found common, everyday phrases and used them in her serigraphs as sacred words. My favorite Corita serigraph is the picture of a loaf of bread wrapped in a plastic cover identifying it as Wonder Bread which, in a liturgical context, is exactly the truth.

I found myself in a conversation with one of the nuns regarding their fading status in the much more conservative Roman Catholic Church and especially with Cardinal McIntyre of Los Angeles archdiocese. They were anticipating, and beginning to plan for, life after they were laicized, having their official clerical status withdrawn by the high officials of the church. She told me they were trying to think and pray their way through a series of major questions.

She said there was a lot of interest in extending their liturgical creativity to discover how to do ministry in the street. I shared that that is exactly what I was working on in Pacoima in my UCC church. She said she'd like to learn from us. I said I'd be glad to work with them on street ministry if they would help us develop our understanding of life of the Spirit and worship. We both agreed to take this idea back to our communities. Within a month they had appointed a team of three sisters to come to my home in Pacoima and meet with seven people involved in our immersion in the barbershops and laundromats and the establishment of our preschool and gang intervention priorities.

We introduced ourselves and talked about our Christian faith at the first session. It took a while to warm up. They were not experienced in conversation where it was not assumed everyone held and practiced the same faith. We were bold to pick and choose among the elements of the faith that appealed to us. They were astounded. We were not familiar that one could speak confidently for all. We wore casual, comfortable clothes. They wore their habits. Those starched, black outfits seemed to take up a lot of space. They seemed bigger than we were.

After two sessions there was warmth and laughter and freedom to raise questions and express surprise.

Those of us from Pacoima had lots of questions as we prepared for our next session. Our seven gathered and sat around the living room waiting for their arrival. The doorbell rang. I opened the front door and there were three complete strangers standing there. Slowly, as my mouth closed, I began to recognize their faces. Their habits were gone. They wore thrift shop dresses. They were "our" sisters but something drastic had happened.

They entered and sat down, seemingly taking up half the space that they usually occupied. This was an optical illusion. We simply asked what happened. They told of the long, secret conversations going on in the mother house. They wrestled with the question. "Does wearing our habits inhibit the ministry to which we are committed?" After much prayer and deliberation their leadership had made the decision. They could, if they felt so called, set aside the requirement of wearing the habit. Nuns who were unwilling to make that move could continue to wear their habits.

We sat in awe as they told the story, as we worked to be comfortable seeing them in civilian clothing. This was such a radical move. I could hardly imagine what deep faith and courage it took. To stand over against their church, to break hundreds of years of tradition and practice surely took great courage and certainty in their faith.

After some further discussion, I asked the two big questions lurking in my mind. "What did you do with your habits? Are they hanging in the closet as a fallback option?"

They looked at each other and one said, "Last night after taking off the habits and putting on our new clothes, we together carried our habits down to the basement of the house and threw them into the furnace fire."

That is surely one of the most astounding moments in my life. I've heard it said, "Don't mess with nuns." I get it. How could I ever have thought that they would leave themselves an out, a backup plan? You step over the line, you stay over the line.

When I moved on from Pacoima and after changes at the IHM college and community, we lost touch. I did, however, interact with several members of the order at other times in my career.

Cross Burning 1966 Ku Klux Klan

In September 1966, articles appeared in the *Los Angeles Times* announcing that a newly organized Ku Klux Klan was going to hold a cross burning in

Soledad Canyon, north of Los Angeles.[11] They invited people to join them. Looking back, it is hard to imagine that in the mid-1960s there were folks who imagined a readiness for the Klan in Southern California. Later, investigation by *Times* reporters showed the funding sources and leadership planning of the Klan rally overlapped with those running a neo-Nazi group and gun advocates. Leadership in our church explored how this Klan rally might require from us a public challenge. How could we raise our voices?

In the background of our discussion, we knew that the residents in the San Fernando Valley were mobile. At that time, one in four homes changed hands every year. People generally did not form deep bonds of trust, community, and common purpose with their neighbors. Most people formed opinions about what was going on around them based on reports from the media, newspapers, radio, and TV. The Klan stories ran without any voice of opposition.

We decided to be that voice. We envisioned forming a picket line on both sides of the dirt road into the hills just north of us where the Klan rally was to happen. We sent an urgent letter to other church people and community groups all over the San Fernando Valley inviting them to join us in saying "no" to the Klan.

As we learned, journalists can extend their coverage of stories by covering the other side. So, the Pacoima Congregational Church became the focus for the third paragraph of stories about the Klan rally. We were what came after "Meanwhile, a group at the Pacoima Congregational Church has announced . . ."

We had print media and a lot of TV coverage. NBC TV put three reporters on the story: Jess Marlowe, later an anchor for local news; David Horowitz, whose career branched off into consumer rights reporting; and a very young Tom Brokaw, later a long-time anchor for the national NBC Evening News. They regularly came to interview and film our preparation and perspective. Horowitz provided my first experience of a mobile phone call from his Thunderbird on his way to Pacoima.

Our efforts succeeded in equalizing media attention to the rally. It was clear that the reporters were happy to give us all the ink and broadcast time they could. We had gathered at the church in the afternoon to brief people about our goal, a nonviolent protest, and about media coverage. We had people do a short version of nonviolent training so that if any confrontation with Klan fans happened, our folks would be equipped to respond. On the Saturday night of the cross burning, over two hundred people with signs opposing the Klan lined the mountain road.

11. *Los Angeles Times*, "Citizen Silences Klan Loudspeaker."

And, with all the attention now focused on the cross burning, the Los Angeles County Sheriff's Department was out in significant numbers to keep the peace. There was no violence. We absorbed a lot of name-calling from buses and trucks ferrying Klan fans up the hill. They burned their cross, made a few speeches but the crowd was much smaller than they hoped for. It was for us an opportunity to demonstrate a public face of the church, a face that took courage.

The story in several news stories on Sunday morning focused on the brave people on the picket line rather than on the rally. I feel we contributed to a more just, peaceful, and welcoming Southern California.

Sunset Strip: Police Confront Youth on Sunset Boulevard

In November 1966 I got an urgent phone call from the Rev. Ross Greek, minister of the West Hollywood Presbyterian Church on Sunset Boulevard. It was one of those calls among a loosely knit ecumenical group of progressive pastors who counted on each other for support. We took risks and phoned each other for help and ideas, when we needed more bodies on a picket line, when things were happening.

Greek's call was a request for help with a developing confrontation between youth, many high school–age, on one side and Los Angeles Police Department and the Los Angeles County Sheriff's Department on the other. Greek's church was several blocks from the hot spot. It offered parking and a good place for clergy wearing clerical collars to gather, get briefed, and scatter out in the crowd to monitor both sides but primarily the police and deputies who posed more trouble. This was sometimes called a ministry of presence. Our hope was to make a visual impact, to be a calming presence for both law enforcement and the young people. Greek asked if I would help plan and lead thirty-minute training sessions for clergy and be one of the spokespersons for the press with him. The mile and a half long stretch of Sunset Boulevard had the best nightclubs, rock and roll stages, and a reputation for various forms of wildness, drugs, and a destination for young people who had run away from home. It traversed the city-county line called the Sunset Strip.

In 1966 Sunset Strip was going through changes in the entertainment available in the area. Some of the changes included new high-end restaurants like Ciro's and commercial establishments. To youth, it was where they found rock-oriented hangouts like the Whisky a Go Go and the Troubadour, which hosted breakout appearances by the Byrds, Buffalo Springfield, Elton John, and the Mamas and the Papas. Increasing crowds of young people were gathering and wandering up and down the Strip. The club owners, whose clients were arriving in long Cadillacs, didn't like all the kids milling around out front. They called for help from the LAPD for that part of the strip that was in the city and the Los Angeles County Sheriff's Department for that part in the county. Ross's concern was that the young people were going to face the violence for which those law enforcement departments were known.

As Greek had anticipated, the cops, weapons drawn, wearing battle dress with helmets and gas masks, marched shoulder to shoulder pushing several thousand young people backward towards the city-county line where the Sheriff deputies, similarly armed, waited. Riots broke out as the kids tried to defend themselves throwing stones and bricks. They were severely beaten, and many were hauled off to jail.

There were times when a single line of clergy stood between the youth and the police, but we could not hold. We did a lot of street counseling with many frightened young people and even a couple cops who hated what they were asked to do. We did press interviews seeking to paint a different picture of who most of these kids were. After months of continued skirmishes, both sides seemed to tire of the exercise. The media stopped covering it and it died out.

Several scholars and groups were interested in this phenomenon, asking who these young people were, what they wanted, and where they lived. On the third day of the clergy presence, I was called by Edgar Z. Friedenberg, requesting that I pick him up at LAX that afternoon and escort him around the strip and the action so he could observe and get a feel for it. I said sure, not knowing exactly who he was. I found out he was an American scholar of education and gender studies best known for *The Vanishing Adolescent*.[12] His work was a finalist for the 1966 National Book Award for Nonfiction.

When I picked him up at the airport, Friedenberg said he wanted to take me to lunch at the airport restaurant in the architectural structure that distinguishes LAX. He said he knew the chef. It was the first I learned about and ate artichoke bottoms. And they were prepared to his specifications. He was the most passionate person I have ever met regarding the truth and beauty of youth and was a committed warrior against all that seek to crush them. He was an astute observer, seeing and commenting on behavior I missed. And I'm a pretty good observer.

A month later he called and invited me to select several clergy who walked the Strip with us to participate in a weeklong conference at Ghost Ranch in northern New Mexico. We were there to join him in describing

12. Friedenberg, *Vanishing*.

and analyzing the Sunset Strip phenomenon. Attending were denominational leadership from several churches and scholars, followers of Friedenberg's work.

Two months later he asked me to join him at the Center for the Study of Democratic Institutions in Montecito, California. For seven hours the two of us were the center of an intense conversation with the whole team of Fellows of the Center. What does this event on the Strip portend? My primary contribution to these examinations was derived from my own curiosity. I had felt a sense of warmth from several of the young men and women over the course of the two weeks of my involvement. I knew something about their stories. I shared what I heard.

When I moved to Santa Barbara in 1984 to serve First Congregational Church UCC I met socially Frank Kelly, then acting director of the center. When I introduced myself, he told me he remembered me. He had been present in that conversation at the center in 1966 about the Sunset Strip event. When I asked why he would remember that eighteen years later, he said he felt we were presenting those scholars with fresh news of great import, that the culture had not evolved but had leaped fully formed into the future and the scholars had been left behind.

People Who Came to Share This Ministry

About half of the Pacoima congregation, thirty people, decided that my ministry was not one they were comfortable with and withdrew. The remaining thirty were steady with the new direction. But departures were not the real story. It is those who joined us specifically because they wanted to be part of this new kind of church.

During my four years at the Pacoima church, I was interested in the people who were attracted to what we were up to and who wanted to participate. We brought in twenty-five new members and had many volunteers who worshiped with us and even gave leadership to some of our projects. Several UCC congregations adopted our nursery school as a mission project, provided a pool of volunteer help and an income stream. Others, including several from the Bible study class at the Church of the Chimes, attended church regularly and provided volunteer administrative support. Fifteen strangers who joined us had first been attracted by the news stories in the papers and TV.

Roger came to see me and explained he was representing a small group of two other seminarians from Princeton Seminary and himself. The group had decided to live together and to work on community development and action in a poverty community in Southern California. They wanted to base their action in a local church and the guys back in Princeton, New Jersey, had deputized him to explore a relationship to a church if he could locate one that met their criteria. They were seeking a church that would welcome their presence and would take their offer of community involvement as an outreach of the church. Our church had achieved a considerable amount of media coverage because of our effort protesting the Klan cross burning and other activities that drew the attention of reporters. They seemed to find our experimentation and expressions of the Christian faith interesting. It was the media attention that drew Roger to this conversation about his little band affiliating with us.

I was excited about the idea. We could do a lot more with their efforts. Their seminary training would enrich my own effort to transform a church guided by theological understandings rather than recent tradition and practice. It seemed like our interests and orientations were compatible. It did not take me a moment to welcome them enthusiastically. A couple of months later, Dick and Lou arrived to join Roger to take up residence in the community and be ready to go to work.

Immediately I found that being criticized by them from the political left was much more difficult for me to cope with than criticism from the right. I had been the critic on almost everyone's left. I had not been criticized from arguments lefter-than-me. Their passionate agenda was to oppose the war in Vietnam. And they brought an "in your face" style of urgency. Whenever I suggested that we use a moderate, gradual approach in our strategy, they said, "We haven't got time for that." They had run the drill of acceptable protest, the letter to congressmen, the letter to the editor, and the regular polite forms of resistance. Our soldiers were still dying, and the peasants of Vietnam were still dying. These three were escalating the protest.

But our church did not have the war on our agenda. When the guys arrived, they ended that omission. Every Sunday and every board and committee meeting was an occasion for argument and challenge about the war in Vietnam. They wore anti-war armbands, buttons, and signs that were unavoidable.

Not long after they arrived, Pete showed up. Pete was the first cultural hippie for most of us. He wore old jeans and sandals, and his beard and long hair were also an affront to those of us used to wearing suits and ties or Sunday dresses to church. Most disturbing of all, he wore a silver earring in his left ear. Pete was a cultural challenge just to look at. When he walked into the church for the first time for a morning service, he was either nothing like anyone had seen before or exactly like the hippies who were considered a blot on society. It took a long time for folks to be relaxed in his presence and even longer to feel his warmth and interest in them. He explored mind-altering drugs. While never suggesting I try it nor making any offers to provide it, he did spend time with me responding in detail to all my questions about the experience he had with different drugs and the difference between using marijuana and acid. Pete earned income crafting silver jewelry, bracelets, rings, brooches, and earrings.

The primary agenda these guys brought was alarm and urgency about the war and intolerance for any who hesitated to speak out against the war. They pushed our church over several months to pass a resolution expressing our corporate opposition. They eventually began to make demands on other UCC churches, then moved on to other denominations. They offered to do teach-ins, debates, whatever to get the issue on the table. They got few invitations. Clergy were not eager to jeopardize their standing in their congregations by getting into that scary political stuff.

So, our anti-war missionaries went to picket in front of the churches, condemning them for their silence. They made it clear that they were from the Pacoima Congregational Church, so my standing among clergy was beginning to lack warmth. A reputation of troublemakers surrounded us all.

The conversations convinced me that the war had to be opposed and that no matter the discomfort that was generated, the war was bad enough to risk it all. There eventually came a time when they proposed an action that I could not support. And they picketed our church the next Sunday. I heard the following week how delighted many of my clergy colleagues were.

Some others were drawn into our church during this time.

Ginny and John participated in many functions and occasionally attended on Sunday. They were from the Church of the Chimes. As was Ann, who worked as our office helper during the week. Ginny and Ann were in the Bible study class. John was an aircraft design engineer who worked at Boeing.

Ed showed up one day saying he was a professional jazz musician and would be glad to help. His employment was as a jazz piano entertainer on cruise ships. He was gone for several months each year. He often played in our services.

Jimmy was an attorney, and he, his wife, Marie, and two kids lived nearby and joined us—though Jimmy kept a nominal membership in the church of his youth, a Black Baptist church in Los Angeles. During the Watts Rebellion we kept their children at our home while Jimmy went into Watts to offer legal services.

Wally, Cathy, and their children joined. Wally was a special agent with the California State Department of Corrections and member of a special unit of agents who tracked down prison escapees. Prison escapees are especially dangerous.

One evening Cathy dropped Wally off at our home for a party. He got a call on our home phone and was ordered to go directly to an apartment building in Van Nuys where there had been a possible sighting of an escapee. He asked if I would drive him down and wait to bring him back if it was uneventful. I said sure. So, I was on the team to go get the bad guy. Turned out it was a false alarm and we headed home. This was my only occasion to drive my car with a man with a gun in the passenger seat.

On the way home Wally said he liked the idea of a VW Bug for an undercover caper. I still have the suspicion that Wally was reporting to law enforcement about our church. He did tell me he had looked up Pete's record. Investigators had determined that Pete was insufficiently organized to be a threat.

I was called upon for pastoral support and a memorial service when Wally and Cathy's four-year-old son, Scott, died falling off a piece of furniture in their garage. That was my first experience leading a service after the death of a child. It was more heartbreaking than usual. And two years later Wally called me again. Cathy had died from an odd accident in a shopping center parking lot. She failed to firmly set the brakes when she exited the car. She was killed by her own car as it rolled backwards. I again provided pastoral support to Wally.

Liz had a passion for women who were victimized. She organized the distribution of birth control products in the ghetto, organized a chapter of Clergy Counseling Service for Problem Pregnancy, recruited me to be listed as a counselor and to offer rides to Tijuana where abortions were safe and legal. She was in church every Sunday though was clear that she did not share our belief. I don't know what she thought it was.

These wonderful people joined the long-time members Eleanor, John, Pam, Doris, Ken, Ivan, Betty, Jane, Paul, Shirley, and others in these projects.

I was invited to join a small group of people in the community who met occasionally for conversation. They were labor union members and had been (perhaps still are) members of the Communist Party. My general understanding of the work of the church as liberation for the poor was interesting to them because of similarities with their socialist orientation. This small group were all white people living in Pacoima. Two worked on the floor in the Chevrolet Assembly plant in Burbank. Another worked as a member of the International Brotherhood of Electrical Workers. Their commitments to socialist analysis held the same sense of the centrality of the poor that was central to liberation theology. All were college graduates and two of the men had multiple master's degrees.

Helen and Dick, one of the couples in the group, shared with me that they were leaving Pacoima and traveling to places around the world searching for a country that was more economically just than the US. They rented out their home. They hoped to sell it and relocate to this new location. They returned after fourteen months of travel reporting they could not find a place that treated the poor any more justly than the US, even though they were outraged with the economic injustices they knew in the US.

I knew almost nothing about labor unions nor the vision and function of the socialism except what I heard in Pete Seeger's music. These long evenings of conversation opened new perspectives for me. They opened my eyes to all kinds of American history that was not taught in schools. How can one have spent sixteen years in public education, kindergarten through bachelor's degree in liberal arts, and never learned the history of labor unions? What kind of history is that? I never read about lynching either.

Police Stories

On two occasions I called for help from the Foothill Division Los Angeles Police Department.

One night I was driving home passing the church, I noticed a light on. I stopped to check it out. When I got to the front door, I saw that the light was coming from the kitchen. I unlocked the door to go in and turn it off. I heard noise from the kitchen and went to the doorway. I saw a high school–age young man was standing at the sink dismembering the cat that hung around the church. He had different parts of the cat in different jelly jars that he had found in the cabinets. He was using two long kitchen knives. When I appeared, he saw me. I said, "Hi" as unalarmed as I could and asked if he would turn off the light when he left. He nodded yes. I said, "Great." I split.

When I got home, I phoned Wally, my friend who worked for the State Department of Corrections. I asked for ideas of what we might do. He said this kind of behavior is often a plea for help and we should get the police involved. He said they have processes for getting youth showing those symptoms into proper care. He said he'd contact the police and would meet me at the church. I was relieved that someone could be rational and have a plan about what I had seen. I wanted to get away from those knives and cat parts in jelly jars.

The police were very gentle once the boy put down the knives. He seemed relieved that someone took charge of his life at that point. He was put in two years of custody and school and therapy. He was released just as we were moving out of Pacoima. As we were loading the moving van, he stopped by the house to say hello. I hoped his time away had been helpful, but I also felt that it was good that we were not sleeping at that address anymore. He did scare me.

The other interaction came on Sunday morning, Palm Sunday in 1968. I arrived early at the church for my setup responsibilities for the fellowship room, including getting hymnals out and placing bulletins where the ushers would expect to find them. When I got to the front door, I found it unlocked. The night before we had hosted a dance for one of the Chicano groups in town. Several folks from the church were there as monitors.

I went in the unlocked door, looked in the worship space, and saw this long, foot wide scrape along the tile floor. It ran from the stairs leading to a raised stage area which we used as the chancel to the door that I had just entered. I surmised that some folks at the dance had taken the consul keyboard and two big speakers that served as the organ for church service. I mean taken, stole, removed, dragged across the floor, out the door, and probably onto a truck.

I first called the choir director suggesting he not count on the organ. Better plan on using the piano. I then called 911, the police. The woman took my identification and location and asked the reason for the call.

I said, "I want to report a robbery."

"Who was robbed?"

"Someone broke into the church."

"If there was no one involved except the criminals we call it a theft, not a robbery."

"Okay, I want to report a theft."

"What did they take?"

"Our organ."

Long pause.

"Your what?"

"Our organ."

"Your organ?"

"Yes, ma'am. We're a church. We have . . . had an organ. We sing. The organ plays."

"I'll send a unit over right now."

"Thank you for your help."

As members of the congregation arrived for Palm Sunday service, they had to walk around a police unit with lights flashing.

Other than that, the service went well.

Movement Leaders Visits

Our home and front yard became a stop for movement leaders. Folks were traveling around the country, often under the radar. I got calls and asked to invite my network of trusted contacts to meet and hear peace and civil rights leaders who were reaching out to make contact with local organizers and donors. These included Berkeley war resistor David Harris just after he completed his prison term; Fannie Lou Hamer of the Mississippi Freedom Democratic Party; members of the Weather Underground who were staying underground; Bob Moses from the Student Nonviolent Coordinating Committee in Mississippi; and Chris Hartmire and several Farm Worker Organizing Committee workers organizing the grape boycott.

End of the Pacoima Story

These four years in Pacoima were years of uprisings in the cultural and political life of the country. Movements for peace and justice arose, challenging many assumptions about life. This church was situated in a special moment in its history. The fifties model of a congregation with Eurocentric roots was no longer a match for the community it sought to serve. After a long, slow but steady spread of the ghetto and barrio and white flight, there were remaining in the church a corps of white progressive members who resisted the flight response to the changing neighborhood. They welcomed progressive ideas and radical action. It was a time when troubling inner-city issues were forcing themselves on the agenda for urban and church leadership. It was a time that the UCC Southern California Conference had funds to support experimental efforts and were able to give a green light to this project. It turned out to be time for a leader with outside-the-box thinking and for experiments that took a little courage to pull off. And I was the guy for that time and place.

The members of the Pacoima church decided to close operations permanently about five years after I moved on. The conference did not have the funds to continue the partial funding and the members were not able to put a financial package together to call a new minister. The church property was sold. They continued to meet in their homes and follow the same worship and mission formats as I had introduced with leadership rotating among the members.

In September 1968 I was invited by my friend Speed to join him as he assembled a staff for the new urban training center in Los Angeles. It was called the Center for Metropolitan Mission In-Service Training (COMMIT).

We continued to live a year in Pacoima and then we moved to Pasadena to establish a kind of commune with Al and Ann Cohen. We bought the house next door to them on South Madison Avenue. Al and I built a deck connecting our homes. We used their washer and dryer. We shared a lot of family life together.

We moved out of Pacoima for several reasons. The hope that was raised in the hearts of those involved in Street Scene was crushed when Governor Ronald Reagan vetoed the grant thus preventing the launch of the project. The disillusionment among those leaders with whom I had worked was, for them, the end of trust in white people and institutions. The disappointment and sense of helplessness led to conversations among them that I was the one who failed and that I should be held accountable. The UCC conference could no longer continue the financial support that paid my salary. And once I had accepted the COMMIT position, the move represented the reduction of an hour from my commute each way.

Chapter 6

Training Clergy and Laity for Urban Ministry 1968–1974

THE 1950S AND 1960S were an exciting time for ministers who wanted to explore forms of ministry beyond the local church. The local church fifties model was very successful, with church attendance high and offering plates showing the generosity of those enthusiastic members. Local churches designated portions of their income for the mission work of their denominations at a regional, national, and international scale. This created an accumulation of funding for alternate and exploratory forms of ministry. Many seminarians were attracted to campus ministry, especially at larger state colleges and universities. Some were drawn to pastoral care ministries and found their vocation fulfilled in private counseling practice or as part of a multi-staff church. Chaplaincy in hospital or prison ministries was available. In my own denomination, the United Church of Christ, our Board for Homeland Ministries (BHM) called the Rev. Donald Stuart to explore a ministry for runaway youth and others in legal, medical, or other distress within the Tenderloin section of San Francisco. BHM placed the Rev. Rick Mawson on the Las Vegas Strip to work with showgirls and other workers being exploited by the mob-run casinos. The Rev. Jack Matlaga was placed in the Mission District of the San Francisco arts community to support struggling artists. Many of these specialized ministries generated amazing stories of saving lives, supporting struggling people in a wide variety of settings.

Another large group of seminarians felt called to overseas mission work. The post–World War II reconstruction in Europe, Japan, and Pacific Island nations was ground for a newer understanding of mission work.

Selling Christianity was replaced by acting Christian in support of indigenous populations' education, agricultural, and civic projects.

Church attendance began trailing off, and, as local church budgets were reduced, less money was being forwarded to regional and national levels of the church. The support for creative, specialized ministry dried up. In 1968 experimental ministries of various kinds were still well-supported. The support the regional church provided to my work in Pacoima was among the last grants from that source.

The specialized ministry that pulled me into its orbit was, obviously, urban ministry, ministry in and for the city. One institutional form that urban ministry took in the late sixties was the establishment of about twenty denominationally funded urban training centers around the country. The first established was the Chicago Urban Training Center for Christian Mission (UTC) in 1965. COMMIT in Los Angeles, utilizing many of the same forms of organizing and training as the Chicago center, was established by six Protestant denominations in 1968. Speed Leas was chosen to be the director. He moved into that position from serving as pastor at the Immanuel United Church of Christ in Watts. He made a plan and put together a small staff to begin work. He invited me to serve as director of theological training. Speed and I had just completed our month of training in Chicago at UTC.

Exploring Black Pluralism at the Chicago Urban Training Center

Four UCC clergy doing urban and campus work had decided together to go to the Chicago Urban Training Center (UTC) in 1968 for the month of October. Our team was: Tom, Speed, Al, and me. The UTC staff curated a mix of about thirty-five persons for each monthlong training session. They looked at who has registered based on public announcement of a session and recruited others to enrich the mix.

Because our group was four white clergy from Los Angeles, the UTC staff invited an emerging Black nationalist leader in Southern California, Maulana Ron Karenga, a professor of Black Studies at Cal State Long Beach and the creator of Kwanzaa, a Pan-African holiday. Three followers of Karenga accompanied him. The UTC staff also recruited three leaders of Dr. King's Southern Christian Leadership Conference to attend: the Rev. Fred Shuttlesworth, the Rev. C. T. Vivian, and the Rev. James Bevel.

The UTC class of the fall of 1968 experienced a three-way conversation for the month: white liberals; Black movement leaders with a non-violent, integration perspective; and a Black separatist movement seeking a vibrant

Black community with its own culture. Since the agenda became the desired future of Black people, we white liberals were spectators, without much of a voice or relevant ideas to contribute. Feeling the depth of these clashing visions of the future, the emotional strength of all the debaters carried many lessons for me. Many of our discussions over those four weeks were arguments between Karenga and the SCLC men. Much of the discussion was about the vision of an integrated society or the vision of a new cultural identity for Black people without relying on white approval. We also debated the efficacy of nonviolence and social change. The program offered exposure to city planners, poor people's organizations, police, the mayor's office, and leaders of several anti-poverty programs as well as, importantly, theological lectures and discussions about ministry to and for the sake of the city. We were given training in community organizing, planned social change, and community power analysis.

Surviving on the Streets of Chicago

The month in Chicago started with a five-day urban plunge. Each of us, operating alone, without money or identification, had to live five days and four nights on the streets of Chicago. This was an immersion experience that exposed us to a brief life without a place to sleep or food to eat or money to purchase them. We were for this brief time homeless and hungry. We had to deal with other people looking for food and a place to sleep. We had to look out for the police and whatever situation came to us. Amazing how few life skills I had to cope with all this.

October 1968 was rainy and cold in Chicago, which made our venture more uncomfortable. I specifically remember the first day at evening commuting time. I was standing on a corner in the Loop in a cold drizzle at the end of the workday. I was not sure where to go for shelter. A big Mercedes turned the corner and drove through a big puddle splashing me head to toe. I saw that guy in his dry business suit, the heater keeping him warm, on his way home. I hated him.

At that time my brother, Karl, was a stockbroker for a large brokerage on Michigan Avenue in the Loop. Having no plan for my wandering the streets of Chicago, I decided to walk by the building where the brokerage was located. Through the large front windows on the street level, I saw a room half the size of a football field with desks lined up in long, straight rows. Brokers were on their telephones. I decided to walk in. The building receptionist, a large, burly man, looked me over. I was amazingly unkempt for only three days and nights on the street. He asked my business. I told him I wanted to say hello to my brother. Karl had no idea I was in town. The burly man sent a messenger and Karl came out and was clearly stunned at my appearance. I told him what I was doing, and he invited me to follow him to his desk which was the front desk in the third row. So, I followed him walking to the front of the room, hundreds of phone calls on pause, many eyes following, and sat, as he indicated, on the chair next to his desk. Karl's best friend there came over at Karl's signal and I was asked to say again what I was doing on the streets of Chicago. Other brokers, bored with their cold calling trying to sell, gathered around. They could not believe somebody would choose to do what I was doing. I held them enthralled. What a great moment of prophetic challenge. After maybe twenty minutes Karl said I'd better go, so we walked back to the rear, and I wandered off down the street. That was a clear violation of the rules of the immersion but clearly a moment I treasure. I turned down offers to give me some money. I believed I had slowed down trading on the stock exchange for a few seconds anyway.

A half hour later crowds were gathering along the sidewalks on Michigan Avenue. I was told it was Columbus Day, a big day for the Italians in town. And there was a parade coming down the street. So, I watched. One band evoked tears. They were playing the song "Georgie Girl." It was a song my daughter, Annie, and I sang. She was eight at the time and I missed her.

I was frightened most of the time.

The first night I found shelter by locating an unlocked window in a church. I slept on the floor in the nursery. I stayed in an all-night movie house another night. And another person on the UTC plunge, who was a community organizer in Chicago, invited me to stay with her at her small apartment on the Near North Side. That was a violation of the rules but a welcome invitation.

Granted, during the plunge in Chicago, I knew it would mercifully end if I could just make through those five days and four nights. To that extent it was play acting, but it did not feel like play acting for those days. I still had to find places to sleep, to find shelter from rain and cold, to experience firsthand the powerlessness and frustration of poverty. I knew that jail would provide some warmth and food but I'm claustrophobic and was not eager to be locked up.

As the members of the October 1968 class straggled into the old church where the UTC was doing its work, home from our days and nights as homeless vagrants, we felt great relief and were eager to tell our stories, to eat and drink, to get a shower and find dry clothes, and to sleep. But we all knew that we had been voluntary visitors to homelessness and the others we saw, with whom we spent time in the shelter and on the street, were not voluntary visitors. It was life for them now. They remain in the corners of my memory. We had lots to discuss upon return to the center and these discussions led to a hunger to understand a lot that we didn't understand about the city. That plunge set us up for all the work they had in store for us as we deepened our understanding of why and how the city functioned and what the church's role was.

I found a small sense of satisfaction that I was able to navigate that time on the street. I remembered reading somewhere that some portion of the homeless population had chosen street life even when more comfortable and safe options were available. I thought about that. There was a sense of freedom that is unique. One lived entirely in the moment. The past was without meaning. The future was too far away. There was only now and several essential questions: shelter for tonight, food now, safety from predators. No car payments, insurance, taxes, bank accounts, mortgages, gutters to clean, no people to worry about or care for, no timecards to punch, no clients to sell sure-to-yield stocks to. Just me, now. Looking for food, safety, a place to sleep. That was it. Not complicated. I was very glad to return to Los Angeles and my new appointment at COMMIT.

Educating Organizers to Lead Social Change

One reason that I was very happy to accept Speed's invitation to join this staff was that I would be able to use my Pacoima experiences to help shape a training curriculum and experiences for other ministers who had a passion to become urban ministry specialists. Our offices and classrooms were on the fourth floor of the United University Church (Presbyterian and Methodist) on the northern edge of the campus of the University of Southern California. My office window provided a clear view of the USC football practice field.

The six years at COMMIT were rich and full of opportunity for me to focus full-time on the social change work for which I had passion. Most of what we were doing was inventing or adapting theory and skills into social change praxis for the church. COMMIT was like an advanced urban studies department of a college. However, unlike a college department, it was a stand-alone organization, supported by grants from denominations, foundations, and fee-for-service consulting.

The board members were representatives of the supporting denominations and faculty from several seminaries. We had a multidiscipline, multiracial staff of women and men who offered a catalog of workshops and consulting services focused on skill-building for community change. Our clients were clergy, lay leaders, congregations, denominational staff, and occasional nonreligious groups. We offered a course in urban problems in the catalogs of three seminaries in Southern California: Fuller Seminary, the American Baptist Seminary of the West in Covina, and the Claremont School of Theology.

Pedagogy: Action Reflection Training

It's easier to act your way into a new way of thinking than think your way into a new way of acting. So goes the slogan of action training and of the plunge or immersion education.

COMMIT offered a curriculum which utilized a method of learning, a pedagogy which is called "action training," based in part on the educational theory of Paolo Freire, the Brazilian educator.[1] He called it praxis. This form of education was a direct challenge to the ways our schooling had been organized all our lives, which was to study an issue or topic, then act. Praxis puts action first.

We helped students learn by immersion experience and reflection on the experience. To help understand poverty, we put students in the hands of the staff of Operation Bootstrap, a self-help project doing job training for men on the streets of Watts. The program had a good record of working with at-risk youth, members of gangs, and those affected by incarceration. Our trainees met with participants in the Bootstrap program who shared their experiences of how racism and poverty had affected their lives. We would spend a couple hours listening to the anger and threats in the stories being told.

These men shared many righteous grievances with feeling, passion, and with anger often directed at white people in general and those in the room as representatives. The people in our group, seminary students and men and women from the suburbs, had a lot of emotional and intellectual material to process at the end of these immersions. That was my work, helping them do theological reflection on that experience. The learning came out of the experience. I would sometimes ask if students experienced the risen Christ on these streets in these confrontations. There were lots of great questions to consider. The learning came from harvesting the meaning of the various experiences of the immersion.

We had specific assignments for groups. For example, it was helpful to know who the most influential persons were in that part of town. We helped participants do a power analysis in a community. We defined a key twenty square blocks in Boyle Heights and gave the assignment of researching who

1. Freire, *Pedagogy*.

were the ten most influential people in these twenty square blocks. The research was done by walking the streets and asking at least twenty-five people
who were the ten most influential people in that area. At the end of the
interview process the next step was to collate the responses and rank the
most often mentioned people.

A member of the COMMIT board, Joseph Hough, ethics professor at
the Claremont School of Theology, volunteered to try out this assignment
to see what his students might experience. He had difficulty getting people
to talk with him. Boyle Heights at this point included a sizable barrio. Joe
didn't speak Spanish. And he wore a white shirt, tie, and sport coat. People
on the street backed away fast when he asked the questions in the assignment. One helpful man at a barbershop on the second day said the word was
out on the street that an FBI agent was gathering names for a gang bust. Joe
saw quickly how his presence in that neighborhood was experienced by the
community. His first effort failed to complete the assignment.

So, with this new information from his first effort, how might he complete the assignment? One idea was to go back to the man at the barbershop
and recruit his assistance to spread word in the community or, even better,
to have him accompany Joe's walking tour helping to translate and authenti-
cate his presence. But how would Joe persuade this man to give this help and
to risk his reputation in the community? There were all kinds of problems
to solve, each of which, success or failure, would yield valuable insight and
learning. These are examples of some forms of action training.

Joe Hough published his research on white racism in *Black Power
and White Protestants*.[2] He then received a major grant from the Cummins
Engine Foundation to select, train, and deploy pairs of seminarians in congregations to develop anti-racism programs. COMMIT was awarded the
contract to provide the training for the students.

Students were selected from several seminaries. We organized a
strenuous urban plunge in Los Angeles, with abundant time for storytelling and the claiming of new truths because of the immersion. We offered
them the planning tools and responded to their requests for skill training.
We used many community leaders from the ghetto and the barrio to help
them deepen their understanding of their own racism and how they were
likely to be seen in Black and Brown communities. And we took them to
Cuernavaca, Mexico, where I had studied the year before. For a month they
participated in various courses and lectures offered by the Centro Intercul-
tural de Documentación (CIDOC) and in the workshops we offered. For

2. Hough, *Black Power*.

us, one of the most important values was for these students to experience themselves as outsiders in unfamiliar dominant culture.

To this day there is still a thriving social service agency in Ventura, California, that was begun by the two students with a group of churches. Project Understanding/Ventura now provides a food pantry, housing, contact and location services, and tutoring. Most of the students had important experiences both in the successes of their work and in the failures.

The foundation found this pilot project sufficiently successful to fund several more years of this model.

Training Community Organizers

Frederick Herzog argued that capacity building for the church's public ministry is a response to liberation theology, to the challenge raised that no theology can be considered Christian if it does not consider the poor central to our reality.[3] Becoming a justice church was fundamental to our faithfulness. The urban training centers were providing capacity for the church to respond faithfully. Our task was to provide experiences and powerful reflection that leads to inclusion of the poor on the personal and institutional agendas for those who see themselves as followers of Jesus.

When the Action Training Coalition met in Southern California, we moved two days of our meeting to La Paz, the headquarters of the United Farm Workers Union. We had some extended conversation with Cesar Chavez. The influential Brazilian educator, Paulo Freire, was in California. We invited him to join us. He and Cesar discussed the methods of empowering poor.

COMMIT employed several community organizers to teach and to lead organizing projects around the region. Rosalio Muñoz was a Chicano activist who is most recognized for his anti-war and anti-police brutality organizing with the Chicano Moratorium against the Vietnam War. Cliff Jones was an organizer in South Central Los Angeles with connections with many leaders in that community. Arturo Holguin had community organizing experience in the San Fernando Valley and focused his work in East LA.

The goal of our community organizing was to build the power and capacity of low-income people, especially low-income people of color, to change the policies and institutions that impact their lives. The skills for this work were part of our core curriculum.

After the immersion experience came the program development phase of our training. As with a variety of other issues we moved at this point to

3. Herzog, *Justice Church*, 21.

a rational planning process which required members of the group to make some decisions about what they intended to do about racism because of their new understandings.

For example, when we worked with a local church over the course of several weekends, we would invite discussion about the various elements where white racism is lodged: within human personality and value systems; within the culture such as films or TV; in the various institutions that operate in our social lives like the police, the school system, and the public library; and in national tax policy or the Food Stamp Program. Racism exists in all these. The task was to choose where the church wanted to focus its efforts.

One helpful step was to analyze the problem and develop a problem statement. If the local school system became the place where the group found racism and chose to address it, we used a planning scheme that asked that the problem be focused by agreeing on who is doing what, to whom, when, and where. Was it a teacher, an administrator, the school board, a group of students? Was it a policy that needed to be changed? What was the specific behavior? Who were the victims of that behavior? When and where did it happen? Who might the helpers or allies be? Spending time defining the problem correctly was important. Eighty percent of the success in social change depends on a careful understanding of the problem.

The next step was defining a goal. What was the effort designed to accomplish? What would it look like upon completion?

There are many planning processes and trainers who can help a group put a plan together. This is a small example of what COMMIT offered in order to build up the capacity for the church in its mission in and for the city.

Conflict Management in the Church

As we gained experience in assisting congregations as they planned social mission projects, we also requested clergy do a better job in planning their own work as administrators and programmers. Speed and Connie had taken courses with the National Training Lab in Bethel, Maine. They adapted the curriculum materials for use with clergy. With this we were able to expand the programming at COMMIT to include management training for clergy.

We found many congregations in significant conflicts that paralyzed the church. Speed began conversations with several local college faculty who were teaching conflict management for corporate clients. We offered training in conflict management and employed the faculty to consult with deeply divided congregations through a weekend of conflict training.

Speed is the most straight up, trustworthy friend I've had. We shared in each other's divorces and remarriages, accompanied each other in figuring out how to best blend families, and we traveled many miles together by freeway and by air to locations to do training programs for a wide variety of clients: local churches seeking to manage major conflict, denominational staff seeking clarity of mission and strategy, white people seeking racism awareness, Black groups seeking empowerment, and many more. When Speed moved to his new position in Bloomfield Hills, Michigan, the family moved from the inner city of Los Angeles to a farm in Michigan. Connie was seeking farm experience, a cow to milk, a grove of peach trees to tend, chickens for fresh eggs, and kneading dough for making bread every day on the wood fired stove. I spent time with them in both places. On one visit to the farm, I helped Speed put a new roof on a section of the house and another visit, I thankfully arrived a day late for watching Speed dig out the septic tank. He probably would have asked me to help.

Regarding conflict management training, I always started with the notion that most people feel that if conflict breaks out in their family or a group to which they belong, it is a sign of failure and breakdown. We found that was not universally true. It was sometimes true but there were other ways of thinking about it. Given our eagerness for diversity in life, it was no wonder that there were a variety of perspectives on almost any topic. Take the simple example of repainting the women's fellowship room. Would you not expect conflict here? For example, conflict over the color. How would such a conflict be resolved? Would the minister have final word? Would the chair of the fellowship make the decision? Would it be the board? Would a consultant be hired to come in to say what the right color is? Would it be put to a vote of all the members? Would that be a majority vote? Or would everyone finally have to agree before the decision would be made? Would people get proxy votes if they wouldn't attend? Would the person with the loudest voice or who was willing to give the most money get to decide?

As Speed began his introductory lecture on conflict, he said that the word "decide" is from Latin. The word *cide* is to cut. "Homicide" is "to cut a man." "Suicide" means "to cut yourself." "Decide" means "to cut off." The purpose of a decision is to end the debate or discussion and choose to move on in the direction chosen. *Robert's Rules of Order* is a conflict management decision process.[4] There are others.

I remember one late evening Speed and I were driving back to Los Angeles from San Diego along the old Highway 395. We had completed the second weekend workshop with a church that had been tied up in a

4. Robert et al., *Robert's Rules.*

massive conflict that promised to split the church. The church leaders felt there was enough desire to prevent that split that they were willing to pay the cost of two consultants for two weekends to work at saving the church. It was hard work. The exercises and process we led them through broke down divisions, led to widening the field of vision on both sides, put everyone through defining the problems according to guidelines we provided, and eventually helped them to enter a collaborative problem-solving process to define goals and objectives for the next six months. It had gone well, enough so for us to feel a sense of satisfaction as we headed north. We did a lot of debriefing of our work on the ride home, to learn from our errors and our successes. Speed was a skilled and effective consultant, not taking sides, not giving answers, but carefully guiding people along the way to a hoped-for resolution. I felt like I was a good helper. We together made a good team. I'm very glad I had this experience and am relatively comfortable when people care enough about our life together to raise hard questions or alternate points of view.

Speed expressed basic satisfaction with our conflict management effort in San Diego. I too felt satisfaction except I came in touch with another feeling. I felt that one side of the division in the church was right and the other wide was wrong! As we drove north, I felt the urge to go back and help the right side win the argument. While being able to function as consultant, at heart I was really an advocate. I often agreed with one side and wanted to help them win. Not a good attitude for a consultant.

I was a much better fit in my anti-war work. From 1970 to 1974 I had a three-quarter time contract with Clergy and Laity Concerned About Vietnam (CALC) to work against the Vietnam War.

CIDOC in Cuernavaca, Mexico: Experience Being an Outsider

After working in the Pacoima community for a year or so, I realized that I had a small sense of connection to the lives of the Black residents going back to my St. Louis experience. But I was totally lost in ignorance with the Latino, mostly Mexican, population. I did not know the languages, the culture, the aspirations, the holidays, or the national heroes. I was clueless. So, I decided to travel to Cuernavaca, Mexico, to study Spanish and culture in Latin America at CIDOC.

Ivan Illich, cofounder of the school, wrote that the intention of the school was to counteract a papal command of 1960 which enjoined US and Canadian religious superiors to send 10 percent of their priests and nuns to South America. Illich was convinced that this project would do more harm than good. He intended that CIDOC would serve as a training station for such clergy and development workers, aiming to educate them about the negative effects of their development and education agenda. The school also offered Spanish language courses.

Genie and I spent a month in this program. We did the intensive language course and much of the of the program presenting the wider political, historical, and economic context in Latin America. Illich made clear that there were liberation forces at work among the poor all throughout Latin America. He wanted church and development workers to be supportive of the bottom-up movements in the cities and the countryside.

A month before we were to depart for our family's long drive to Cuernavaca, Genie and I were invited to a supper with Illich in the Long Beach apartment of Norm and Nan Self, campus ministers at California State University. He was to deliver a lecture sponsored by the campus ministry at Cal State Long Beach. We had lots of questions.

We told him that we planned to extend our journey by driving from Cuernavaca south down the Pan-American Highway to Oaxaca for a four-day visit, and on south through the Mexican state of Chiapas, into Guatemala and to the capital, Guatemala City.

Our only reason for the last destination was that we had met at a party in Woodland Hills an au pair, Maria, a high school student from Guatemala City. When we said we'd be in central Mexico she suggested that we drive down to Guatemala and meet her family. Why not? If we were on the adventure road, we might as well keep going. It was 1,900 miles driving from LA to Cuernavaca and another 1,500 miles more to Guatemala City. Same distances home.

Genie asked Illich at the dinner about the rumors of left-wing revolutionary forces at war with the army in northern Guatemala. She asked whether we might at some point drive up to meet them. Illich smiled and encouraged her to have the courage to be a good tourist.

It took a good equal amount of bravery, self-confidence, and naivete to move around in adventures like this. Especially it was problematic to do these things with three elementary school–age children. At the time I found myself convinced that I could handle whatever the journey put in our path. I was just that confident. I am a little in awe of all that when I look back on it. My kids were six, eight, and ten.

Our first evening in Oaxaca we walked to the *zocalo* to find dinner. We looked around and saw nothing familiar until someone saw a small shop that advertised pizza. With a great sense of relief, we headed straight to it. Looking at the menu we recognized no words except pizza. I pointed and held up one finger. Coca Cola? I held up five fingers. What I learned was that the pizza I pointed to, and which was placed before us on the table, was eel pizza. It looked terrifying but when starving, one is less choosy.

The first moon landing, July 20, 1969, occurred while we were in Cuernavaca. With other members of our host family, we watched on a small black and white TV. We could hear Walter Cronkite's voice narrating but drowning out his narration were Spanish speaking scientists making their own commentary. All of us were thrilled with the story.

We did find Maria's home and met her family in Guatemala City. My kids gave their American football to Maria's brothers. We got a *balón de fútbol* in return. We stayed two nights in a massive old Colonial Hotel. Our sleep was interrupted by the sound of machine gun fire. At breakfast at the hotel nobody seemed to know what was going on. They also didn't seem to care, or they didn't want to talk to us about it.

As good tourists, we visited the spectacular Lake Atitlán, one of the world's most beautiful lakes that lies at five thousand foot elevation. It is surrounded by volcanos of twelve thousand and thirteen thousand feet all around the lake. These were Sierra Madre mountains like we've never seen before. And we spent time in the markets in several remote villages including the one in Chichicastenango. Some of the time while Genie and the kids wandered the market, I would find a place off to the side to photograph the scene. I had a great long lens on my thirty-five millimeter camera. I could fill the view finder with a face one hundred yards away with a beautiful, sharp image.

Of course, we did not know until we got there that two sections of the Pan-American Highway in Guatemala were not paved. The highway had been cut through the ragged mountains. In two sections, there were boulders the size of our car rolling down the steep hillside picking up speed until they rolled across the road. Seemed like this happened every few minutes. They could have crushed our VW. The skill was looking up where the boulders were when they are starting their roll and timing my dash down the road before or after the boulder rolled across. One was a mile-long section and there was a lot of stop-and-go timing between rolling boulders. They were rolling as we drove south and still rolling as we were coming back north. We were careful and managed to get through those stretches of highway unharmed.

Coming back through southern Mexico, we were hit by a very powerful rainstorm. Small rivers turned into torrents. They were dangerous. We came to a small earth-packed bridge over an angry stream. By the time we arrived, the flooding stream had begun washing out the Pan-American Highway's one-lane bridge. Campesinos stood by helplessly and watched their bridge being washed away.

After some quick map-work I figured out that if I could not get my family and car across this bridge before it washed out completely, it would take at least six days to go back to a cutoff and journey another more eastern route along the eastern shore by the Gulf of Mexico to get home. My sense of challenge arose and took over decision making. I told Genie and the kids to get out and run across the bridge as fast as they could as some villagers were doing. Then I backed the VW up, threw it into first gear, spun the tires throwing dirt in a fan behind me, and drove the car as fast as it could across the remaining single lane.

We made it. After the crossing I got out of the car and stood in the drenching rain and more fully realized just how dangerous it was to trust we could run and drive across it. There were some cheers by those watching.

My world view was challenged and changed by the experience of study at CIDOC and the auto travel through Mexico and into Guatemala. I found I was again a naive American liberal with not a clue about the world—the world as experienced by people who were poor and living in the southern reaches of the central Americas. My respect for our country, already at a low level because of the Vietnam War and increasing rates of poverty, was made even lower. We had heard lectures and conversations about the United Fruit Company exploitation of the poor and indigenous people on the banana plantations and about the coup d'état orchestrated by the US State Department and CIA removing the democratically elected socialist president Jacobo Arbenz of Guatemala in 1954. At CIDOC there were two men who had been in the Arbenz government and several who were in the forces opposing the imposed military government. These sources and eyewitnesses helped me see new truth about the US and its interests.

We visited historical places to learn the significance of what happened there. We stood in ruins of the house in Anenecuilco, Morelos, where Emiliano Zapata was born in 1879. At the entrance to the church in Dolores, Mexico, we heard the story of El Grito de Dolores (the Cry of Dolores), which occurred on September 16, 1810. On that day, Roman Catholic priest Miguel Hidalgo y Costilla rang his church bell and gave the call to arms that triggered the Mexican War of Independence. It explained why every city and village in Mexico has a Dieciséis de Septiembre Street.

Cinco de Mayo, widely celebrated because it's a good day to drink margaritas back home, is an annual celebration held on May 5 to observe the commemoration of the Mexican army's victory over the French Empire at the Battle of Puebla on May 5, 1862, under the leadership of General Ignacio Zaragoza. And I feel I had at least a small grasp of the amalgam of Christian and Indigenous beliefs shaping Dia de Los Muertos, the Day of the Dead.

We visited the beautiful colonial city of Puebla because that's where the Volkswagen assembly plant is and where I had work done on our car.

This venture gave me so much background for better understanding our Pacoima neighbors. I affirmed I am terrible at language other than English. This was true with German in high school and college and now with Spanish in Mexico. Genie was good at formulating sentences to contribute to the conversation such as it was. I had a better ear for distinguishing sounds and words. I got what they said to us. She responded, which was helpful in many situations.

Note on Writing Inclusively

Speed and I wrote two books together, bringing our different perspectives into harmony.[5] I'm a storyteller. Speed understands how parts interact, the technology. On his own he studied and became skilled at watch repair and TV technology. In retirement he's taking an online course on programming, wanting to build a database. In the chapters of our book projects, they read as if you could repair a church like you could repair a watch. Look for symptoms. If you have symptom A, turn to chapter 7 for instructions on how to make the repair. My job was to find stories that illustrated the steps. My chapters were stories end to end. He had to find the critical path through them, the steps that lead to solving the issues.

Speed and I committed ourselves to write *Church Fights* with inclusive language and by including stories where the minister was a woman. This was new to us, and we both found that we had not yet learned to think and speak inclusively, so it blocked our writing. To make any progress on a book we thought would be helpful in the life of the church, we decided to write without barriers just to get a first draft done in a timely way. When we had that done, we hired a woman, an outspoken and well-known feminist, to edit the book to make it read smoothly and inclusively. She did a great job, and in the acknowledgements, we wrote a generous word of thanks to her for the work she did for us.

The book went off to the publisher. With no experience nor commitment to inclusive writing, the copyeditor rewrote it back to all male-centric language and illustrations. They set the plates to print and sent us copies of the galley proofs. When we blew up over the reediting of the book, they said they'd be glad to reset the type, but it would delay publishing three months and cost several hundred dollars. We had no grant for the project, worked on our own time, and were barely making it on the salary of an underfunded

5. Leas and Kittlaus, *Church Fights* and *Pastoral Counselor in Social Action*.

church agency. No way could we find those funds. We both were moving on to new jobs and had no time to further fight so we gave up and told them to print it. Of course, we did not remember to delete our gracious thanks for the editor who worked hard to create the inclusive style of the book. When the book came out, it was greeted with great enthusiasm around the church and in seminaries. But our editor saw herself being thanked for the thoroughly sexist language in the book. We apologized and shared the story but that did not heal the hurt and embarrassment. She never spoke to us again. Can't say I blame her.

In 1973 Speed was invited to join the staff of the Institute for Advanced Pastoral Studies in Bloomfield Hills, Michigan. It was a significant opportunity and he accepted it. I served as executive director at COMMIT after his departure and pursued opportunities for social action advocacy work. Funding from the denominations began to dry up and I could see that specialized ministries like COMMIT did not have a sustainable future.

Chapter 7

Organizing Against the War in Vietnam 1970–1974

CLERGY AND LAITY CONCERNED (CALC) was a loosely connected network of about fifty religious based anti-war chapters around the country plus a New York national office. It was the primary vehicle for church leaders to express their opposition to the war. CALC had the capacity to bring several hundred thousand people from the religious community to Washington for demonstrations.

Local and regional groups were autonomous and did their own fundraising. The national office organized events often in Washington and joined national coalitions in support of demonstrations. It invited local chapters to participate, and it provided resources for use by the chapters. My task was to organize within the religious community in Southern California to oppose the war in Vietnam. I also served as West Coast field organizer in support of groups from Denver to the West Coast.

It may be difficult for readers to imagine the conditions in the church and society in which the peace movements worked. The war in Vietnam continued to divide the institutions society normally relied on to provide stability: the family and home, the church and university, the business community, the government, and civil society. If the reader has not experienced this turmoil, my account may seem weird. The sense of crisis, desperation, and division that led some to set themselves on fire, to face a lifetime in prison, to plant bombs in the restrooms of the US Capitol, and to live out their lives in Canada and elsewhere are rehearsed in reading and watching available resources.[1]

The Organizing of a Religious Based Anti-War Strategy, January 1966

The push to begin an organization to mobilize clergy and laity in an anti-war movement began with a call by the Rev. Dr. William Sloane Coffin Jr., chaplain at Yale University, speaking in New York at a press conference in January 1966. He publicly announced the formation of the National Emergency Committee of Clergy Concerned About Vietnam. This was largely a New York–based group, and it organized impressive demonstrations in New York with groups around the country following their lead. They helped plan and publicize the International Days of Protest for October 15–16 which attracted one hundred thousand people in sixty American cities and over a dozen foreign countries. Encouraged by success in local activities, the New York emergency committee began to discuss the possibility of expanding the New York group into a national organization. Several clergy met in the Union Theological Seminary apartment of President John C. Bennett. A formal leadership group was formed, statements about the war were drafted, and calls went out across the nation for clergy to mobilize their congregations around support for an indefinite bombing halt and negotiated settlement.

The continuing positive responses to their effort led to the employment of an executive director. In May 1966, the Rev. Richard R. Fernandez, former campus minister at the University of Pennsylvania, began work. The organization's name was changed to Clergy and Laymen Concerned About Vietnam (CALCAV), and a couple years later to "Laity" and shortened to CALC.

In January 1967 CALC announced a mobilization of religious groups to take place in Washington, DC. This was the second mobilization for the organization. The event convened at the New York Avenue Presbyterian Church in a worship service presided over by Coffin. Several of my anti-war friends and I flew from the LAX to Washington, DC. Two thousand people attended the event.

I was asked by Fernandez to read the Old Testament text in the service. The text was Isa 2:4: "He shall judge between the nations, and shall arbitrate

---

1. There are many accounts of the war available including Ken Burns's PBS series, which provides little coverage of the peace movement, and films such as *The Movement and the Madman* and *The Boys Who Said No.*

for many peoples; they shall beat their swords into plowshares, and their spears into pruning hooks; nation shall not lift up sword against nation, neither shall they learn war anymore."

It was an energetic, overflowing crowd. For many of us it was the first time to be in an anti-war crowd that large and noisy. Many were not church people. Almost all were against the war. It was standing room only. The pews, aisles, and stairs were filled. When the time came for the reading of the Isaiah lesson, I stood at a microphone on the right side of the chancel. I began to read. Suddenly a young man walked up next to me and started yelling. I wondered what was happening and what I should do. It was clearly an effort to disrupt the service. I held the microphone in one hand and the Bible in the other. I decided to keep reading and he kept yelling. When I came to the end of Isa 2:4, he was still yelling. So, I read verse five and then verse six. I thought to myself that there was a lot of Bible to go and I'm up for continuing to read all twenty-two verses of that chapter and further until the guy quit yelling.

No one moved to take him off the stage. It was a moment of uncertainty. I kept reading. Finally, the crowd caught on to what I was doing and started applauding, then rose to their feet in applause. The yeller quit. He had no plan for what would happen if the reader did not yield. He slumped off stage. Coffin explained to the crowd that the right-wing, pro-war fundamentalist minister, the Rev. Carl McIntire, and a group of fifteen followers had come to Washington to disrupt the CALC gathering. Coffin said we should give McIntire "all the respect he deserves." That was a mixed message. Coffin invited McIntire to come forward and share his views, which at this point were primarily about obeying the law and being patriotic. Coffin asked McIntire why St. Paul was in and out of the pokey so often. The disruption collapsed.

Mine was a tiny contribution at that point, but it is fun for me to vastly exaggerate the scene and turn the story into a Homeric epic with me as Odysseus. I had stood alone at the point of a battle between the fundamentalist and the progressive armies. I held my ground, and the battle (if not the war) was won. We may all have our fantasies of heroic victories. This is mine. Talk about mythic immensity! I went back to Los Angeles feeling I'd helped.

On June 23, 1967, a massive demonstration was held in front of the Century Plaza Hotel where President Johnson was to stay on his way back from a visit to Vietnam. He was to speak to Democratic Party leaders to raise money. Five hundred US military were dying each month and 40 percent of the American population still believed in sending more to fight in Vietnam.

A loud ten thousand protestors came to the street that night. The police captain had estimated one to two thousand would show. The police made up for their lack of proper preparation by violence against American citizens practicing a constitutional right. Fifty-five were arrested and scores hospitalized. The *Los Angeles Times* headline called it a police riot. This was a year before the police riot around the Democratic Convention in Chicago.

Scale Paralysis

When we tried to imagine what we possibly could do to stop this war, we felt helpless. We had already written to our representatives and senators and to the White House. We had signed petitions galore. The power was way out of balance. Every night on CBS the trusted news anchor Walter Cronkite told us of the waves of bombers and the numbers of deaths.

The war makers were so powerful, and the range of our power was so tiny that we were convincingly powerless. I saw it as a problem of scale. The scale of our power was so small, compared to administration and military, that we felt paralyzed. I named it "scale paralysis."

The Ann Arbor Conference 1971: Seeking to Organize a National Movement

A phone call came one evening in late May 1971. I had just spent the last two days in a peace march to the Federal Building in Los Angeles. The caller was Dick Fernandez, director of CALC in New York. I had seen him in operation at the Washington religious mobilization. He was calling at the recommendation of Bob Bonthius. Him I knew. Bonthius was director of the urban training center in Cleveland, Ohio. We had become friends at Action Training Network meetings.

Dick said that CALC needed help planning a national conference in Ann Arbor, Michigan, scheduled for August 17–22, 1971. Bonthius had said he would be glad to help with that task if Fernandez could persuade me to join him as a coleader. Dick said it would be at our usual hourly rate plus expenses. I agreed. But it was not about the money. It was about using my organizing skill to strengthen anti-war efforts and to experience a greater scale of power, helping diminish my sense of scale paralysis.

A few days later I sat on my front porch in a phone conversation with CALC staff in eight cities around the country. I was moving through levels of scale. From the streets of Pacoima to the whole of Southern California. This was an invitation to move to a national scale operation. I was becoming part of something that was way bigger than my small personal power, something that felt almost as large as the problem we wanted to solve through political means: ending the war. It was my first conference phone call, and I already experienced this sense of expanded range of influence.

Bonthius and I clarified on phone calls our purposes and roles and what planning system we would use as consultants. We led three conference phone calls with the NY-CALC conference planning committee. The staff had not been introduced to a rational planning process before. Usually, Dick made the decisions or a group brainstormed for hours until everyone caved into an idea.

The purpose of the Ann Arbor conference was for CALC to evaluate its effectiveness in reaching the religious community, establish program priorities on both national and local levels, and develop a long-range strategy for pursuing social change.[2] To publicize the conference, ten members of the national and field staffs visited forty-two cities in thirty-two states and paid advertising was placed in several national magazines.

Over four hundred people from more than forty states attended the Ann Arbor conference. Half of them were not affiliated with CALC.

The program consisted of small discussion groups on issues ranging from war crimes to electoral politics to amnesty, action training sessions that demonstrated organizing techniques and tools, evening services of worship, and celebration. Speakers such as Harvey Cox, William Sloane Coffin Jr., and others helped focus our minds on our moral responsibilities. Dave Dellinger of the Peoples Coalition for Peace and Justice and Fred Branfman of Project Air War addressed perceptions that the war was ending as well as the topics of US covert wars and economic justice. Several ideas were generated and several of them were used by national staff for programming. The plan of the conference was to ratify two major campaigns that CALC at all levels would cooperate on.

Stopping the Makers of Cluster Bombs: The Honeywell Campaign

The question for anti-war organizers was how now to stimulate alarm and energy for protest to end the war. As President Nixon withdrew American troops from Vietnam, he began a major bombing campaign. The American public was relieved to have their sons and daughters in uniform coming home. And the US military was happy to have another form of waging war that kept most of its continuing troops out of harm's way. No more daily body counts. No more photos of death and agony of American troops.

2. Hall, *Because of Their Faith.*

CALC considered the anti-air war program, but it was abstract and didn't grab a person's alarm in the same way.

Bonthius and I led an exercise of strategic planning for the National Steering Committee. We were looking for an enemy close at hand. How about the corporations that were making money off the war? We spent some time exploring that question and developed some criteria for choosing a corporation for our attention.

We wanted to choose a corporation for the focus of a new phase of anti-war campaigning. We wanted to present a new target for our anger and moral outrage, a corporation that could be credibly accused of acting immorally while using church invested funds, including pension funds, to make money from the war. One that had made and sold consumer items that could be boycotted.

We listed some obvious corporations and discussed them in terms of the criteria.

The winner was the Honeywell Corporation. Honeywell manufactured the cluster bombs used widely in the air war. The cluster bombs were clearly presented in a new slide show, *The Automated Battlefield*, which was in circulation among anti-war church groups around the country.[3] A cluster bomb is a form of air-dropped explosive weapon that releases or ejects smaller submunitions. Commonly, this is a cluster bomb that ejects explosive bomblets filled with metal shrapnel that scattered at explosive force, that are designed to injure or kill personnel. My image was that a cluster bomb was about the size of a bathtub and was filed with baseball size bomblets. One bomb after releasing the baseballs could spread burning shrapnel over the size of three football fields. Cluster bombs pose risks to civilians both during attacks and afterwards. Unexploded bomblets can kill or maim civilians and unintended targets.

The horror of the cluster bombs was hard to watch. The last several slides showed the American corporations that were involved in making money for stockholders by manufacturing the weapons and technology in the slide show.

Honeywell, after some quick research, was found to be on the buy list for church investment strategies. My pension from the UCC was benefiting from the war through its investments in Honeywell. So, there was both a personal connection to the war and an opportunity for strategic action at the Honeywell shareholder meetings. And Honeywell manufactured a range of consumer photo equipment. I had a nice thirty-five millimeter Honeywell camera.

3. Prokosch, *Simple Art of Murder*.

I organized the picketing of the Lake Avenue camera store in Pasadena. I briefed the camera store manager that we were not seeking to boycott the store but to inform people about the connection of the Honeywell brand to the terrible weapons being used in the war. My sign indicated that the store sold many good thirty-five millimeter cameras in addition to Honeywell.

What had clinched the deal making Honeywell our corporate target was that 90 percent of congregations had Honeywell thermostats regulating their heating systems. A speaker could get to this point in a presentation, walk over to the wall of the fellowship hall, and slap an anti-Honeywell black ring on the wall around the thermostat right there in front of everyone. People asked for a personal supply of rings to be used at the office, the home, and other public places.

That conceptual decision made, the details of the various dimensions of this effort could be developed. The Honeywell Campaign was launched. It flourished. Anti-war people attended and spoke at shareholder meetings, picketed camera stores, and pasted anti-war signs on HVAC controllers in thousands of churches across the country After relentless pressure from groups across the country, Honeywell spun off its munitions development and manufacturing to a new corporation that Honeywell founded, United Technologies.

New York-CALC Staff Organizational Development

Another element in our contract as consultants was to take place immediately after the conference. With an increase of funding available, several new senior CALC staff had been to the conference. Bonthius and I were asked to lead an organizational development training session with the entire NY-CALC staff. Who was responsible for what, what teams within the staff would work together, who answered the phone, who took direction from whom, how were disputes resolved?

We spent a day observing and interviewing the CALC staff in their office. This was the picture we observed. All staff had desks in the same large room. In the center of the room was Dick's desk. It was round, clearly the center point of all creation in that space. Everyone was eager to know what he was thinking, planning, who he was talking to and about what. Dick is one of the most charismatic people I know. I want to know who he's talking to and about what even now fifty years later. His phone would ring, and everybody stopped to listen. Everyone assumed people who called him were important to the anti-war movement and to world peace. Everyone in the room drew meaning and energy from him.

The next day at a retreat center, Bonthius and I gave feedback on what we learned and observed and offered several models about a modest structuring of the staff. Of course, no one wanted not to sit close to Dick's desk, but we finally worked out a plan.

From that came some long conversation with Dick in which he asked me to take over the CALC work in Los Angeles and build a stronger organization. He also wanted me to be the western region contact person for national CALC in the area from Denver to the West Coast.

Organizing the Los Angeles-CALC Steering Committee

Dick wrote a letter to the incumbent LA-CALC director relieving him of his duties.

Since I was not well-known among many clergy I reached out to Bob Vogel, longtime and highly respected peace secretary of the American Friends Service Committee in Southern California. He agreed to help me build a good steering committee who could rally different cohorts of the religious community in the region and who could help fundraising for our work. Vogel saw the opportunity to enlarge peace and anti-war energy in the religious community in our part of the state.

The congregation that was doing the most active anti-war work was All Saints Episcopal Church in Pasadena. They had organized a Peace Operations Center in the church. The Rev. Dr. George Regas, the rector, had preached a series of sermons condemning the war. He was direct, clear, and forceful. And he offended parishioners. But he would not let them go. He pursued them, invited them to make their case for the war, and he would debate, discuss, inform, persuade, and listen to win them over, and he was largely successful. So, there was no doubt where All Saints stood on the war. There were lots of clergy who wanted Regas's freedom but were not willing or able to pay the price he was willing to pay to speak his understanding of the gospel and its relationship to the war and then to insist that people stay in relationship with him to pursue the truth of the matter.

Vogel and I visited Regas and presented him our proposal for building a region-wide, religious, community-based anti-war movement using All Saints as a base, holding our new steering committee meetings at his church. Regas was excited to support the plan personally and to make the church available. I had no mailing list, no phone tree, and little constituency.

Vogel and I made calls to fifty or so clergy over the next several weeks, adding names to the list of supporters, looking for talent we could use. The fact that Regas was on board helped a lot.

My responsibility as the new LA-CALC director was to organize a new steering committee. I invited the top three anti-war activists from each of the denominations plus faculty from the Claremont School of Theology (CST). Regas was chair. At our first meeting, which was held at All Saints Pasadena, there were twenty-one people present. After some personal introductions to get a feel for the scale and passion of this group, I gave a brief introduction to CALC its purpose and history. Since national CALC was committed to fund our initial organizing period, primarily for my salary and office expenses, the committee needed to agree on a plan to raise program money. The Rev. Buckner Coe, senior minister of the Claremont UCC, said we should each tithe to CALC. He didn't get support, so, in his usual stubborn way, he dug in saying he would block moving to any other agenda item until we agreed with him. It went on for a half hour. Dan Rhodes, professor of ethics at the Claremont School of Theology, finally leaned forward and looked Coe in the eye and said, "Buck, I gave you a ride from Claremont to Pasadena, the whole thirty miles. If you don't let us move on this agenda, don't trust us to develop a funding strategy, then I'm not driving you back to Claremont. You can walk!" Silence, laughter, the tension broke. Coe said, "OK, I'll trust we will be serious about our fundraising responsibility. I still think my plan is the best, but thirty miles is too far to walk."

I loved it. We were able from that point on to have hard conversation and debate. We were in it together and we all wanted to stop the damn war. We had differences about how to maximize our protest and we resolved the differences so we could move on together. And they were a wonderful fundraising team.

The next big break for building our LA-CALC organization came in a phone call from Dick. He told me that Coffin was in North Vietnam leading a CALC-organized delegation of church leaders from the US. Coffin had agreed to a speaking tour to report on his experience and views with CALC groups in three areas of the country.

Dick offered us four days the following month if I could find places for him to speak. That's a great way to build a constituency, to create a mailing and phone list. I did advance work setting up dates for Coffin to speak at churches and synagogues in the San Fernando Valley, in Claremont, in San Diego, and a couple places in Los Angeles. I booked him on three radio talk shows, one in San Diego. I offered Regas the opportunity to have Coffin preach on Sunday morning and again at the Sunday evening rock mass that All Saints hosted once a month. I agreed to the request from the Pasadena Presbyterian Church that Coffin would meet with clergy and lay leaders on Sunday afternoon.

It was so easy to set these up based on Coffin's reputation, but mostly because we would be his first stop in returning from North Vietnam with a delegation of American anti-war leaders. We would be hearing his first reports.

I had tried to set Coffin up at a nice hotel near where we lived in Pasadena, but he wanted to sleep on the couch at our home. Our daughter, Ann, started flute lessons before I left to drive Coffin to San Diego for a day and a half. When we returned to our home at dinner time, I was in the kitchen making drinks. I heard this soft, somewhat wobbly flute playing "Twinkle, Twinkle, Little Star" back in the living room. Daughter showing off for Dad. Suddenly our old piano sounded like the complete Los Angeles Philharmonic in accompaniment behind the lovely flute solo. Coffin had to get into the act.

Like a good organizer I took sign-up sheets to every one of the events where Coffin spoke and put them in the hands of people who were evangelical about collecting signatures and contact information. When I put Coffin on the plane for his next stop, I had the largest mailing list of any CALC chapter.

Serving on the New York-CALC National Steering Committee

While I was doing this regional organizing, I also flew to New York for regular meetings of the National CALC Steering Committee at New York Theological Seminary where the Rev. George W. "Bill" Webber was serving as president.

Since religious communities, liberal to conservative, are slow to act corporately, many members of the national and regional staff and clergy in local congregations were ready to act against the war long before the bureaucracies that employed them processed motions or declarations. That delay tied their hands. CALC was a parallel organization dedicated to ending the war. The denominational staff could express their personal commitments without having to wait for the resolution of massive, diverse church bodies. It was carefully noted on letterheads, pamphlets, and press releases that each person's denomination was "listed for identification purposes only" for the opportunity to work publicly against the war.

Webber served on the CALC Steering Committee, and the seminary provided meeting space, office space for National CALC, and single bedrooms for those of us who traveled into New York for the meeting. At our monthly meetings we worked to keep track of what was happening around the country with the affiliates, with diplomatic and peace group efforts to end the war. And many of the CALC programs were conceptualized here.

The organization began publishing a newspaper, *The American Report*, for general educational purposes and for sharing ideas and event news. Beginning in 1965, CALC called press conferences to support dissent, organized telephone calls across the country for a "Stop the Bombing" campaign, organized many national mobilizations in Washington and elsewhere, published several books, attended Dow Chemical stockholder meetings, planted seeds for the divestment campaigns, and organized a worship service at the National Cathedral at the time of the Mobilization. They set in motion a "Set the Date" campaign using the skills of many public relations volunteers and a follow-up "Unsell the War" campaign which ran TV commercials across the nation. On April 4, 1967, CALC organized the worship service at the Riverside Church in New York where the Rev. Dr. Martin Luther King Jr. gave his anti-war speech linking poverty and war as evils in America. In April 1972 CALC began the Honeywell Campaign.

The War: Turning Hearts and Minds

From the sixties through the nineties Bill Coffin was a force of political activism based in progressive theology. These are two of my Coffin stories.

During the four-day post-Vietnam-trip tour around Southern California, I experienced his speaking and preaching to overflowing churches and synagogues; his argumentation in small groups; his forceful presentation of facts, circumstances, and moral criteria for action for all those days; and his telling of funny and poignant stories. I came to realize that he had the persuasive power and charisma of an evangelist. I saw hard-line business leaders change their view on the war while listening to Coffin. These were moments of conversion, not just against the war but to lives reoriented to peace and justice. I know that may seem overstated, but it is what I saw.

On Sunday afternoon, after he had preached at All Saints Episcopal Church in Pasadena, I had arranged for him to meet with a men's group gathered by the Pasadena Presbyterian Church. About twenty-five men along with the pastor gathered in a large, expensively decorated apartment. The host was a woman active at the church. Her husband was not a believer. He hovered with a scotch-on-the-rocks back by the bar while Coffin sat on a footstool surrounded by the men and told his story. After describing his views of the war, he focused on the destruction and suffering from US bombing he had seen in the Vietnam cities and countryside. He described several small Baptist churches in the Vietnam countryside that had been bombed out. The men asked what they could do. Coffin thought for a moment, then challenged the men to act in contrition for all the death and destruction our country was pouring down on North Vietnam by paying for the rebuilding of these churches. At that time the Pasadena Presbyterian church was raising several million dollars to rebuild its own sanctuary which had been damaged by an earthquake. What an outrageous challenge amid a group of high-power, pro-war business leaders.

The host's nonbeliever husband back at the bar wiggled the ice in his glass and said, "By God, I'll pay for one of them."

Later I was given a sizable check from that nonbeliever and several others for rebuilding the churches.

After Coffin flew on to the next part of his speaking tour, I reflected on what I had witnessed and experienced. He was another person, like Regas, who was not satisfied with letting people hold their views but instead directly challenged them. Both were clear that some views about some matters were, in the light of the Christian faith, wrong and needed serious challenging. I was deeply impressed by the power of this man with a powerful speaking gift, his passion grounded in the Christian faith. I saw a possibility that might set off another great awakening in America.

I wrote a proposal that got surprisingly wide support among denominational leaders before it was crushed.

The Proposal: Billy Coffin, Evangelist

I called it "Billy Coffin, Evangelist." The paper was about four pages long and described the formation of an evangelism organizing team based on the Billy Graham model. The Coffin organization would do evangelistic campaigns in three major metropolitan regions a year, hold four-day campaigns in each city, and gather crowds in football stadiums, baseball stadiums, or in large indoor venues. There would be mass choirs from the progressive churches and monthlong door-to-door visitations throughout the region weeks prior to the events with volunteers from the progressive churches inviting everyone to attend. There would be an honorary sponsoring committee of denominational, business, and political leaders, and a permanent core staff which Dick Fernandez and I would lead.

Coffin's preaching at these mass events would conclude with a call to conversion to a new life as a follower of Jesus, to a life of feeding of the hungry, visiting prisoners, clothing the naked, and supporting widows, orphans, etc.

After my four days of watching and listening to Coffin on his return from Vietnam, I had not a single doubt in my mind that he and we could pull this off and that it would set a new course for Christianity in America. Sometimes I just want to change the world. I was full of it. This could do it.

Dick saw the possibilities immediately and elaborated the proposal. He approached top level denominational leaders to test out the idea with seasoned church leaders who could spot a loser of an idea fast. Within a week he got signatures of supporters and sponsors including the president of the National Council of Churches, the president of the United Church of Christ, the stated clerk of the Presbyterian Church, the presiding bishop of the Episcopal church, the head of the United Methodist Council of Bishops, and others.

Dick sent Coffin the proposal. After two days Coffin invited Dick and me to come New Haven to discuss the proposal. I felt we had accomplished the biggest step. Coffin had read the proposal and did not laugh at it or throw it out. I flew to Philadelphia. We drove to Coffin's home in New Haven. We had a long afternoon of discussion walking through the proposal. It was still very sketchy, but the skeleton was easy to see. We discussed what the permanent structure would need to be, the full two-year scenarios for each target city, and what funding sources looked promising. Dick reported on the enthusiastic support of the denominational leaders. We spent the largest part of the conversation on the call to conversion that would happen at the close of the service. Like the Graham evangelism model, we agreed that a call to a new life in Christ was necessary. This evangelism was the core theological idea. We saw a call to come forward to the chancel rail as a sign of willingness and intention to live a new life based on a self-giving love for God. We were unable to come to an agreement on the exact language for this call but shared the conviction that it was important.

We did agree that those who came forward for the new life would have to be greeted with an organized reception, a renewal of their baptism, and a set of next steps for each of these people. We knew that the local community had to step forward with organization to carry this energy and these people forward. The preparation of the local community would need to include the follow-up program.

Dick and I left Coffin's home after four hours of serious talk. We had the feeling that he was on board with us. It was getting exciting. This could happen. We had a lot of work to do.

A couple weeks later Coffin went to an island off the coast of Maine as he regularly had done for the summer. He shared the proposal with several of his longtime activist clergy colleagues who had summer places there. They talked him out of it. They convinced him that it was all about his ego, and they raised questions in him as to whether he had the power in his preaching to make this succeed.

Dick and I had no doubt that this would have generated a massive new energy for Protestant Christianity in America and would have planted a new vision for the life and work of the church, of Christianity calling us to responsibility for peace and justice and, as the concern grew, about sustainable living. And we had no doubt that Coffin could have pulled off his role at the center of this energy. We had no doubts that the two if us could have put together and maintained the massive organizational support required. We would have relied on so many progressive colleagues around the country whom we knew from anti-war organizing. The potential for the organization was already out there around the country. We just had to build it. And the hunger for the message was there. I am so sorry the guys in Maine talked Coffin out of it. They may have saved us all from massive embarrassment if we tried and failed but they may have denied another religious awakening in America.

I've had many great ideas that I could not get off the ground.

This was the best one.

The Rector and the Rabbi to the Paris Peace Talks

The next major opportunity for expanding the anti-war work came when I learned that the CALC national office had arranged for a delegation to visit the Paris Peace Talks, which had been going on for some time. These talks were a four-way negotiation designed to end the war. It seemed endless. Representatives of the governments of North and South Vietnam, of North Vietnam's soldiers in the South, and of the US sat and chatted awaiting direction from their governments.

The CALC delegation was thrilled with firsthand briefing by all sides of the negotiation and with the updates they were given by all sides. The CALC delegation failed to include any western region delegates. So, I asked if they could set up another such visit for two Southern California clergy. After a series of follow up calls I got word that they would find it useful to have another delegation and that I should recruit.

Vogel and I went to see Regas again. He was interested. Then we went to visit Rabbi Leonard Beerman of Leo Baeck Temple in West Los Angeles. He was interested. Beerman was outspoken in his opposition to the war, and he brought the credential authority of being a former marine.

I scheduled a phone call with Gerhard Elston of the New York CALC staff who was arranging the visit. I asked him to brief Regas and Beerman to reassure them that this was a serious venture. They met in the COMMIT office, and we had a forty-five-minute phone conversation. They were comfortable with the arrangements, and they were convinced that CALC could set up meetings with the delegates from North and South Vietnam.

The deal was, of course, that Regas and Beerman would be willing to make three joint reports of their trip at times and places I would arrange. They agreed. And they had to pay all expenses. Agreed again. A window of time was established for the delegation to depart Los Angeles.

When they returned, they drew very large, enthusiastic audiences not only at the events I set up, but in many other venues including joint appearances in each other's congregations. Their anti-war messages were very powerful, Beerman in a cool, analytic, prophetic voice, Regas at his passionate best. The rabbi carried to every program one of the bomblets that fell from the cluster bombs. He pulled it out of his pocket and held it so all could see. He talked of its purpose, the indiscriminate death it rained down. The image burned into one's consciousness. The delegates representing the North Vietnam government had provided the little unarmed cluster bomb to him to bring home.

We had sign up clipboards on every occasion. As the mailing list of our chapter of CALC grew, fundraising for our program was not difficult. And we were getting a lot of media attention. CALC began to be perceived as an important religious anti-war voice in the region.

Taking West Coast Anti-War Protesters to DC 1972

On May 8, 1972, President Nixon intensified attacks on North Vietnam through a renewal of massive bombing, a naval blockade, and the mining of Haiphong Harbor. Responding to the President's order, CALC called a May 16 emergency demonstration in Washington.

The announcement led me to talk with Regas. He agreed he would support our LA-CALC in organizing a major delegation to Washington for this emergency demonstration. He would encourage All Saints members to participate. My office was the place to call if one was interested in joining the trip. I reached out to the Northern California CALC group and invited them to join us.

I took my COMMIT credit card to the travel agency we used and said I wanted to charter an airplane. That was new for me. We filled the plane with Californians. A group from Northern California flew down to connect with our flight. That brought Professor Davie Napier, Professor Robert McAfee Brown, and others into our delegation. I rented a bus to transport us between Washington Dulles Airport and the assembly point at a Washington church.

At the departure point from All Saints, our group boarded a chartered bus to drive to the airport. Regas had agreed to be our contact point at home if there were any emergency. He also, looking almost embarrassed to say it, pointed out a woman in the thirty-person All Saints contingent and said he hoped I would keep my eye on her because she was a major donor to the church. Then he apologized.

This felt like an emergency. There was little orientation: some policy updating and directions for the day, lobbying and civil disobedience if the situation arose. CALC had maintained moderate political positions and expressions of resistance. There were more radical groups who wanted to join and influence this large and mainstream group, but the leadership worked to stay in touch with and to speak for its mainstream constituency. There were also constant efforts from within the organization to take on issues not connected to Vietnam. CALC kept its focus.

About 450 people attended. In small teams we visited congressional representatives urging support for the bill to cut off funding. One group did a sit-in at a representative's office. Another group was evicted from the Senate gallery for shouting "end the war" during a Senate session.

The largest demonstration began around 3:00 p.m. when we began a sit-in worship service in the Capitol rotunda. The singing, anti-war speeches, and prayers lasted nearly three hours. The acoustics, I remember, were terrific, with the big dome and hard surfaces all around. We sounded pretty close to the Mormon Tabernacle Choir in my humble opinion. Virtually everyone cooperated when Capitol police began making the first 120 arrests, avoiding any further incidents. Among those arrested was Coffin, who took charge of the process. He first spoke to those of us sitting on the floor, about two hundred of us. He said we were about to be arrested and taken to the jail. He said it was no dishonor if some decided they did not wish to participate and that they should get up and move away. And he told us that the Capitol police standing with their billy clubs and helmets were not our enemies. They were doing their job and we should treat them with respect. We had a couple ways to be arrested when it was our turn. We could simply follow the directions of the police or become passive, go limp, and let them carry us. Then he turned to face the police and said we were now ready for them to do their duty, but they should know that we hoped that they might think about why we were willing to be arrested, the cause that brought us together. He said we hoped their hearts might be changed by our small sacrifice.

I suffered my first experience with claustrophobia in that van carrying five of us off the jail. I knew that all the air was being sucked out of that rolling prison cell. I knew I was about to die of asphyxiation. I couldn't breathe. I contemplated the thought of banging my head into the wall to knock myself out. Knowing that all this was not real didn't relieve me of my high anxiety.

Overnight housing had been arranged by CALC staff for the one overnight for those who needed it. But all our crowd from California participated in the arrests in the Capitol Building. We were taken in groups of five to the DC jail in DC police department paddy wagons. I did, as Regas had asked, keep my eye on the All Saints woman. She clearly was up for going to jail. I never worried about her. Her anti-war passion was pure. She wanted the war to end. She was willing to make this sacrifice and who knows what more.

Men and women were in different parts of the jail. Coffin led the men in hymn singing. Having been choral director at Yale, he made us sound better than one might expect. He seemed to know all verses of all the hymns we sang. Most of us were really scared, being in jail for the first time. At times someone would start reciting verses from one of the Gospels. When his memory failed him, one of the other incarcerated took up the recital. I was convinced we could have assembled the whole book of Matthew if we had a couple nights.

Dr. Benjamin Spock was in the cell next to mine. Professors Harvey Cox and John Cobb Jr. were across from me. The cells were fitted for two men, upper and lower bunk, a metal toilet, and washbasin were on the wall opposite the gate. There were five of us in my cell. But sleeping was not part of the plan.

At 2:00 a.m., one of the men yelled for us to stop making noise and listen. When it became still, we could hear the women singing hymns off at some distance. The sense of scale and solidarity was powerful.

Our only nourishment was two pieces of bread each. I ate one and put one in my pocket. Several others of our group did the same.

In the morning we were transported to a courthouse. Dick had worked overnight to secure for us legal representation from supervised third year students from Georgetown University Law School.

There was a lot of energy in the anteroom of the court. A volleyball game broke out with a wrapped up piece of paper. We were asked to decide how we wanted to plead. Guilty, not guilty, or nolo contendere.[4] The Cali-

---

4. A plea by which a defendant in a criminal prosecution accepts conviction as though a guilty plea had been entered but does not admit guilt.

fornia group had to factor in that our plane home was scheduled to depart around four that afternoon. Not guilty meant a trial hearing would set for appearance in a couple weeks. Nolo contendere meant a hearing would be set sometime in the future. I chose the latter as did most of our crew. Our plea was accepted by the court, and we were dismissed a few at a time. We learned a couple months later that the charges had been dropped.

I waited outside the jail for my buddy Al. We walked from the jail to the Russell Senate Office Building. We sat in the Senate dining room, ate breakfast, and told stories. A few others from our group joined us. We had all saved bread from our jail cell. We also decided to take a stack of bread slices from the Senate dining room. We created a great ending to our journey.

I kept in touch by phone with Regas and he regularly made reports to those who stayed home and worried. I phoned him to say all was on track for our departure from Washington. Then I proposed our idea. We were bringing home bread from the DC jail and the Senate dining room. I suggested he bring wine to greet us and lead a Eucharist service right there in the airport. It would unite those who stayed home and those who made the journey. He loved the idea.

So, when our plane arrived around 7:00 p.m. at LAX, it was diverted to a different terminal, different from the one where our family and friends expected to meet us. It turned out that so many people had showed up to greet our plane that the airport authorities had to accommodate the crowd. They had time to divert planes from one terminal and sent us to that now empty one so our crowd could all greet us as we walked off the plane. There were cheers and tears for that short journey that held so much potential risk.

Regas convened us with one of the public address systems used to announce flights. We had a brief interfaith service of unity and common purpose. He welcomed us with profuse praise for our witness and courage and thanked the spouses, partners, and supporters for their prayers, concern, and funds. He invited Beerman to read from the Jewish Bible and make some remarks. Regas told us how proud he was of our anti-war effort, had one of the women from the church tell us what it meant to her that we had made this flight, and then he served the bread and cup using the bread from the DC jail and from the cafeteria in the Russell Senate Office Building and the wine he had brought.

During the passing of bread, a group of armed, uniformed airport police showed up. They were there for public safety and to protect property. They had no clue what our group was doing. They had been told that we were a bunch of peaceniks who had taken over a whole terminal. One of the people in our group knew the head of security at the airport, the man leading the armed police. John Colburn, a fellow Turk, went over to explain what was happening and what we were doing, an interfaith worship service with some of the most distinguished religious leaders in Southern California. He said we'd finish in a few minutes and would leave promptly and in an orderly fashion. The police stepped down.

Coe, senior minister of the Claremont United Church of Christ, was moved enough by the experience and his passion to end the war that the next Sunday he wore sack cloth and poured ashes over his head in the pulpit. In his sermon he condemned the war in the strongest words and phrases of the prophets of Israel condemning the unfaithful king. He said he would not preach again from that pulpit until the war ended. The congregation had better double their efforts and effectiveness.

There was a move in the church to call a congregational meeting and enter a vote of no confidence in the minister. Coe insisted that they do that and two Sundays later after the service there was a motion of no confidence put before the congregation. After heated debate the final vote supported him 80 percent to 20 percent. But for him that was not sufficient. He resigned.

These experiences moved us, changed us, and emboldened us to consider actions that we, being a polite people, would have never considered previously.

The War Continues: We Resist to the End

I asked Dick about his prodigious fundraising to keep so much action financially supported. He said that the problem CALC was trying to solve, the war, was every day on the front page of newspapers around the country, above the fold day after day. He didn't have to sell the problem. He had to sell the solution. CALC's program consisted of organizing in the religious community, providing the opportunity for religious leaders to put their names out as anti-war activists, fund raising, providing training for laity and clergy as they entered the peace movement, and organizing big demonstrations focused on nonviolent resistance to the government's policy of war in Vietnam.

While I was developing and expanding our visibility, we offered various kinds of support to several local peace groups in the faith community. Members of the Steering Committee were available to be speakers. We had several people who were helpful in developing programs. We cooperated with other peace groups in sponsoring protest events. I developed an understanding of how to work with media to get them to cover events and spread the impact of our action. It became clear that newspaper city desks were looking for events to assign reporters and photojournalists. In a press advisory my job was to put before them a half-page description of what we planned to do next, giving them all the relevant details, big names of speakers, and a contact person, usually me, to call for further details. We put out many press notices and had special letterhead printed for that purpose. I understood we were helping the journalists do their job while they were helping get our story and message out.

Jane Fonda in My Office

I returned a phone call from an organizer of a planned mass march that was to take place on April 13, 1973, on the USC campus. The caller wanted to discuss my joining the leadership of the planning process and whether I would be able to turn out a large number of clergy and lay people who opposed the war. We talked for a while. I was confident that, by that time, I had built enough credibility, infrastructure, trust, and had enough contacts that I could say yes, I could produce such a response. Our people would join eighty other anti-war groups, thousands of protesters who were being mobilized for that evening. The key organization at the center of the planning process was the Indochina Peace Project located in Santa Monica, founded by the radical anti-war organizers Jane Fonda and her husband Tom Hayden.

At the end of the phone conversation, after we agreed on several collaborative next steps, we traded office and home phone numbers, and I asked her name. I had been talking now for nearly an hour and a half with a very savvy organizer whose name I already knew well: Jane Fonda.

The morning after the demonstration, I received a phone call at my USC office from Fonda. She was deeply appreciative of the presence of so many clergy and lay people. She felt they had made the critical difference in the tone and nonviolence by the demonstrators. And she wanted to thank all those I felt were especially important to the turnout of the religious community. She wanted to telephone them to say a personal word of thanks. Fonda was looking for a list of maybe a hundred leaders. I was stunned by this spirit of appreciation and this act in such a personal way.

Fonda said her offices were full of volunteers working on the same project. She wondered if I had some place she could use to make as many of those phone calls as possible from my list. My own office was available for the rest of the day because I was leading a training session in our assembly room. Clergy from around the region were coming together to work on career planning, another kind of training we offered.

Fonda parked where I suggested and came up to the office. She was very pregnant. She settled into my desk chair, pulled the phone onto her lap, propped up the list I had assembled, and began dialing and expressing thanks to surprised clergy all over Southern California.

Meanwhile, a half hour later, I gathered my training group around the big table in the assembly room. Little did they know what was going on just on the other side of one of those office doors near where we met for the career planning session.

In the middle of the afternoon session, the door to the hallway and stairs opened and there appeared before the startled clergy, who were deep in reflection upon their careers, a uniformed campus cop. He looked angrily at me standing there in the front of the group and asked what must have seemed like the stupidest question in the world. He asked, "Is Jane Fonda here?"

I knew I could only answer the truth. I said, to the astonishment of the clergy, "Yes." The cop said that the administration, as she well knew, had banned her from the campus because of her outspoken anti-war views. Her car had been "made" in the parking lot and he was dispatched to find her and remove her from the campus.

I walked over to my office door. All eyes were following. I opened the door and there she was, feet propped up on my desk, working her way down the second side of the list, protruding stomach making her look awkward, pregnant, frail, and innocent, talking on the phone.

She excused herself from the phone and said, "I heard. I'll be on my way, officer." He said he'd wait outside to be sure she complied. She thanked me for the opportunity to make these calls. She apologized to the group for the distraction and departed.

Say what you will about Jane Fonda, this is the picture I hold close.

I've had friends over the years ask me if that was really Jane Fonda who called.

Transition to the Next Work

The Paris Peace Accords were signed in June 1973. Dick resigned as executive director of CALC the same month. The work of the regional field staff tapered off and the LA-CALC Steering Committee decided it had done its job and disbanded. The signals were clear that I needed to consider new employment.

I was invited to attend the final banquet in New York at the time of the closing down of CALC. It was attended by over a hundred people who felt connected to each other through CALC. Great speeches were given by Coffin, Brown, and the Rev. Richard John Neuhaus. Dick paid tribute to those who were the key parts of the national CALC team. He introduced me and said I was "the best planner in the peace movement." That was surprising to me and amazing coming from a guy who had been in the room with many peace movement leaders over the years of the war.

It was a time of change all around. There were a lot of other concerns to be addressed. Where might I find work to continue this quest for peace?

Another door opened for me, one for which I had little experience, but which offered great opportunity to bend the direction of US policy, to bend it in directions outlined by the social policy of my church, the United Church of Christ. I agreed to represent the United Church of Christ in Washington, DC, as director of its lobbying and public policy office beginning in the spring of 1974.

Saigon fell to North Vietnamese forces on May 1, 1975. The heavy load on the human spirit we had born had been lifted by the sight of that last helicopter leaving the closed US Embassy in Saigon.

While living in Washington, I stood a few times looking at all those names on the wall at the Maya Lin–designed Vietnam War Memorial on the Mall. I again felt so empty, so hopeless for humankind. The artist's design, that big slash into the ground and the names, opened my heart to the pain once again. I do not want to forget that the nation asked so many to pay so dearly for so little.

Chapter 8

Lobbying in Washington, DC, for Peace and Justice 1974–1984

I WAS A HIRED lobbyist. From March 1974 until August 1984, I served on the national staff of the United Church of Christ as director of the Washington, DC, Public Policy Advocacy office. This turned out to be the longest continuous period of service of all the positions I held.

The Rev. Larry Schulz called me from New York inviting me to consider joining the staff of the Office for Church in Society (OCIS), a national agency of the United Church of Christ. He was particularly interested in my considering the position of director of the Washington Office. We agreed to meet in my office at COMMIT in Los Angeles later in the week.

Larry had been a seminary classmate at Chicago Theological Seminary. We had become friends there and stayed in touch since. He was new to his position of director of the Office for Church in Society (OCIS) and was assembling a staff of social change activists with a particular set of skills.

I began to realize how ignorant I was about my church at the national level. I pulled into my office the big rolling two-sided chalkboard and began to list all the questions I would need to have answered before I would know if I were interested in such a major cross country move for my work and my family. I covered the front and the flip side with questions. When Larry arrived for the interview, he patiently walked through all my questions and gave helpful and politically weighted answers. Larry's mentor, Ray Gibbons, had been powerful in defining the importance of working for peace and justice at the national level of the United Church of Christ, founded in 1957, the result of a merger between the Congregational Christian Churches and the Evangelical and Reformed Church. In more recent years, UCC President

John Thomas characterized the UCC as often being a "first responder" on critical social issues. My view was that Ray Gibbons and his team back in the 1940s laid the groundwork. I was eager to enter that work, to live up to those traditions, to help my church play the largest role possible in the continuing work of justice and peacemaking.

As soon as he returned to New York, Larry phoned and offered me the position of director of the Washington, DC, office.

A friend said I was now going to the proverbial belly of the beast. Many friends thought then that all the world's trouble was caused by actions in Washington. They hoped I would fix things. In my experience to that point, I had sat with white youth trying to find their identity and purpose, with a powerful group of 1950s housewives breaking out of that confining space. I had walked the streets of the ghetto seeking friendship with young men hanging out on Van Nuys Boulevard. I had functioned as a coach to other clergy called to social change work. I had spent three years organizing within the religious community against the war in Vietnam and participated in acts of civil disobedience. I had studied and taught planned social change theory. Now I was going to the center of the policy world where, if one could bring about change, it would bring a massive change affecting a lot of people. Ever naive and confident, I was going to Washington where the grown-ups mix it up.

When Genie and I decided it was time to share this news with our kids, to tell them that the family was relocating to Washington, we hoped they'd be thrilled. When I got home on the day we were going to share the news, Mark said he had an announcement. He told us with great excitement that, a dream fulfilled, the football coach had invited him to come out for spring football practice at Blair High in Pasadena. I then announced we'd be moving to the Washington, DC, area that summer. What a letdown.

I announced my resignation from COMMIT and other projects I had been doing. Genie and I agreed that I'd fly east in March 1974 to begin work and to house hunt. She and the kids would stay in Pasadena until the semester ended in June and then I'd fly back and drive across the country with them.

A farewell party in early March 1974 was held at the Pasadena home of the Rev. Bill Persell, rector of St. John's Episcopal Church in downtown Los Angeles. Joe Hough was the master of ceremonies for what essentially was a roast. I was touched by how many dimensions of my work in Los Angeles were present that night: several corporate executives who had been involved in the anti-war movement, in urban ministries, and in civil rights work; most of the Young Turks; several former gang members from Pacoima and

Los Angeles; clergy and movement colleagues; and folks we met in Cuernavaca at CIDOC.

Joe did charge me to urge the bigwigs in the east to commit to have meetings out here in the West, which they just don't seem to see as part of the country. He said he had badgered one committee of National Council of Churches to hold a meeting in the West. They finally did—in Cincinnati!

I flew from LAX to Washington Dulles on March 22, 1974, a Friday. Bill and Grace Moremen, members of the Young Turks in Los Angeles, now living near Washington, met me at the airport. Bill was senior minister at First Congregational Church UCC in Washington. At my request they had rented a studio apartment for me at the Capitol Hill Suites, 200 C Street SE, which was furnished with a kitchenette including a table and two chairs, a bed, and a bathroom. It was within walking distance of 110 Maryland Avenue NE, where the UCC office was located. I bought a small black and white TV that I sat on an upside-down plastic wastebasket. On that little TV a few nights later, Bill, Grace, and I watched Hank Aaron hit his 715th home run, breaking Babe Ruth's all-time home run record.

On Saturday and Sunday, I walked around the neighborhood. The metal banging and pinging that woke me up in this new time zone was the construction of the new James Madison wing of the Library of Congress being built across the street from my apartment building. I found the Avenue, a stretch of Pennsylvania Avenue east of the US Capital, lined with small shops, bars (The Hawk and Dove and The Tune Inn), restaurants, a barbershop, and the notable Trover Shop Books and Office Supplies. It was a neighborhood for those who lived on Capitol Hill and, during the work-week, a place to catch lunch and a quick off-site meeting. There seemed to be a very sophisticated, smart bunch of folks milling around the bookstore. It was a great pickup spot for singles on the hill. But the conversations I picked up seemed focused on policy and legislation. I went back to my apartment feeling not only lonely for my family but that I was shrinking in size and importance. I was a very uninitiated rookie entering a whole new ball game, the rules of which I had not a clue. And I knew this might be a serious opportunity to make a difference in the world. So, at age forty, I was a rookie again.

I did buy a copy of *The Washington Post* and quickly learned to love it. Editor Ben Bradley, Woodward, and Bernstein were in full journalistic investigative power. *The Post* displayed headlines about the indictment of several Republican Party and government officials. Nixon was at the end of his rope. The Vietnam War was still dragging on. The protests were massive and, for many long-time anti-war protesters, becoming violent. The

Weather Underground were bombing buildings. Peaceful protests were, for many, no longer having an effect.

I did marvel at the location of my new job. It was in the United Methodist Building at 110 Maryland Avenue NE. It had been apartments but was in transition to office space. First Street NE was the eastern edge of the capital grounds. My office was across the street from the Supreme Court! The north side of our building was Constitution Avenue. Across the street that way were the offices of the US Senators. There were two Senate office buildings when I first arrived, the new one and the old one, called "the new SOB" and "the old SOB."

I saw that this location, so close to the Capitol, to the court, and to the senate offices, was prime real estate. Being able to walk to the Senate and House office buildings, the court, the Library of Congress, and the Capitol itself was amazing. How did the Methodists manage this when so many corporations would pay millions for this access? In the early twentieth century, the Methodist Christian Temperance Union had petitioned the government for space and received the grant of this prime turf. However it happened, I appreciated the United Methodist Board of Church and Society for welcoming an array of denominational Washington offices and staff. Only the lobbyists for the military had better access to the Senate offices. They had offices inside the old SOB.

The UCC/OCIS office was on the second floor directly over the National Council of Churches office. After a time, I learned that North Carolina Senator Sam Irvin of Watergate-hearings fame was retiring and moving out of his apartment on the top (fifth) floor. I arranged for us to move up there because there was more space—three bedrooms, two bathrooms, a large living room space with a fake fireplace, a dining area, and kitchen plus several large closets. We'd have rooms for separate staff offices and space for staff and small group meetings. It also had the advantage of being on the south side of the building facing the court. The north side faces the Senate offices and, at the time, the Hart Senate Office Building was under construction and the construction noise was deafening. The only problem on the south side was the rumble and smell of the idling tourist buses on Maryland Avenue blowing diesel fumes in the air, keeping the buses cool while the tourists visited the court.

My introduction to the staff I was to direct could not have been more embarrassing. Bright and fresh on Monday morning, wearing my best suit, I walked the four blocks past the Library of Congress and the Supreme Court to the Methodist Building. I found the UCC office on the second floor. With a great deal of dread and excitement, I pulled the door open and stepped up to the desk of the receptionist. She glanced up at me like greeting a stranger was somehow painful.

I said, "I'm Paul Kittlaus." I guess I expected a drumroll or something. Nothing. No recognition on her face at all. So, I then said, "Larry Schulz has appointed me the director of the UCC Washington office."

After a long pause she said, "We haven't heard anything about that." My heart sank. I asked for a conversation with whoever oversaw the office. She got up and disappeared and came back and said, "Mr. Dudley will see you now."

Thus, I met Tilford "Ted" Dudley

He greeted me with a lack of warmth but politely. Maybe in his mid-seventies, I thought. He took me to his office, a large room with a stately desk placed in front of an ornate fireplace. He said that he was director of the UCC Washington Office. There was no vacancy.

I had quit my job, sold my house, moved across the country, and my family was following shortly!

So, we talked for a while. Larry had failed to alert the Washington staff that he had appointed a new director and that I was coming that Monday. Ted and I both saw the situation we were in, felt no animosity toward each other, but clearly were sitting in the middle of a dilemma that we decided would be solved at the staff meeting called for Wednesday. Larry and the others on the New York staff were coming down to join the Washington staff. In the meantime, I saw Ted as an enormous resource for a rookie lob-byist. He enjoyed telling stories, which fit the best style of transferring his knowledge and experience to my empty brain.

My friends and colleagues were generally in the same age cohort as me. In our arrogance we were not convinced that previous generations had been politically radical enough. Else what explained the mess we were deal-ing with? Suddenly, in realizing who Ted Dudley was and how far back he had been at work on an agenda like mine, I was humbled. It gave me a new perspective that this new colleague had finished Harvard Law before I was born and had come to Washington to work for FDR!

At the all-staff meeting on Wednesday, when confronted with his em-barrassing oversight, Larry tried to avoid making a clean decision, which he worried would alienate either Ted or me. His indecision was alienating both of us.

He proposed to call Ted director of the office and me coordinator of it. Neither of us knew exactly what any of that meant but decided to let it ride. Ted had plans to retire soon. I didn't have a clue about what was going on around me in Washington, so Ted and I decided he would apprentice me, and we could collaborate on any decisions that needed to be made. We were both okay with that and felt we didn't need to confront Larry around a decision he didn't want to make.

Home Search: Family and Nixon's Resignation

I rented a car and spent weekends with real estate agents looking at homes for sale. I liked one three-bedroom, custom-built house in Alexandria, Virginia. It had the advantage, I finally figured out, of being within sight of the Potomac River. I found that I was constantly lacking orientation as I moved around looking at homes. I was used to seeing the mountains in Southern California. They confirmed for me that I knew where I was, where north was. But in most of suburban Virginia and Maryland I was disoriented. I finally found what I thought was the right home for my family. Mark would be in high school, Adam and Ann in middle school. In Takoma Park, Maryland, I bought an old four-bedroom, two-story home on Maple Avenue. It had an unfinished attic and a full basement. Such features were unheard of in California. It was going to be an easy walk to the promised construction of the Takoma Park Station on the Washington Metro rail system. Metro would zip us down into Washington and to Union Station at the foot of Capitol Hill. From there it was an easy four block walk up the hill to my office. Genie, the kids, and I drove from Pasadena to Maryland. We moved into that house in June 1974.

Takoma Park had a distinctly countercultural vibe. Mayor Sammy Abbot, supported by the city council, had declared Takoma Park a nuclear free zone! The wonderful, old-timey Fourth of July parade forbade any motorized vehicles and went right past our home.

Instead of graduating from Blair High School in Pasadena, named for William Blair, who was elected president of the Pasadena Unified school board at the same time he was the editor of the *Pasadena Star-News*, my kids graduated from Montgomery Blair High School in Silver Spring, Maryland. It was named after the twentieth postmaster general of the United States.

A momentous event opened before us on the night of August 9, 1974. Mark had been invited to play football by the coach at Blair High School in Pasadena. It had been his dream. But our move to Washington meant he was denied that chance.

It was a wet, gloomy, and humid night that August evening. Our family sat in front of our TV and watched the speech from the Oval Office by President Nixon announcing his decision to resign. The heavy weight of those terrible years suddenly seemed to lift a little. When all the commentary was done, I turned the TV off so we could chat as a family and then move the kids off to bed. Mark looked at me and said, "OK, Dad, can we go home now?"

This would be the home where my marriage would end. I would choose to take up residence in an apartment in March 1976. I worked to continue to be present in my children's lives. After five years of separation, I concluded that I was being a better parent from the outside than from the inside. I filed for divorce.

I was clear that our children deserved the best I could give them and that any issues I had with their mother must be kept between her and me. It was never about the children. I know this could have been handled differently. With some therapy and with what wisdom I could muster, I chose to avoid discussing the issues and to concentrate on telling them how much I loved them. And I chose to keep as close and involved in their lives as I could be. Perhaps one day they, I hoped, would come to understand.

Learning the Public Policy Job

My learning curve was steep as I settled into the routine in this new public policy work. I picked up *The Dance of Legislation* by Eric Redman one evening at Trover Books.[1]

It was considered a classic description of the legislative process. In it, Eric Redman draws on his two years as a member of Senator Warren Magnuson's staff to trace the drafting and passing of a piece of legislation, S4106, the National Health Service Bill, with all the maneuvers, plots, counterplots, frustrations, triumphs, sheer work, and dedication involved. He provided a vivid picture of the bureaucratic infighting, political prerogatives, and congressional courtesies necessary to make something happen on Capitol Hill.

I took it home and read it cover-to-cover in one sitting. It helped me begin to understand this new work of mine. I needed to learn that dance he described and to come to understand in depth the process and the points of influence in the process. I needed to learn the content of legislation and to know the social policies of the United Church of Christ. Was I to freelance and claim that whatever weapons system I might lobby against was the belief of the church that paid my salary? Was I bound by some set of rules of representation? Who decided what we were to advocate?

The Rev. Walter Fauntroy, a Baptist preacher in Washington and the first official nonvoting delegate representing the District of Columbia to the Congress, often said that politics is working to turn what one believes into public policy. I used that statement in many briefings for visiting church

1. Redman, *Dance of Legislation.*

groups. It is an easy way to talk about the connection between faith understandings and the function of government.

After a review of the actions of General Synod, I proposed that these resolutions and pronouncements provide the guidance, the social policy. The General Synod of the UCC had for a long time been debating and voting positions on controversial societal issues. Biblical and theological resources had informed the discussions. These positions could easily be claimed to be a consensus of a broader representation within the church.[2] Our staff began to assemble a policy book of actions of General Synods as far back as we could find records without awakening the angels in the UCC archives. From that point on, any testimony we wrote, any newsletter reports, any media releases all were justified in this four-inch thick, three-ring binder Red Policy Book. It became well-worn over the years, as new pronouncements were added and old statements researched.

There was the legislative process to learn: which committees dealt with which issues, what their timetable was, what bills were to be considered, where the points of influence were, and who might be allies and who enemies on a particular issue.

There were the details of issues of importance. What weapon systems if any should we oppose and why? What level of federal assistance to families with dependent children were we proposing and why? How much was the right amount for the Food Stamp Program or the farm subsidy program?

Once the legislation was passed by a committee, then what? Who decided how much money should be attached to the program? How about the other body (House or Senate) if the bills were different in the two houses? How would they be reconciled? Would the president sign the bill? When it was signed into law, who wrote the rules and regulations that determine how the law is implemented? The questions went on and on.

This was a very different skill set than I brought with me after a career in pastoring, community organizing, peace movement organizing, social action, and conflict management training. And of what use was a seminary education in such a setting? Are there ways of writing testimony with theological content that could have meaning in the kinds of policy discussions that permeate the hall and hearing rooms?

The skills needed for success as a lobbyist were not ones that fit me well. But I did have useful skills for that work. I was an excellent talent scout for great staff colleagues, who were substantive issue people, able to marshal

2. There are polity issues that need to be understood if one is interested in this question. In the UCC any official unit of the church, a congregation, a board of a church, or the General Synod, speaks for itself. No unit is bound by the pronouncements of another unit. Each unit speaks to the church and not for the church.

persuasive arguments and build coalitions, and great fun to be around. I felt I was a good talent manager, able to support and defend the work of our staff, to communicate appreciation for their hard work, and to interpret their efforts to our board and the wider church. I brought a lot of experience organizing grassroots campaigns in support of or opposition to legislation.

When I was making the get-acquainted rounds of UCC national staff, I visited the office of the Rev. Howard Schomer, an executive on the staff of the Board for World Ministries. His title was "secretary for world issues." I could never imagine what size ego one must have to introduce yourself as world issues secretary without laughing your head off. When I was ushered into his office in New York, he was on the phone speaking in German. He called out to his secretary in French. He sounded frustrated. When he hung up, he looked over at me and said, "Would you believe it, both of our Mercedes are in the garage."

I immediately thought, "I'm going to like this national staff work." Of course, there never was even one Mercedes in my driveway.

Assembling a New Staff

Larry asked that I evaluate our continuing staff and make changes if I thought it important. My first hire was for the first face one would see coming into the door of our offices, Aida Bound, office manager. Before Aida, coming into our office was like entering a library. After, it was like entering the set of *Saturday Night Live*. She brought what I believe we mean by a vibe. She was terrific and helped us all do our work better and enjoy each other more.

Civil Rights and Civil Liberties

In 1975 the country was still digesting the righteous claims of the civil rights movement. Congress had been adjusting various civil rights acts over the past decade. We needed to be engaged in this process. The constant need to protect the constitutional guarantees of civil liberties was a long-time commitment of our church. These two related issues were combined into a portfolio and the best candidate for that job was already on our staff. He was the Rev. Barry Lynn.

Barry had come to work in our office a year earlier in a short-term position supported with special funding. The Synod had passed a resolution in support of gaining an amnesty for Vietnam War resistors. The position was created to support that resolution. Barry had recently completed his theology degree from Boston University and was eager to do policy advocacy work in Washington. Larry and I interviewed him for this position over the phone and were both convinced he was an outstanding candidate. He was bright, passionate, and wanted to make a difference in the world. He was ordained UCC so was basically familiar with our systems.

Over the years that Barry worked in our office, he transitioned from the amnesty issue to the civil rights, civil liberties portfolio. Along the way he completed a four-year evening program at Georgetown University Law Center and passed the DC bar. He is married to Dr. Joanne Lynn, a medical doctor whose career has focused on palliative care and gerontology. Between them they covered the fields of law, medicine, and theology. I suggested that Joann also take up being a mortician and then they would offer birth to death services.

One major campaign that Barry waged was to oppose the legislation requiring male citizens upon attaining their eighteenth birthday to register for the draft at the local post office, thus providing the Selective Service System with convenient contact information should a military draft be needed to raise an army quickly. The proposed legislation carried stiff penalties of both fines and jail time if a young man moved, like going away to college, and failed to register at his new location. Our church argued that constituted an infringement of civil liberties. Barry waged a one-person campaign against this bill including a series of debates on college campuses with the director of the Selective Service System, General Lewis B. Hershey. This was an illustration of one skill of a policy advocate. We had to know the issues as well as those we debate against.

In the early eighties, we took a different look of what might be possible in the civil rights portfolio. We hired Faith Evans. He had a very different background. He was born in Brooklyn, New York, and was abandoned on the street to fend for himself. Faith joined a gang, broke the law, and was sentenced to prison. When he was released from an upstate New York prison, he was given a train ticket back to New York City. He knew as he traveled south that if he went all the way back, he would soon return to the survival tactics which landed him in prison in the first place. So, he got off the train not knowing where he was. It turned out to be Troy, New York. He found help, and quickly a wife and some kids and a job. Then his wife abandoned him. Faith became a single parent.

He was determined not to push his kids to the street, as had been his own story. He joined the local Welfare Rights Organization. His organizing skills were so obvious that he soon was moved to Washington, DC, to join the staff of the National Welfare Rights Organization. He eventually found his way into collaboration with church leadership working on poverty issues. He connected with my boss, the Rev. Dr. Yvonne Delk, who brought him into our office where he filled a valuable spot among all of us highly educated, middle-class achievers. He showed us what achievement looked like against much greater odds than the rest of us on staff had experienced. What was important for him was not what the executives were thinking in any organization but what the secretaries and custodians were thinking and feeling. Thus, he especially connected with support staff in the national church, other allies or even competing agencies, and among support staff in the Congress. From them he learned who was a jerk, who has serious power, who's trending, who to listen to, and how to find the weak spots in an organization. Getting to know and find Faith's skills and perspectives added great value to our staff.

Foreign Policy and Military Spending

In 1977, the Tenth General Synod of the UCC meeting in Washington, DC, was the setting for a heated debate about what policy the Synod would take on the question of boycotting investments in corporations doing business in South Africa during the apartheid period. Gretchen Castle Eick first came to my attention as she debated World Issues Secretary Schomer on the floor of the Synod. Schomer had been the President of Chicago Theological Seminary when I graduated. He was a formidable figure who had been leading the corporate responsibility effort of our church. His view was to avoid confrontation with the corporations like Caterpillar Corporation. He was regularly engaged in meetings with corporate executives negotiating an understanding about their role in South Africa. Gretchen and her group were insisting that the time for negotiations was over and that the UCC needed to divest from these corporations. Gretchen's passion and knowledge of the complex issues persuaded the General Synod to overwhelmingly support her side of the debate. The UCC General Synod urged the Pension Boards and other bodies investing church money to divest from a prepared list of corporations. Her victory was very impressive.

I was looking for someone to join our staff with a portfolio in foreign policy and military spending. Gretchen was obviously a deeply engaged volunteer with many of the skills for policy advocacy. She mobilized facts, made policy points in passionate statements, did outreach to gather allies, and really wanted to make a difference in the world. As the spouse of a local UCC pastor, she knew the UCC, she had learned the social policy making process of the church, and she would learn the public policy process of the government. She was thrilled at the invitation to join the staff. Gretchen used her writing acumen to craft complex testimony for the Congress and to interpret it to local church members.

Over her years in our office, she became an expert on weapons systems, many complex foreign policy issues, and human rights issues that ended up on her desk. And she was great at building coalitions of religious and other groups who shared these policy positions.

Economic Policy and World Hunger

I had responsibilities for health care, economic justice, energy policy, and world hunger. When I would brief visiting clergy and laity who were interested in what "their" Washington office was up to, I would use these big categories of issues. "My responsibilities are the economy and world hunger." And I would think to myself, "How pretentious!"

The economic policy work during my tenure focused on the huge problem of rapid inflation during Jimmy Carter's presidency. That was coupled with the cutoff of oil from the Middle East, leading to long lines at the gas stations and unhappy residents. During Reagan's presidency we focused on protecting the safety net.

Throughout my ten years we also had a series of other staff colleagues as interns, clergy on sabbatical, and positions funded by special offerings within the UCC.

Bible Study: Look, I'm Normal, Said the Gay Guy

I organized a weekly early morning Bible study in my office open to others in the religious policy advocacy staffs. We had around fifteen regular participants. We'd ponder a lectionary lesson for what it might yield to us about our lives. This happened during the time I was wrestling through my anguished divorce decision. How will a divorce affect my three children? I looked for help in these lessons and discussions. On a morning when, perhaps I was beginning to be irritating in my indecision, a member of the group, the man representing the Metropolitan Community Churches, which had its primary outreach to the gay and lesbian community, said, "Look Paul, I grew up in a broken family. My parents divorced when I was the age of your children. Look at me now. I'm normal." This comment still amazes me. How long had we been telling gay men that they are abnormal, living in sin, and going against God's law? And here he was, spontaneously holding himself up as normal, as a model of how healthy my children will one day be. Turns out he was right.

The Washington Interreligious Staff Council (WISC)

The most functional ecumenical enterprise I have experienced was the Washington Interreligious Staff Council (WISC). Up to thirty-five of us met together on Wednesday morning in the National Council of Churches (NCC) conference room. Almost all were Washington-based staff of mainline Protestant denominations with representatives from Roman Catholic, Jewish, and other religious advocacy groups. It provided a rich treasure of support for our work.[3] The longer-term staff mentored the younger/newer staff. WISC provided an enormously helpful conversation for learning concepts, policy, contacts, and advocacy language. These meetings deepened my knowledge of issues. I learned lobbying skills from these colleagues.

Most Washington-based denominational offices had one or two staff. The Friends Committee on National Legislation (FCNL), the United Methodists, and the UCC offices were multiple staff operations. We all were committed to work ecumenically and to give leadership where invited. Our office's view of our mission was different from many others. We wanted to bend policy in the direction of our social policy. Our staff spent major time cultivating relationships with Members of Congress and their staff. We got out of our offices, walked across the street into the Senate offices and hearing rooms, went over to the House side, and talked to people. It was hard, shoe-leather work. We sat in hearings to deepen our grasp of the issues. And since we were a larger staff, we could specialize our focus.

I was surprised that many of the denominational offices were not charged with making a difference or engaging in advocacy. Their task was to monitor and report. They read *The Washington Post*, *The New York Times*, and the *Congressional Quarterly*. They listened carefully to the reports on Wednesday morning. They wrote reports and articles for denominational newsletters and spoke at national and regional meetings. But they did not engage in the lawmaking effort. The UCC tradition was to engage and make a difference.

I developed one clear frustration. After a lot of work, we would often be unpersuasive with legislators. And they would, after all our testimony, for example, cut allocations for the Food Stamp Program, which provided important nutrition for families living in poverty. After such a failure, some

3. The following denominations and faith groups had Washington based, policy-focused staff: the Presbyterian Church USA; the United Presbyterian Church in the USA; the United Church of Christ; the United Methodist Church (who owned the building in which many of our offices were located); the Friends Committee on National Legislation; the Mennonite Central Committee; the American Baptist Office; the Lutheran Council; the Maryknoll Fathers and Brothers; the Religious Action Center of Reform Judaism; the Conference of Catholic Bishops; and others.

colleagues would sit back and find comfort in the old saying "We are not called to success but to faithfulness." To which I would blurt out, "You can still eat in your faithfulness, but the food stamp recipients won't." In that circumstance I was clear we were called to success on behalf of the poor.

Some interns in our office felt that their job was to cut through the legislative verbiage and tell the "truth." If they saw a member of Congress who served on the appropriations subcommittee on military spending, they wanted to yell face-to-face that "you are murderers!" The interns felt that we weren't blunt enough. I asked how long it would be for them to have their second appointment with that member.

A question often asked was how we in the Protestant staffs in Washington cooperated with the sizable Roman Catholic and Jewish advocacy groups. On hunger and welfare issues we worked very closely within the task force structure. But on abortion issues, for example, the Protestants and Jews worked together. The Catholic advocates went another way. And on foreign policy questions touching on Israel, especially military aid bills, the Catholics and Protestants worked together and often against the positions taken by the various representatives of Jewish organizations. We had some hard discussions when we tried to address the issues that separated us. In this way I could understand why Congress has very formal structure to the debate style. They refer to each other with great respect. They might say, "My esteemed colleague is wrong on this question." The reason for this formality is that opponents on one issue might be on the same side of the next issue.

The Interreligious Taskforce on US Food Policy: World Hunger

Two major issues that occupied the church lobbying work after the Vietnam War were world hunger and human rights.

Many of the denominations were raising a generous amount of money to fight hunger at home and abroad. In most cases a portion of those funds was designated for public policy. The Rev. Dr. George Chauncey, head of the Washington Office of the Presbyterian Church US (the southern Presbyterian Church) quickly envisioned the creation of a special task force on the public policy of the hunger issues.

George was successful in inviting the denominations to contribute funds to create the Interreligious Taskforce on US Food Policy. The task force operated as one of the WISC task forces. The funds were used to staff an office and to hire researchers and advocates who worked as a team with the denominational staff. George served as chair of the task force and as supervisor of the staff.

George hired Janet Vandevender for the position of staff director of the Interreligious Taskforce on US Food Policy. She was responsible for coordinating an evolving staff that included task force employees plus interns, sabbatical pastors, and clergy assigned from the participating denominational staffs. Together, working with task force members, the staff coordinated local church member education and lobbying efforts, did issue analysis, tracked legislation, drafted testimony, lobbied, and sent letters to congressional and committee offices. These letters, signed by heads of denominational offices, urged various kinds of action: passage of proposed bills; amendments that, from our perspective, would strengthen the bills; opposition to other proposed amendments; etc. The office provided the support for all this activity.

In 1963, four years after my ordination to ministry in the United Church of Christ, I experienced a vocational call to ministry, to focus on issues of poverty and racism. It was a strong vocational definition and the 1960s were rich in opportunity to engage these issues. In the US the War on Poverty was a package of legislation first introduced by President Lyndon B. Johnson during his State of the Union address on January 8, 1964. This legislation was proposed by Johnson in response to a national poverty rate of around 19 percent.

A powerful word from Latin America gave new energy to the church's critique. The gathering in September 1968 of the Latin American bishops of the Catholic Church in Medellín, Colombia, expressed powerfully a commitment to address poverty: "A deafening cry pours from the throats of millions of men, asking their pastors for a liberation that reaches them from nowhere else. 'Now you are listening to us in silence, but we hear the shout which arises from your suffering,' the Pope told the 'campesinos' in Columbia."[4] There is much biblical support for a focus on "the least of these." This social analysis brought new perspective and new intellectual categories for our work. The Medellín bishops' conference marked a turning point for Latin American Catholicism, with the concepts of "liberation theology," "structural sin," "preferential option for the poor," and "Christian grassroots communities," born during those debates.[5] It was a watershed moment for Latin American Catholicism.

George was an impressive colleague, able to analyze public policy issues from a liberation theological perspective and to write articulate, hard-hitting testimony within a theological framework. George would often do

4. "Medellin Document," 1.

5. "Medellin Document," 3–6.

the first draft for testimony that, after review by other members of the task force, was delivered by a member of the task force. George's skillful prose lifted why the churches are involved in such matters.

Family

Genie Holmes and I were legally separated in 1976 and, five years later, divorced.

Janet Vandevender and her son, Ben, a one-and-a-half-year-old, came to Washington as part of our developing relationship. In August 1977, during Ben's summer month with his brother Aaron and dad in Tempe, Arizona, Janet got a phone call reporting that Ben had drowned in his dad's backyard swimming pool. We flew out together for a memorial service and to spend time with Aaron. Janet and I were married at the First Congregational UCC in Washington, DC, in 1981 and moved to a home in Takoma Park, Maryland. Aaron spent summers and Christmas holidays with us. He graduated from California Polytechnic State University San Luis Obispo and Lewis and Clark Law School.

All three of my children lived with their mom and graduated from Montgomery Blair High School. Mark graduated from the University of Massachusetts and earned a masters from Brown University. Adam graduated from the New School in San Francisco and Ann from Boston University.

In the fall of 1977 Janet began the evening law program at Georgetown University Law Center. It was a four-year program and classes were scheduled four nights a week at the Law Center, just a short walk from our offices on Capitol Hill. So, weekends were heavy-duty study periods. Lugging a backpack full of law books was a heavy load.

I enrolled in a master's degree in the political science program offered by the George Washington University. All evening classes were taught at the Library of Congress down the street a block from the United Methodist Building.

I graduated in 1981. Janet graduated in 1982 and became a member of the District of Columbia Bar in 1983.

Living in Washington: Enjoying the National Symphony and Willie Nelson with the President

Janet and I enjoyed tickets to the National Symphony concerts at the Kennedy Center. The music director at that time was Mstislav Rostropovich, an exiled Russian citizen. He was one of the greatest cellists of the twentieth century. Rostropovich fought for art without borders, freedom of speech, and democratic values, resulting in harassment from the Soviet regime.

Because of the notoriety of so many people in Washington, if I kept my eyes open, I recognized people from the nightly news. One evening Janet and I found our seats, great seats, on the orchestra level of the Kennedy Center for a performance of *The Messiah*. I noticed that our seats were the fifth and sixth in from the aisle, and that the first four seats stayed vacant almost to the dimming of the lights. I knew the signal. It was common practice for people of note to stay in a special lounge until minutes before curtain time. Then they'd hustle down the aisle and slip into their seats almost unnoticed. So, the seat on my right and the other three were about to be inhabited by some elite, important persons. I watched for the hustle in the aisle. Into the seat next to me was suddenly Robert McNamara, former secretary of the Defense Department during the Vietnam War. Next to him were his wife and their friends.

If there was one person I blamed for the prolonged, disastrous Vietnam War, it was McNamara. I worked my butt off for several years along with millions of others trying to change this guy's mind. I blamed him for the deaths of most of those whose names are on the Vietnam Memorial. Now he and I were bumping each other's elbows off the armrest.

It was hard for me to enjoy the great music. But I waited. I knew the text well enough to know we were about to hear the angels announcing, "Glory to God in the highest, and peace on earth, goodwill towards men."[6] I could not help but glance to my right at McNamara. He was sound asleep.

It was also easy to tell when the president was attending a performance. There were a bunch of well-dressed, well-built men running around with earbuds, talking into their sleeves.

We were at the Kennedy Center for a performance of choral music by the Robert Shaw Chorale from Atlanta. Should have known. Atlanta is in Georgia. President and Mrs. Carter had to be there. And we were at the Merriweather Post Pavilion for a big Willie Nelson and Friends concert. His big hit at the time was "Georgia." There were those big guys doing their thing protecting the president. The president and Mrs. Carter sat three rows in front of us.

In addition to our immersion in country music outlaws, introduced by the Lynns, I expanded my own enjoyment to bluegrass and became aware that the Washington area was a mecca for bluegrass music. The primary live venue in the country for bluegrass was the Birchmere, a bar

6. Handel, "*Messiah* Oratorio Libretto," movement 17.

and performance space in Alexandria, Virginia. Every Thursday night the Seldom Scene played to sell out crowds. Others like Vince Gill and Emmy Lou Harris played the Birchmere long before they were famous. The NPR station, WAMU, operated by American University, was NPR news and bluegrass all day and night. The Sunday morning show was named *Stained Glass Bluegrass*.

I got completely soaked up in my heavy immersion in bluegrass during my recovery from a series of surgeries following a fall from our roof. I was home for several months as the healing was going on in my broken body. We had a good high-fidelity radio and record player. I listened to music all day. I took long naps sitting in my chair. I read. I took pain pills. Standing was a major effort taking almost more strength and balance than I had. Only one leg was usable. So, selecting a radio station in the morning meant that was going to be it for the day. There were then no remotes for volume and tuning. Bluegrass was the only music that was never depressing, bluegrass music never varied much in volume. The songs told funny stories and were entirely tolerable at worst and uplifting at best. I could not say that for classical, pop, or jazz. Nothing but bluegrass as they said on WAMU. I would not try to stand up until I had at least three things I needed to stand up for, the bathroom was reliably number one on that list.

We quickly learned to enjoy the Maryland special dining experience of crab, coleslaw, and beer. I drank the beer. Janet drank something else. We had a Chesapeake Crab House nearby. They'd throw the boiled crab on a table covered with brown wrapping paper. They gave us the necessary hammers and nutcrackers. It was hot and spicy. My mouth burned. The juicy coleslaw and beer were medicine. One can't be dainty cracking crab legs and sucking the meat out. The restaurant had a big, waist-high, metal trough with several faucets of water and piles of paper towels. It was close to a full bath. And a cultural event.

Our favorite restaurant was the Foundry in Georgetown on the second floor of a converted foundry. Our favorite table was the one by the big window looking down on the first lock on the Chesapeake and Ohio Canal and a bronze bust of Supreme Court Justice William O. Douglas who was instrumental in the restoration of the canal. I learned to love Jack Daniel's on the rocks with Janet drinking her scotch, watching the snow fall on that scene below.

I became an avid Washington Redskins football fan and a fan of the University of Maryland basketball team coached by Lefty Driesell and of Georgetown University coached by John Thompson. I easily shifted college athletic conference allegiance from the Pacific Eight Conference to the Atlantic Coast Conference. Our home baseball team was the Baltimore Orioles.

Two Super Bowls with one a victory, one world series championship, three final fours with Georgetown winning the tournament in my ten years.

Carter Years

The Carter years made it possible for me to experience "access." President Carter reached out to the religious community when he came to office in 1977. Anne Wexler was the White House director of the Office for Outreach. Phil Spector, a young attorney on Anne's staff, was assigned liaison to religious groups. Phil did not know his way around Protestant Christianity and asked me to help orient him to situations involving the church. He served the president well in making and nurturing connections with our offices. Phil attended parties at our apartment. He would take my calls in his office at the White House.

I had "access," including this close contact in the White House. Access really means that when I called, my contact picked up. Phil would ask me for help with something and I would ask him for help. The receptionist in my office would buzz me and say, "The White House switchboard is calling." I always took the call. I had the same sense of inflation when I climbed in a cab and said, "The White House, East Gate, please."

On March 13, 1979, the phone rang in our apartment at 12:30 a.m. It was from the White House switchboard inviting me and a guest to come immediately to the White House. Buses were waiting to take us to Andrews Air Force Base. President Carter had successfully completed shuttle diplomacy between Israel and Egypt. Air Force One was due to land at 1:45 a.m. and we were to join the welcoming party to greet the president as he arrived in the middle of the night. We cheered as the president disembarked. News cameras rolled and flash bulbs flashed.

In September I was invited to the North Lawn of the White House as Egyptian President Anwar El Sadat and Israeli Prime Minister Menachem Begin signed the Middle East Peace Accords that won them the Nobel Prize for Peace.

I received an invitation to a gospel sing and picnic on the South Lawn of the White House to be held on Sunday afternoon September 9, 1979. The invitation indicated I could bring a guest. I phoned the outreach office and was authorized to bring two guests. Janet and my daughter, Ann, joined me. It was a delightfully sunny day. On the South Lawn, the White House staff put on an old-fashioned picnic of southern fried chicken, mashed potatoes, coleslaw, and iced tea. The gospel singing was outstanding. We mingled with political, corporate, show business, and media figures. Ann saw the

Secretary of Labor Ray Marshall talking with Roger Mudd, the CBS-TV News anchor. She said, "He's my mother's boss." Genie was working in the Occupational Safety and Health Administration (OSHA) in the Department of Labor. Ann went over and introduced herself and chatted about life in the Department of Labor.

The president named Donald McHenry as UN ambassador. I received an invitation to the September 23, 1979, swearing in. The invitation indicated I could bring a guest. After the swearing in in the East Room, Janet and I went through the receiving line. When she shook hands with the President, she thanked him for the wonderful gospel sing and picnic two weeks earlier. He said, "Aren't you sweet?" She hangs on to that.

I chatted with Vice President Mondale in the receiving line. I told him about my flight in a small plane flown by his brother Mort Mondale who was head of the state teacher's union in Minnesota. A year previous, Mort was flying us into the Minneapolis-St. Paul International Airport after a debate on the military draft at a school in a small town in western Minnesota. The teacher's union president and the church lobbyist debated two guys from the American Legion. Mort had met my flight from Washington and flown us to the debate that afternoon. When we were taken back to the landing strip, a fifty-yard-long grassy field, we found that the temperature had fallen enough that ice crystals had formed on the wings of the small plane. So, we walked around the plane rubbing the ice off the wings with our gloved hands. Seemed low-tech to me. We took off from the grass strip with only the headlights of the car that drove us there lighting the strip. When we were airborne, Mort discovered that the landing lights were not working. We had wing lights but when we got to the Minneapolis airport, landing lights were considered crucial for the control tower to fit us into the sequence of planes strung out along a glide path for landing. Mort radioed the tower and described our predicament.

They carefully instructed him where to enter the lineup of planes descending toward the runway. Mort was nervous which didn't help my confidence. We headed from the side straight at the line of planes approaching the runway. We banked left to enter the line. All seemed fine until Mort got the idea that our slow plane was going to be overrun by the wide body passenger jet just behind us. As soon as our wheels hit the runway he cut to the left to taxi onto the infield and get out of the way of the fast-approaching monster. He almost tipped the plane over in that maneuver. We bumped along on the grass and were met by several emergency vehicles that had been sent in the event we needed medical assistance. That seemed thoughtful. We taxied on in and I met my flight back to DC that night thinking, "Just another day in the life of a lobbyist."

I was telling this shaggy dog story to Walter Mondale in the receiving line. By the time I was well into this story to the vice president (a mistake to try to tell a long story in a receiving line) the president was listening in. At the end of the story the president said to Mondale, "I see it runs in the family." I have no idea what that was all about but they both enjoyed it.

After two years in office the president had found himself weighted down by inflation. This became a major issue for the White House. Economists analyzing this inflation determined that it was being driven by inflation in hospital costs. How to bring down hospital costs, to contain them, was the question. The domestic policy staff under Stuart Eisenstaedt gathered a working group to develop proposals on inflation in the hospital costs. The working group met Thursday mornings in the White House Mess, the dining room on the lower level of the West Wing. It was staffed by Navy personnel. Thus, the name mess as in mess hall where the military take their meals.

I was working on health care issues and was invited to be a member of the working group as the representative of the religious community's concerns. Every Thursday morning for two months I took a taxi to the Pennsylvania Avenue west gate of the White House, showed my driver's license, watched while the armed White House policeman checked my name on the schedule for the day, walked down the driveway to the entrance to the West Wing, then was ushered down to the mess. In those meetings I came to know the Washington representatives of the American Nurses Association, the health insurance companies, the American Medical Association, the labor unions, and other interested stakeholders seeking to reduce hospital costs. The legislation that we hammered out was introduced with many cosponsors and passed and signed into law. It was called the Hospital Cost Containment Act of 1977. I was learning how the process works and how to argue our points when we had access to the conversations in the legislative cycle.

On the more comprehensive legislation on health care, Carter ran on a ticket advocating universal, single-payer health care. Senator Edward Kennedy was chair of the powerful Health, Education, and Labor subcommittee in the Senate. He advocated that health care is a right and not a privilege. In Carter's first two years as president, he had a Democratic majority in the both the House and the Senate. The opportunity for the country to move to universal health care as a right was never better.

Except Senator Kennedy and President Carter were rivals within the Democratic Party and waged a competition for leadership in the party. The Senator's efforts in health care reform were focused, as was his constant theme throughout his career, to secure universal health care within a single-payer system. Most Washington offices of religious groups supported universal, single-payer health coverage. So, working with Kennedy's staff was a natural alliance. He called on us and we called on him in the dance of this legislation. My phone would ring with a request from Kennedy staff to come over to his office for a meeting of a small group to discuss options in the developing legislative horse trading. Sometimes we discussed how the bill should be written or how to tighten up some provisions. On occasion, the question was how we get a particular senator's vote. Can we move him to support? His support is needed for passage.

One day as he entered the room, Kennedy said, "Seems like you guys are like the volunteer fire department up in New England. Somebody rings a bell, and you all drop everything and show up." He expressed his appreciation to us. On the other side, when I was hosting a particularly important group of visitors, I could call his office to work out a time for him to come across the street to spend a half hour with us. He was unusually generous in this way. Most senators and members only give face time to constituents—folks who vote and have influence in the home state or district.

The opportunity to achieve a universal, single-payer system was bungled. I worked with three people from that Thursday White House group to try to keep the negotiation between the White House and the Senate sub-committee, between Carter and Kennedy, on track. Carter shifted strategy and withdrew from going for the whole universal plan and began offering the congress pieces of the plan in separate bills. Kennedy was furious, believing that the only thing that had a chance of passage was the whole package. The game was over.

I noticed that high-powered lobbyists pocketed handfuls of matchbooks that were on the table by the door of the mess. The matchbooks had the presidential seal on one side and the words "The White House" on the other. To show off one's "access to power," the game was to put a couple of these on the coffee table at home or the office whenever you had a meeting or threw a party. Of course, I took a few. I was deflated as I was enjoying a party at a friend's house when I saw on his coffee table a matchbook that said "Air Force One."

In August 1980, I was invited to come to the White House when the newly elected Prime Minister Robert Mugabe of Zimbabwe was welcomed in a state visit. This reception provided my favorite moment in the White House. Of the two hundred people gathered in the East Wing Ballroom for Carter's presentation of Mugabe, most were African American church leaders, leaders of several prominent human rights and civil rights groups with a focus on Africa issues. It seemed to me that about 90 percent were African American men. I saw only one person I recognized, the Rev. James Joseph.

I had first gotten to know Jim when I was on the urban training center staff in Los Angeles and he was chaplain at the Claremont Colleges. Jim and Joe Hough worked on racism issues and our center was contracted with to provide anti-racism training to seminary students. Jim had been appointed by President Carter as under secretary of the Department of the Interior and later served as US ambassador to South Africa. We chatted until applause broke out as the President, Prime Minister Mugabe, and a small entourage stepped on to the platform.

The president stepped to the microphone and gave a very detailed, gracious, and glowing welcome to Mr. Mugabe, the first democratically elected prime minister of the country of Zimbabwe, former colonial Rhodesia. There was sustained applause. Mugabe stepped to the podium and replied to the president's warm welcome by making his own glowing tribute to the president. He made his point as clear as he could when he said, "You know, Mr. President, that the symbol of my political party in Zimbabwe is the cock. The cock symbolizes strength and cleverness in battle. And I want to say to you, Mr. Carter, that you are the cock of the United States!"

In a moment of stunned silence Mr. Carter's face glowed a deep red and then there was uncontrolled explosion of deep, long, very loud laughter. Carter's face went to deep purple. We all fought to control our laughter and to bring ourselves back to appropriate behavior. Mr. Carter warmly thanked his visitor, and we were invited to a receiving line and refreshments. Jim and I agreed we'd have to look a long time before we found another moment like that.

It is fair to ask what besides feeding my ego was the importance of all this access. I was not a policy wonk. I did not carry in my head proposals for policy language and budget data. But I loved legislative strategy (who needs to talk to whom and by when) and connecting people. Bill McKinney, president of Pacific School of Religion, once called me "a connected guy." I was not a reliable source of detail policy information, but I knew who was and could make the connection. Thus, from my own perspective, I spent time at the various events widening my circle of contacts ("building my rolodex" in the jargon of the time). I believe I was able to bring into play the religious community agenda and our perspective and data on a wide range of issues.

If I had to make the case in testimony or a sign-on letter, I had to prepare carefully and stick to the stuff I had prepared. If I wandered off the ranch, I was very unreliable. More than once when asked questions after delivering testimony for which I had no answer, I quoted a friend who said to a senator, "I've already told you everything I know and then some." It was normal in congressional hearings to run into areas where more research had to be done to provide a solid response to a query. At such times additional answers could be inserted into the hearing record. The record of the hearing is kept open for a period for such additional information. The point was to build a record that was thorough and accurate. It's helpful to have grown up enough to know what I could and could not do and be comfortable with that wisdom.

My experience with members of Congress was that they were intelligent, committed to doing their work conscientiously, and basically friendly. And they were loyal to their folks back in the district. The three basic questions I heard in relation to any legislative proposal were the following:

1. Will this help our country?

2. Will this help the people in my district?

3. Will this help me get reelected?

When I went to Washington, I thought I held a cynical view about politicians and office holders. What I assumed about all of them was based on the reported outrageous behavior of a few of them. When away from campaigning, and away from reporters and cameras, most of them, in my experience, were thoughtful and interesting people. Even a very conservative member of Congress. We had a nice chat one afternoon about whether the blue sky is best in North Carolina or in California.

It was also clear that they were very dependent on their staff. It is impossible for members to be informed on all the issues on which they had to cast votes. They probably had a few issues that they brought with them, issues they cared about out of their own experience: agriculture for the members from Nebraska, water policy for Utah and Arizona, or homelessness for members from big cities, for example. Their first vote on the floor might be on food stamp authorization or aid to Israel. They relied on staff to brief and guide them, and they formed friendships with colleagues who had similar values and constituents and followed their guidance. So, for a lobbyist, it was important to get to know the influential staff. Each member was assigned to several committees and subcommittees and usually sat through hours of testimony from experts. They got educated on the narrow set of issues that came before that committee.

My daughter, Ann, was in Washington working for Congressman Ted Weiss from Manhattan. She had a desk, a typewriter, and a bachelor's degree. The staff director told her to draft a speech for the congressman to deliver on the anniversary of the Roe v. Wade decision, January 22, 1985. That's all she got. She had a couple days to research and draft it. Ann researched what the congressman had previously said in his annual floor speech on that day. And she had to research what new developments had happened on reproductive health issues. She had to suggest, given his past statements, how he would position himself on any new issues.

With that she drafted the speech. The staff director stood over her shoulder for a few moments reading, then said she had to complete it in twenty minutes. When Ann rushed to the end, the staff director snatched the paper out of the typewriter and handed it to Congressman Weiss who walked over to the House Chamber and gave the speech.

I had several reactions. Pride most of all. But I also wondered what kind of government we have when my just-graduated daughter wrote a speech that was delivered by a congressman, a speech that showed up in the *Congressional Record!*[7]

I learned some years later listening to Andy Young that Jimmy Carter, as he was preparing himself for his run for president, asked Young, member of Congress from Atlanta who was a UCC pastor and a former aide to Dr. King, to help him learn foreign policy issues. Young, having served on the staff of United Church of Christ Counsel for Christian Social Action earlier in his career, pulled out his file of foreign policy pronouncements and resolutions adopted by General Synod of the UCC and gave them to Governor Carter. Carter read them, making our theological work and issue analysis his first briefing on foreign policy.[8]

I reflected on this wonderful story. Having spent ten years working with staff colleagues to draft resolutions for five General Synods and having represented many of those position papers in my policy advocacy, I was astounded that some of them might serve the purpose of starting the education of one who would become president.

In 1980 I was at the midway point in my ten years (1974–1984) as a lobbyist for the United Church of Christ in Washington, DC. I did not understand that the public policy world was about to change, that a new and painful inequality was being plotted and the deals were being cut. And I cared a lot about this change. I lost my access to events and to policy discussions with domestic policy staff at the White House in the 1980 election.

Party at the End of the Known World: The 1980 Election

On November 5, 1980, Janet and I hosted an election night party at our apartment at 800 4th Street SW. Our guests included several senate staff

7. Weiss, "Statement on Abortion."

8. From author's notes of remarks by Hon. Andrew Young, 15th General Synod of the United Church of Christ, Atlanta, GA.

members, several lobbyists for groups like Bread for the World, and staff from the National Council of Churches, the Lutheran Council, and others.

It was a strange evening. First, the TV networks announced projected results of the presidential race before our guests arrived. Polls in the Eastern Time Zone were closed by 7:00 p.m. while the rest of the country was still voting. The major networks and their polling organizations had determined that Reagan would overwhelm Carter and declared him winner as the polls closed in the East. Voters in the Midwest and on the West Coast stayed home. The 1980 election, in addition to sending Carter back to Georgia, altered the Senate by defeating eleven senior liberal Democrat senators. The new Republican majority was fifty-three to forty-seven in the Senate in the 97th Congress.

Second, as we ate and drank and chatted, we watched the results in congressional races roll in from around the country. It was an evening during which we felt that the world we had known was suddenly disappearing and a new world, yet undefined, was taking its place.

Former Vice President Walter Mondale later told me that the peak of the liberal project in America was the 89th Congress (January 1965 through January 1967) when there were sixty-eight Democratic senators, most of them seasoned, big-government, thoughtful liberals, in the Senate and a 295–140 Democratic majority in the House. And Lyndon B. Johnson was in the White House. Mondale that under those conditions "you could get some good things done."

And the third and very personal reason it was a strange party was the unemployment that faced some around the room. Around midnight we turned off the two television sets, gathered our chairs in a circle, grabbed another round of refreshment, and talked about what all this news might mean to us personally. Losing your job on election night makes for an unpleasant party. Both the senate staff persons in attendance lost their jobs because the senators who appointed them lost.

For those of us who were lobbyists, we would have to start all over again to develop contacts. It was back to square one. New congressional members and staff had to be cultivated, new working and personal friendships formed. We knew there would be far fewer in the Congress who would be interested in our ideas. The current staffers, many with whom we had developed close working and personal relations, would be packing up. Carefully nurtured contacts and useful relationships were not useful anymore.

I began to realize what I was about to lose.

1980 Ronald Reagan: Government is Now the Problem

It was 1980 and a windy and cold November evening in Washington, DC. I stood on the corner of First and Constitution NE waiting for the M2 bus to take me back to my apartment in Southwest Washington. It was the end of another workday on Capitol Hill and Senate staffers were streaming out of the Russell and Dirksen Senate Offices Buildings across the street from the Methodist Building where our offices were located. Cold wind gusts burst up the hill making for serious discomfort. I had my wool cap, gloves, and overcoat collar pulled tight.

But something was different this evening. I saw eight stretch limousines parked along First Street between the Senate office buildings. I hadn't before seen a bunch of limousines like that in DC. Jimmy Carter had been president for four years and limo passengers were not his people. These limos turned out to be a sign of things to come.

My claim that 1980 was the year that changed everything is based on my deep commitment regarding the poor, "the least of these." What was changing that night was the emergence of a transformation to Reagan's campaign promise of smaller government, one that gave breaks to the rich and corporations and slashed open the safety net for the poor. The New Deal of Franklin Roosevelt, the Fair Deal of Lyndon Johnson, and most of the programs of the safety net were targeted for elimination. It was about the role of government.

In the presence of those limos parked on First Street and the corporate executive passengers now meeting with the newly organized Senate with a large Republican majority, I saw the beginnings of this new inequality in America. Ronald Reagan had trounced President Jimmy Carter on November 4, just a week earlier. The Electoral College vote was 489 for Ronald Reagan to 49 for Carter. That was a lot more than a message from the people. It was a rejection. As I saw that late afternoon, the agenda of government was about to become the agenda of corporate America. Those limos transported important corporate leaders who were—as I contemplated their limos, uniformed drivers sitting in the warmth of the car heaters, motors humming low—meeting with senators, primarily those who would be the new Republican chairs of Senate committees. They were outlining the agenda for the 96th congress. Corporate America had bought that future through contributions to election campaigns and now those they elected were being shown how to say "thank you."

The time after the election and before the swearing in was a time of transition. The other party had come to power and the governing party was stepping down. The outs were coming in and the ins were looking for work.

Homes around the District were up for sale and eager buyers worked with eager real estate agents.

It had happened four years earlier when Carter defeated Gerald Ford. New Democrats came to town, many with a Georgian accent. The Republicans went home or found positions in lobbying firms. Janet and I, with tickets from Congressman Andrew Young, had stood about twenty yards from the podium when President Carter took the oath on the East Front of the Capital. Jimmy and Rosalynn Carter, in a very populist move, had walked much of the way down Pennsylvania Avenue to the White House after he had taken the oath. But that was another day. This was the Republicans' turn to form the administration and reorganize the legislative branch.

I remembered how surprised I had been in 1976 that friends I had worked with in various offices and coalitions began talking of their applications to the Carter transition team. I was learning how the system worked. Many of them became appointees of the new administration to various positions in the government. For example, Judy Stone, in the Presbyterian office, joined the staff to the Highway Safety Commission director Joan Claybrook. The giant bureaucracies that make up the US government are filled with permanent civil service staff, but with each change of administration, presidential appointees are layered across the top of the permanent staff. Most of the government does not change with a change of ruling party. Only the top level does. Most of what the government does is routine. In my experience on the hill and in my relationship with some of these civil service folks in our local church, I developed great respect for them. Most of them were attracted to government service as a way of serving people and their country. They did their work with competence and dedication.

I had read in my study for my political science degree that during the time after WWII, Italy averaged three changes in government every year for almost a decade. But the country chugged along without interruption because only the top one percent of the government changed with each change in administration. It's almost like that in the US, and I came away feeling that it serves us well. I heard stories about the Nixon administration trying to politicize the Internal Revenue Service and make it an instrument of political manipulation, but the IRS attorneys, civil servants, straight up, loyal, and acting on what was best for the country, made it impossible. Presidents could appoint their political friends to the top positions, but they could not remove the civil service layers below. Those folks knew the laws they were in place to implement and did not wish to jeopardize the country or their employment. I found the federal work force reliable, hardworking, and having the best interest of the country as their value.

The Lobbying Paper for the Presbyterians

"Does the church through its Washington based staff, turn its social policy into the nation's public policy?"[9] In 1981 I was approached by Dean Lewis of the Presbyterian national staff with a request that I prepare a paper for them as a background document as they considered merging the Washington offices of the northern and southern Presbyterian Churches, a relic of the division over race issues at the time of the Civil War. They would pay a stipend for a paper reflecting my take on how well the Washington offices of the denominations were doing the job they were set to accomplish and any suggestions I had on how they might reorganize and refocus that public policy work. Putting a sharper point on it, Lewis asked, "Does the church through its Washington based staff, turn its social policy into the nation's public policy?" In the assignment, I wrote, "The general issue I am working on is 'influence'—in other words, the way in which the official positions taken by Protestant denominations do or do not—can or cannot—have influence on public policy broadly understood."[10]

The approach I took was to look at the last seven years asking myself to identify any specific instances that I could, in good conscience, make the case that our efforts made a real difference, that public policy was different because of the work the Washington Interreligious Staff Council and its members did. I meant that to be an exacting standard.

The passage of a piece of legislation was somewhat of a miracle and had fingerprints all over it from so many competing forces. Opposing interest groups bombarded congressional offices with advice. Lobbyists from powerful corporations offered advice and cash support for reelection campaigns. A cocktail party at a nice restaurant with an open bar hosted by the American Electric Car Association could raise hundreds of thousands of dollars and be very persuasive for a member of Congress whose vote is crucial on an amendment in committee. Our ability to mobilize good arguments, brilliantly stated testimony, and a few letters from constituents seemed a thin reed on which to place any hope that we could actually make a legitimate claim that we had made something happen.

But I was satisfied that there were six times in my seven-year service that we made a difference. Given the thousands of hours of combined staff time the churches paid for to support all these staff colleagues that may seem like a small result.

To be specific about my claim I wrote the following:

9. Dean Lewis, letter to author, January 5, 1981.
10. Kittlaus, "Evaluation and Proposal."

I would argue that the following policy outcomes are a direct result of the religious lobby's intentional action, and that this action was necessary within the context of a lot of others' actions to produce the effect.

1. The adoption by the 96th Congress of the amendment to eliminate the purchase requirement in the Food Stamp Program.
2. The adoption by the 95th Congress of the Human Rights provisions in the Development Aid bill.
3. The adoption by the 96th Congress of the Grain Reserve bill.
4. The adoption by the 96th Congress of the Full Employment and Balanced Growth Act (the Humphrey-Hawkins bill).
5. The fifteen-month delay within the 96th Congress in funding the draft registration program promulgated by the Carter administration.
6. The action of the Conference Committee in the 96th Congress to include no funding for the rehabilitation of the chemical weapons plant in Pine Bluff, Arkansas.[11]

Given this, I asked what did we do uniquely or especially well that contributed to these outcomes? After reviewing these efforts, I concluded that there were several identifiable elements, capabilities we exercised to bring about our desired result. Without reconstructing the entire paper, I list here those capabilities necessary to success in most lobbying effort on the part of the denominational staffs working together. We had created these capacities from time to time but had never created permanent organizational structure to apply to all legislation.

Capacity One: Master the detail of the policy area. Have our staff know as much as congressional staffers about all the details, relevant research, and important political currents that come into play as the bill is shaped.

Capacity Two: Develop arguments in support of all the changes we advocate and spend whatever time is necessary to get to know by name and phone number all the key players in the process. Press our argument in all the key discussions.

Capacity Three: Set up an active media operation. See media journalists as allies to get our message out.

Capacity Four: Use the vast network of social action church-oriented members to hold their senator/member accountable on our issue.

11. Kittlaus, "Evaluation and Proposal."

Focus on states and districts relevant to the situation. Provide advocacy training, press packets, legislative updates, and mobilization alerts.

From these conclusions I developed the notion of a successful lobbying campaign by the mainline religious community that tied together all four of the capacities. This model was helpful in thinking in fresh ways about the skills to look for in the hiring of new staff.[12]

Rethinking the Theology That Informs Our Advocacy

For what should we advocate? It became clear to me that the policies we advocated were based on a general opposition to more military spending and a general support for more spending on the poor, homeless, children, and otherwise marginalized. But in our testimony, we were not able to offer much in the way of a constructive vision about military spending and foreign policy and even less on management of the US economy and its complex dynamics that created or ended jobs and prosperity for people. Our testimony and our action alerts to our networks of people around the country usually opened with a theological or biblical statement that we called our "rationale." But it was at times proof texting, pulling quotes out of the Bible to suit our position.

I brought these concerns and a proposal to our board of directors, and they set about developing constructive responses that became multiple year projects. We asked our theologians and biblical scholars for guidance. Professor M. Douglas Meeks taught theology at Eden Seminary and was a member of our board, and he drafted a paper on the economy drawing on biblical and theological sources. After wide circulation and review he eventually expanded the paper into the book, *God the Economist*.[13]

Meeks began his paper with a definition of economy. "The Greek word from which we derive economy, *oikonomia*, is a compound of *oikos*, household, and *nomos*, law or management. Economy means literally the law or management of the household. Household relates to the production,

---

12. Community organizers and policy advocates work on very different rhythms and calendars. And they need different skill sets to be effective. Lobbyists work within the flow of the congressional legislative calendar. Organizers are not bound nor guided by that. For example, it made no sense to gear up on food stamps if the agriculture bill wasn't up for renewal until next year. But a community organizer works on a different flow of energy and timelines, normally determined by the readiness of a group to plan an event. I realized I had moved into a different ball game again moving from organizing to lobbying. Organizers are playing football; lobbyists are playing baseball.

13. Meeks, *God the Economist*.

distribution, and consumption of the necessities of life."[14] "As the introduction to almost every contemporary economics textbook shows, one of
the most basic assumptions of modern economics is scarcity. Scarcity, it is
claimed, is the universal presupposition of exchange relationships."[15] But
with "God as Economist . . . a radically different assumption" holds: "If the
righteousness of God is present there is always enough to go around. From
manna in the desert, to Jesus' feeding of the multitudes, to the Lord's Supper, the biblical traditions depict the superabundance of God's spirit as the
starting point of God's household and its practice of hospitality."[16] Meeks
worked out the implication of this new assumption and helped us frame our
testimony with these insights.

The work on developing biblical and theological understandings of
our task in relationship to the foreign and military policy was assigned to a
development team. This work went on for several years after I left the Washington office. My successor, Jay Lintner, staffed this process. The chair, Dr.
Susan Thistlethwaite, president of Chicago Theological Seminary, drafted
their findings and eventually it was published as *A Just Peace Church*.[17] The
team turned the classic Roman Catholic just war theory, the clarification of
conditions that establish the right to go to war, on its head. The peace theology team asked what conditions within and between nations foster peace.

Kirchengemeinschaft: The UCC and the German United Churches (East and West) Partnership

I boarded the U-Bahn at the Zoo station in West Berlin, heading into East
Berlin. It was 1981, eight years before the Berlin Wall fell. Two years earlier, the Rev. Christa Grengel and the Rev. Reinhardt Groscurth had come
to my Washington, DC, office to explore how the UCC and Evangelical
Church of the Union (EKU) in Germany might work together to implement a UCC General Synod resolution on peace and partnership among the
three churches. At the end of our conversation, they invited me to come to
Germany for a month as their guest, two weeks in West Germany and two
weeks in East Germany.

The division of Germany at the end of the World War II and the erec-
tion of the Berlin Wall had closed travel and communication between East
and West sectors and had, as a result, cut off communication and created

14. Meeks, *God the Economist*, 6.
15. Meeks, *God the Economist*, 12.
16. Meeks, *God the Economist*, 12.
17. Thistlethwaite, *Just Peace Church*.

two different church bodies across the northern portion of Germany. East and West German pastors could no longer talk together. Travel across the border was allowed only for East German church officials like Grengel. West German citizens could travel in the East only following very restricted guidelines. With the UCC, a working group on these connections had been functioning for years. The group had been the source for and energy behind the Synod resolution, which was called Kirchengemeinschaft, roughly translated an official "church fellowship." The UCC-EKU Working Group coordinated official interactions among delegates from the three churches.

When I stepped off the subway at the Friedrichstrasse station, it was a relief to recognize Grengel. I did not want to be lost in East Berlin. For the following two weeks I was immersed in the reality of life in East Germany. It was under the control of the Soviet Union and had a socialist economy. My eyes were opened to many unexpected values, like ensuring that education was provided to the children of workers (largely at the expense of educating the children of professionals); that music was a central feature of family life so most people played instruments, sang, and kept the organs in the churches in superb condition; that health care was excellent and readily available; and that democracy began on the factory floor as workers chose candidates for elected office.

In the capitol building of the East German government, Grengel and I met with state secretary for Church Affairs Klaus Gysi. He made clear that in socialist doctrine, the church would wither away but in Germany it was very healthy. He admitted that it was a dilemma for the government. He pointed out that East Germany was the only Soviet-dominated nation to deal with a majority Protestant church. All other states had predominantly Eastern Orthodox (Russian) or, as in Poland, Roman Catholic churches. Gysi indicated that the key difference was that the Protestant church believed it should criticize the government. "And," Gysi said with a warm smile for Grengel, "they do it very well." The issue being debated at that time was the government policy on conscription. The church was pressing for conscientious objector status as an option. The church was the only institution that had not been integrated into the soviet system.

In a gathering of East Berlin medical doctors one evening, I talked about my work in Washington seeking better government policy for disarmament, peace, and justice. One of the doctors said about the disarmament issue, "It would seem that you are not very effective." I had to agree. The US military budget kept going up. But I said, "let me show you the argument we had to solve. Maybe you can help me." I took a paper napkin on the coffee table and drew wiggly lines down the middle of the paper. I said this was the Berlin Wall, East Germany on the right side of the line and West Germany on the left. I told them that the most recent justification given by our US leaders for deploying more missiles along the left side was because of the buildup of Russian troops on the right, ready to invade the West. I drew a black arrow thrusting from right to left on the napkin. A three-star general had recently testified to a congressional committee that we must be capable of defeating the invasion from the East.

I asked the folks to formulate an answer to counter that argument. The man who had challenged my effectiveness turned the napkin 180 degrees and said, "We are told the same thing. The West will invade. Thus, the defense." We did not come up with a successful response to our military leaders.

Youth groups with whom I met wanted to see maps of the West, to learn if I had known John Lennon, and asked if everyone wore Levis (which they pronounced "levies").

My experience in West Germany was much more familiar, with churches functioning in many ways like the churches in the UCC. Two major differences struck me. The first, that the state taxed everyone for funds to meet the budget of the churches. There was no stewardship campaign effort. Second, I became acquainted with the ecumenical academy which gathered different portions of the country (labor, business, church leaders, legislators, the military) to plan policy for the country.

When I returned from this trip, I met with the UCC-EKU Working Group to report on this extensive visit. I had developed several proposals for next steps. One of those, taking a group of UCC pastors to East and West Germany to plan further peace activities among the three churches, resulted in my leadership of such a group to Germany in 1982.

I'd share one other profound personal experience. I returned to DC full of the experience of living with different values in the East, simpler materialistically yet in many ways richer in daily cultural experience and in security. Shortly after I returned home, Janet and I went to a new mall in Georgetown. Its glitter of expensive shops, jewelry, fancy shoes, and eating establishments with vast menus was overwhelming to me. We had to leave so I could become reoriented to the life I live.

The Campaign Opposing President Reagan's Second Budget

Ronald Reagan had moved into the White House in January 1981 and caught everyone on Capitol Hill by surprise by proposing a budget that severely cut a wide range of federal programs that support the poor: housing, medical care, income support, food and nutrition programs, most of the elements of the so-called safety net. Congress adopted most of these changes because advocates for the poor, including the churches, were completely caught off guard.

In December 1981 Judy Stone, a former staff member of the Presbyterian office, asked me to meet someone she thought I would want to know. He was Robert Greenstein, who had been director of Food and Nutrition Service in the Department of Agriculture during the Carter Presidency. Among the various assistance programs, the Food Stamp Program was the largest nutrition assistance program administered by the United States Department of Agriculture (USDA). The program is now called the Supplemental Nutrition Assistance Program (SNAP). The goals of the program include "raising the level of nutrition among low-income households and maintaining adequate levels of nutrition by increasing the food purchasing power of low-income families."[18] In 1981, it had roughly twenty million participants. He had been very sympathetic to our efforts to expand the program to cover more malnourished children and adults.

Like all political appointees, Greenstein was replaced when Carter left office. Reagan appointed his own staff. Bob was in the process of founding the Center on Budget and Policy Priorities. The center would provide analysis of and proposals for the federal and state budget issues and impacts on hunger, welfare, and other safety net programs as well as on military spending.

Sitting in my office that cold and snowy December Friday afternoon, Bob spelled out what he had learned from his sources at the Office of Management and Budget. This was the new set of proposals in the president's budget for consideration by Congress in 1982. They were planning a round of even more severe cuts to the safety net for the poor. It was a disaster and completely antithetical to what we had been working on for decades. Bob has a way of delivering fact after fact after fact in a dispassionate speaking voice and I found my stomach tightening and a deep moral cry forming in it. "They can't do that!"

I asked Judy why she brought Bob to my office with this terrible news. She said she hoped I'd do something about it. I sure wanted to. I thanked them and said I'd work on a proposal and would get back to them.

What was occurring to me was that this might present an opportunity to try out my newly minted "campaign model." The whole plan appeared in my mind. I could see all the moving parts, all the buy-ins I would have to negotiate. I went to my handy Selectric typewriter and spelled it all out. This was not the first nor the last time this has happened to me, to see a complex plan with goals, strategies, timelines, and leadership needed. This was a large-scale enterprise and with the most at stake. I was ready to organize

18. See fns.usda.gov.

a national interreligious campaign to deny President Ronald Reagan his second budget cuts in programs for the poor.

A slogan came to mind: "The Poor Have Suffered Enough." I first went to my boss, the Rev. Dr. Yvonne Delk, executive director of the Office for Church in Society, and pitched the idea to her. The plan called for her to give significant leadership. She was ready.

After that, the next step was to present the idea as a moral battle to my WISC colleagues. It was a fight that needed to be waged and that required a shift in working style and priorities for all of us. If it were an "Emergency Campaign," as I presented the idea, we had to set aside normal schedules and assignments and focus entirely on addressing the emergency. Yvonne worked with her peers, the heads of the national offices of social action agencies, to bring them into the plan. I went to New York to the NCC building to accompany her in the recruiting effort. They all agreed that they would release their Washington-based staff from regular assignments, staff meetings, reporting, and travel requirements. They also agreed to make headquarters staff available to travel as part of the grassroots organizing. And, very importantly, they agreed to commit financial support to the project.

I worked with the Washington-based staff. We agreed, after some hard negotiation, to merge several of the WISC task forces so that we could plot together across the range of issues being threatened. It made no sense to get a committee to deny cuts to the Food Stamp Program if another committee doubled its anti-poverty program cuts. Bob wrote articles for us and joined me in a round of speeches to groups we gathered in Washington and in the Midwest. Bob also wrote brief analytic pieces that we published with the "Emergency Campaign" identification.

We needed a field strategy. I called Dick Fernandez, UCC pastor living in Philadelphia, with whom I had worked through Clergy and Laity Concerned About Vietnam. CALC had very effective field strategies with chapters all over the country. Dick agreed to come to work with us on a part-time basis.

We needed a media strategy including a publication, a regular newspaper, to keep people around the country energized and informed. I called Lean Howell who had just completed his leadership as editor at the magazine *Christianity and Crisis*. He agreed to lead the publishing every two weeks of a newspaper that we distributed free through all the outlets we could find. National offices were energized by the campaign and sent out packages of this publication all over the country.

Dick and I gathered twenty-five denominational headquarters staff in my office in the Methodist building. They came from New York, Indianapolis, Chicago, Louisville, and Valley Forge. We presented the details of the

Emergency Campaign and, given their new freedom to work on the campaign, we proposed they each plan to travel (on their own budgets) to four cities in the month of April. We had listed fifty cities we hoped to reach, and they each picked a set they would cover. In picking a city, they had to know someone who would serve as the local organizer and coordinator of local action. Several raced to the chalkboard to cross out the cities they wanted. Then we spent an hour trading local contact names and contact information in the cities. Advance work had to be done to prepare for their visit. The traveler would ask a local contact to pull together the others to plan in advance the visit. We shipped eight boxes of our newsletters, bumper stickers, buttons, and flyers on "How to Call a Press Conference" to a contact person in each city. Dick was clear you couldn't have a campaign without bumper stickers and buttons!

Probably the best speech in support of the campaign, other than Bob's describing the impact on the poor of the proposed budget cuts, was Yvonne's "Code Blue" speech at the IMPACT briefing in 1982. With perhaps eight hundred people from the religious community assembled in the House Office Building, she described how in hospitals when the code blue call goes out, all hospital personnel know that a major life-threatening situation has occurred, and they should be prepared to respond with full readiness. She issued a code blue on the threat to life that was about to happen to the poor and rallied that room full of folks to work on the Emergency Campaign. It was a stirring moment.

This was a unique type of organizing, to figure out how to bring together significant advocates from within the national staffs of denominations that share the similar concerns and goals, to pool financial and network personnel to work together for a short period of time with a very specific goal to accomplish, a goal that justice demanded.

In his second budget (1982) the president had asked for $22 billion in additional cuts in food stamps, Aid to Families with Dependent Children, rent subsidies, etc. over the next three years. At the end of the budget process Congress granted only $3 billion in the means-tested programs we hoped to protect. In the end of this budget process the president got only 17 percent of the cuts he sought. On this statistical basis we reported that our Campaign was 83 percent successful in our goal. That was reason to cheer.

Of course, our Emergency Campaign was part of a much wider political force seeking to prevent the cuts. Unions, school systems, welfare rights organizations, and many other groups worked alongside us. I attended some coordinating meetings with the intent that when the reluctant members and senators were identified along the way, we could join efforts in concentrated action both in Washington and in the field. After the federal budget was adopted, we celebrated what felt like a major accomplishment on behalf of the poor and we settled back into the old routines.

From my personal perspective, this Emergency Campaign ranks at the top of my professional accomplishments. It was a perfect moment. I knew my way around Washington and the legislative process and the media. I'd hung out with enough good policy advocates and analysts, watched closely at how people advanced their ideas. I had the academic exposure to research and historical perspectives. When Bob and Judy had walked in the room that winter afternoon, the perfect cause for the religious community presented itself and I was able to put the pieces together and bring enough people into it to make it happen.

Another reason why I could move quickly was that I was serving as chair of the Washington Interreligious Staff Council and of the Food Policy Taskforce, two major pieces of the puzzle that had to put resources to work. And soon I was chairing the committee managing the campaign. A couple of days after he started accompanying me to many meetings as we developed the details for this work, Dick asked me, "Paul, do you ever go to meetings you don't chair?"

Several years after I moved from Washington, I was back attending a conference. I saw Bob Greenstein again. He said he missed me because I was a great catalyst for action.

A Sample of Congressional Testimony

Senator Mark Andrews, US senator from North Dakota, chaired a March 14, 1983, subcommittee hearing, the announced purpose of which was to offer testimony on the questions of the effectiveness of the federal food and nutrition programs and their relationship to the citizens of this country whom they are intended to serve. On the panel of witnesses were Dr. Jean Mayer, president of Tufts University, a noted food and nutrition researcher; Kentucky senator the Honorable Walter Huddleston; Dr. Edward Brandt, assistant secretary for health, US Department of Health and Human Services; John Bodie, deputy; the Honorable Ted Wilson, Mayor, Salt Lake City, Utah, on behalf of the US Conference of Mayors; Nancy Amidei, executive director, Food Research and Action Center; myself, listed as director of the UCC Washington Office and offering testimony on behalf of the Interreligious Taskforce on US Food Policy; and Barbara Howell and Janice Patty, Bread for the World.

We sat together at a long table facing the raised platform on which the committee members sat behind their table. We had our names on plaques in front of us so the senators could address us by name. We each had a microphone and a glass of water.

I felt that if this testimony were to be delivered as well as it was written, it might positively influence the way the senate committee dealt with the hunger issue. If that turned out to happen, it would confirm my sense that this public policy work can make a difference, can bring food to the table of hungry people. It could actually be an important thing to be doing.

Each of us brought to the table a perspective on the question before the subcommittee: How effective are the government's food and nutrition programs?

My testimony that morning had two points. One was to offer our theological framework for thinking about these important questions. The opening addressed that point.

> Based on our biblical faith and our understanding of the traditions of the church, it is our belief that God is a God of justice who promises to establish justice in history and to demand that those who are claimed by God to work for justice.
>
> And we believe that while God loves all people, and through that love seeks justice for all people, God makes what theologian John Bennett calls a concentration of love on the needy. Equal concern for all requires unequal attention when unequal need exists.
>
> We believe that God judges nations by the standard of justice. The divine standard is not the size of the nation's gross national product, the beauty of its worship places or the frequency of its prayer breakfasts. The divine standard is justice, which means, first and foremost, how a nation deals with the weak, the needy and the vulnerable.
>
> For the God of biblical faith, the litmus test of whether a nation is just or unjust, of whether its economy is fair or unfair, is always the question: What is happening to the poor?
>
> The current public policy toward the poor of this Nation leads many of us to conclude that by this exacting standard, America is to be judged harshly.[19]

Our second point was to respond to a growing interest among legislators to move the care of the poor from the federal budget to voluntary, charitable institutions such as, and especially, the church. Our argument was that this thinking was moving the care of the poor from justice, as secured by the government acting on behalf of the whole people, to charity. That would be putting the poor at the mercy of the whims of charitable

19. *Hearing before the Subcommittee*, 57–58.

donors. Ronald Reagan was president, and he favored reducing the cost and responsibilities of government as they related to those with low incomes. He often said the government is not the solution but is the problem.

I said in my testimony,

> I think finally the question for us is to look at whether we are a nation which deals with its poor principally through the mechanisms of charity or principally through the mechanisms of justice. . . . [We see it] is a matter of justice. The poor need to be fed. They need to be fed in as many places as possible, and the government acting on behalf of the community of persons in this nation was going to be the instrument through which that justice was implemented. Now the vision of this particular administration seems to be that we want to reduce that, and we want to shift it back to the realm of private charity, which means that for us major portions of the population, those particularly who are weak and vulnerable and poor, will survive only if those people who have material wealth are also morally perfect, that is, willing to give charity. And that is a very thin reed, even with the best that the churches can do to address that problem. So, I would say the churches, of course, need to do more, have done a lot, but there are not the resources in that kind of charitable direction to meet the current need.[20]

To address the question of the capacity of the churches to take on the responsibility of feeding the poor, I used an illustration from an interfaith group in Philadelphia.

> A group of clergy counted the number of congregations that are listed in the phone book, the number of religious local church congregations, and compared that total number to the number of dollars that would not be coming to Philadelphia for a variety of means tested Federal programs as adopted in the budget 1 year ago, and discovered that it would take $50,000 for each congregation to match the number of dollars that the city of Philadelphia and its various means tested programs were being deprived by the changes in the Federal budget. Well, it is clear that that kind of resource is simply not available in the voluntary way in the lives of local congregations.[21]

As is the custom in a congressional hearing, the hearing record shows verbatim the testimony I delivered and my answers to questions. The record

20. *Hearing before the Subcommittee,* 59–60.
21. *Hearing before the Subcommittee,* 59.

also shows a much longer version of the testimony that I submitted "for the record" plus a letter written after the hearing in response to questions later raised by Senator Jesse Helms from North Carolina, chair of the full Committee on Agriculture. His staff reviewed the testimony and felt some additional probing was necessary. We responded in detail, with facts and with respect.

Our most regular newspaper exposure was in *The New York Times*. Economics and health care writer Robert Pear wrote dozens of stories about our Emergency Campaign and other work.

> The Rev. Paul Kittlaus director of the Washington Office of the United Church of Christ, appearing with Senator Kennedy, said that feeding the hungry was not just an "option of charity," but an "obligation of justice." Thus, he said, while churches have spent millions of dollars on food assistance, "ultimate responsibility for assuring that each person has access to a nutritionally adequate diet rests with the people as a whole acting through the Federal Government."[22]

We created helpful exposure in a column in *The Washington Post* by syndicated columnist Carl Rowan. He wrote in conclusion for a column in 1983,

> President Reagan ought to talk to Paul Kittlaus and the other religious leaders who pray nightly over the suffering of this nation's needy before he makes a decision to ask for four more years in the White House.[23]

Departure from Washington

A question began to take shape in my mind regarding how long I wanted to continue in this public policy ministry. I knew I had one of the most unusual and important positions that the church could have offered to someone with my vocational calling, commitments, and passion. Yet, I began to see the limitations of that life that became more and more important to me. A major part of this was having had the experience of envisioning how the denominations could work together in the Emergency Campaign. Washington and headquarter staff and budgets were organized in a common effort that had all four of the capabilities I had identified. I grew restless with the limits of the deployment of public policy staff by the churches. Each

22. Pear, "New Drive on Hunger."
23. Rowan, "Reagan's War."

one wanted their own eyes, ears, and hands at work in Washington. There was some cooperation but not with the effectiveness that we experienced in the campaign. That there was so much duplication, overlap, and unfocused activity became a barrier to my own energies. I was becoming a grump and needed to move on.

But something else was at work in me. It had to do with reordering my relationships with people. I was a policy advocate as was nearly everyone else I knew or hoped to know in Washington. That reality and identity put certain restraints on relationships. What had value in a new relationship was how it enhanced my reach and influence as an advocate. And I was evaluated by others with the same focus. I was someone important if I could help someone advance their cause and career. When I was no longer helpful, the need for the contact dropped. It got tiring. I was tired. Some people were contacts and some were friends. This was all out of balance in Washington.

Injury: Surely You Should be Dead or a Quadriplegic

My final six months on the OCIS staff in Washington were dominated by my recovery from a January 1984 fall off the roof of my house in Takoma Park, Maryland. This included a month in the orthopedic unit of the George Washington University Hospital and months at home with physical therapy, additional surgery, and several changes of cast. My departure was not how I might have envisioned it, given crutches and weakness. But the farewell parties were full of warmth and expressions of thanks. I felt I was giving up a vocational prize, an opportunity to make more social change than I would have in any other ministry. If solving poverty were my goal, the job I had for ten years could not have been a better place to work.

The fall off the roof has meant six major surgeries with a titanium rod in my left femur and plates on either side of my left ankle. I used to love to walk and run. As I traveled around the country from Washington meeting with church people, I kept a record of the many cities, towns, and countrysides where I had run. Janet and I used to walk miles on the beach at Nags Head, on the outer banks of North Carolina. Barbara and Leon Howell welcomed our rental of their place on the beach. Now running was done and walking was painful and awkward. I used to love walking and talking but I now had to pay attention to my strides which made conversation flow difficult. My surgeon said I surely should be dead or at least a quadriplegic from that fall. So far, I am neither. I do get crabby occasionally.

On January 20, 1984, I climbed up a ladder to the back side of the roof of our home in Takoma Park. I was seeking to retrieve *The Washington Post* on the front side. There were clumps of snow on the back side as I climbed to the peak. There was black ice down the front side which I did not see. I bumped my butt off the peak and slid from about two and a half stories high down the ice and off the front of the porch roof and fell another twenty feet to the frozen ground.

At the hospital I watched the 1984 Winter Olympics. I watched athletes slide down iced winding channels in an event called the luge. I had done that without the sled.

I also watched Superbowl XVIII with John Rother who decided my room at GW Hospital was as good a place as any to watch. Redskins lost.

I had many visitors from our church and from my colleagues in WISC. One woman stood with her hand on my shoulder and told me how much closer she felt to me as I lay so helpless and in pain than she did in the United Methodist Building. She said I showed little vulnerability at work. She said it was clear I was always eager to offer support, ready to let anyone cry on my shoulder, but never in a million years able to show my need. I've thought about that for a long time.

After the first week of the several long surgeries, I suddenly had difficulty breathing and my temperature and pulse rate spiked. I was rushed to the cardiac unit and attached to a heparin drip, a blood thinner. I was diagnosed with a blood clot in my left lung. They were chasing other potential clots, which, in the brain or the heart, could be fatal. As the heparin drip dripped into the night, I phoned my kids to chat.

Thinking about this episode in my life I am reminded of the orthopedic surgeon who made it possible for me to walk again. I thank Dr. Panos Labropoulis for his amazing reconstruction work that made it possible. One orthopedic resident said most surgeons would have amputated the leg given how busted up the femur and the tibia were. And I am reminded of how Janet did her work and half of mine during that time and spent hours at my bedside. And I give thanks to my boss, Yvonne Delk, and my UCC colleagues helping me recover.

If you ask, as some do, what happened, I must admit that climbing up on that roof the morning after an ice storm was one of the stupidest decisions I've ever made. I've made other stupid, reckless decisions but escaped paying a price for them. This time I paid for all of them.

I was in Washington for ten years, 1974 to 1984. During that time the US had four presidents: Richard Nixon when I arrived in March 1974 until August that year, Gerald Ford from then to January 1977, Jimmy Carter until 1981, and Ronald Reagan four years until I left to head back to California. For those ten years our office functioned with typewriters, telephones, and the US mail service. I led a team to explore desktop computers and they were ordered and were delivered in 1984 just after I left for California.

The Washington Metro rail system was opened in 1976. Before that, I had ridden the bus from Takoma Park or Southwest DC to Capitol Hill. After that I walked down to the Takoma Park Metro Station and rode the rails to Union Station and walked up Capitol Hill to the Methodist Building.

I entered the Pastor Seeking Church process. At the end of the eight-month search process, I was called to the First Congregational United Church of Christ in Santa Barbara, California. I had come to feel that the next period of my ministry should be as pastor and teacher in the context of a congregation. I yearned for the Sunday worship leadership, experience serving communion, the teaching, weddings, memorial services, baptisms, visiting the sick, and all the other rich and important moments that make the story of a local pastor.

Chapter 9

Pastoring in Santa Barbara 1984–1992: Homelessness and Peace Mission to Germany

FOLKS IN WASHINGTON WHO heard that I had accepted a call to serve a church in Santa Barbara said it sounded like an oxymoron given all I had focused on poverty and justice. But one can't drive along the beach or by the public parks in Santa Barbara without seeing homeless encampments. Santa Barbara churches were first responders, early to form helpful responses to the expanding homeless population.

We were surprised at the leftward tilt of Santa Barbara politics when we were looking at a possible relocation. The Santa Barbara oil spill that occurred in January and February 1969 in the Santa Barbara Channel was the largest oil spill in United States waters at that time. It now ranks third after the 2010 Deepwater Horizon and 1989 Exxon Valdez spills. It remains the largest oil spill to have occurred in the waters off California. An estimated eighty thousand to one hundred thousand barrels of crude oil spilled into the channel and onto the beaches of Santa Barbara County. Pro-environmental politics was established. In 1992, the city was represented in both statehouses by progressive legislators and in Congress by a progressive Republican congressman.

A friend suggested I look at the First Congregational Church of Santa Barbara. I pictured myself unsuited for high glamour. Of course, there was a lot of high glamour in Washington but that was not where I lived or worked. This friend had been raised in that church and indicated that they were quite liberal. I asked for my profile to be sent to the Santa Barbara search committee and got a phone call almost immediately from the chair of the committee. He invited me to take the next step, which was a phone interview with the committee.

And the next day I slid off the roof of my house. So, I did the phone interview sedated from my hospital bed. Janet had passed on the news to them that I was in for a period of rehab, that I was in the hospital for the phone conversation. I do not remember the interview. But afterward, they invited Janet and me to fly out for an in-person interview.

They were not in a big hurry and their interest in me was high. They waited out my month in the George Washington University Hospital and arranged our visit for an appropriate time after I left the hospital. Of course, I was not in good shape to present myself as a vigorous, desirable candidate. They knew they were going to see a guy on crutches, needing lots of rest and otherwise not ready for prime time. By the time of the trip, I was outfitted with a walking cast on my left leg. But another medical complication had arisen. After a couple days at home from the hospital there was a sharp pain in my left wrist. X-rays showed that the scaphoid bone in my left wrist had broken in the fall. I was outfitted with a fingertip-to-elbow cast on my left arm. The point of the cast was to immobilize my left thumb in a position like I was hitchhiking or giving a thumbs up. To walk I needed crutches, but I could not operate a crutch with this cast on my arm.

The physical therapists quickly showed me that I was not the first to have this problem. They fashioned for me a platform crutch. I bent my elbow and placed my cast arm on the platform attached to the crutch, used Velcro to secure my arm to the platform. I was able to lift and move the crutch by using my shoulder and arm muscles. Off I went. Slowly and wobbly.

I was told that it takes a week to recover for every day one spent lying inactive in a hospital bed. I had thirty days in bed. After the several weeks upright, we flew to California. We rented a car at Los Angeles International Airport. My right foot was fine, as was my right arm, so I could share driving with Janet.

My first meeting with the search committee was at the church, where we introduced ourselves and chatted about the church and its history. We adjourned and gathered again for dinner at a Mexican restaurant across from the beach. It was lovely. A breeze off the Pacific Ocean was cool and fragrant. I could hear the seagulls' squawking argument. We had found that the cast which immobilized my forearm and my hand with my thumb sticking out like I was permanently hitch-hiking did not allow me to put my arm through the sleeve of my suit jacket. Janet had to rip the seam to make it possible. But we decided we would just carry the jacket into the restaurant. So, without the jacket on, I crutched awkwardly into the restaurant. Janet said a word of apology, explaining why I was in shirtsleeves. All the men from around the table took their jackets off in an act of solidarity. I learned it was a relief to them, not a sacrifice.

The various interviews went well. They had arranged for me to preach in a nearby church so they could evaluate that part of my craft. I offered to do the children's sermon also and I was a knockout with the kids. In the middle of the adult sermon, I ran on empty for energy. I could not stand another minute, so I skipped four eloquent pages and, sweating and white-faced, I sat down. They decided I sold myself on the kid's sermon. They could see my struggle and said they were relieved when I sat down rather than pass out.

The only awkward moment in an interview was a question to Janet. Did she plan to serve tea at the monthly weekday women's fellowship meeting? As a newly minted attorney, she said she planned to be employed and would not be available in midweek mornings to pour tea. She said that the compensation package for the minister was not enough to live in Santa Barbara. We had agreed she would work. To put a finer point on her point she offered she would be glad to serve tea to the ladies if they paid the minister enough so she would not have to work.

The oldest and the youngest member of the committee seemed to have doubts. They did not prevail. The committee voted 100 percent to present me to the congregation as their candidate for senior minister.

A Secret is Shared

The chair of the search committee took me aside for a private conversation. He reported the committee's agreement to put me forward to the congregation as their candidate. He said he was also charged by the committee to share information they felt I needed to know before I agreed to accept their nomination.

He said that some in the congregation had learned from a reliable source that the previous minister had been arrested for soliciting sex with an undercover policeman in a local park at night. It immediately came clear that my task as the new senior minister was going to be very different from what I had pictured. This was a major act of clergy sexual misconduct.

Still, after all these months, many in the congregation were unaware and feeling confused by his sudden unexplained departure. He was popular and had worked successfully to bring new members into the congregation. He had revived the church by his evangelism. There were many variations of the racy story among those who thought they knew. It was a story that triggered strong emotional reactions, outrage, and eagerness to share.

That's where matters stood for the me if I accepted the call to be the new senior minister: a divided congregation without full disclosure of the facts, with rampant rumors and broken trust. The scale and nature of my task was going to be difficult, and my pastoral gifts were going to be challenged. I agreed to accept the challenge. I was confident that I could help the church do the work it needed to do to be able to move on.

I said to the chair of the search committee, "Let's move forward." He was happy that their work was complete in the search phase, to find the best candidate available and informing me, that candidate, of the damage within the church that would affect the early years. And the secret did not scare me off. Their job now was to sell me to the congregation. Shift from buying to selling.

The next morning several members of the search committee took Janet and me to the Brown Pelican for brunch before we drove back to LAX for our flight home. The restaurant on the sand at Hendry's Beach was only a couple steps removed from being a beach shack. Tables and umbrellas, blue sky, blue ocean fifteen yards away, the sounds of sea gulls and of waves pounding on the beach, bronzed young men and women walking their dogs on the long beach, old folks walking along holding hands, having to put the saltshaker on the menu to keep it from floating away in the breeze, the salty smell of the Pacific Ocean, eggs benedict, mimosas, and new friends. One of the women said, "We didn't think you would say no to all this."

The next stage was for us to return to Santa Barbara for several days to be presented to the congregation as the committee's recommendation as the new senior minister. We attended several receptions and enjoyed hospitality for meals at several homes. I preached a sermon at the church on a Sunday morning. Immediately after the service there was a meeting of the congregation. The committee made their case why I was the one. I offered a few words about why them, that church for me. I responded to their questions, and we were asked to depart to another location in the church while the congregation talked further and voted. When I heard a loud applause coming from the sanctuary, I knew the vote was a strong yes.

In the early fall after resigning our jobs, selling our home, and enjoying farewell parties, we moved from Takoma Park, Maryland, to Santa Barbara into the manse, the home owned by and situated next to the church.

This was not a congregation that catered to the elite of Santa Barbara, no movie stars, no fabulously wealthy international personalities. Its members were schoolteachers, lawyers, business owners, librarians, and professors from University of California at Santa Barbara, Santa Barbara

City College, and Westmont College. They were all from somewhere else. Many of them had bought their homes before Jet Propulsion Lab (JPL) in Pasadena located a major think tank, the Santa Barbara Research Center (SBRC) in Goleta. Other science research think tanks had followed. And Santa Barbara became a thing. Real estate skyrocketed.

I began work in the fall of 1984.

In addition to all the normal responsibilities I threw myself into, I worked a major percent of my time on the problem of a divided church. It was an important time to help people work through their fears, outrage, and sense of betrayal and to look for understanding and a sense of forgiveness.

At this point in time clergy sexual abuse had not come into widespread awareness. In contrast to the current resources, including study guides, protocols, and legal guidelines and processes, there was none that I could find when I needed it.

The conference minister knew of at least one previous episode of such behavior in another church by this minister. Why had he not informed our search committee? He said he was not protected in the law. If he shared what he knew to be true in a previous church with a search committee, any search committee would certainly reject the candidate. The candidate would likely bring suit since no charges had been filed against the minister, no conviction on the record. Everything was hearsay except for the fact of the arrest. To make the story public and block the minister from further employment is serious and to fail to be transparent is also serious.

A lot has happened about these issues since that time. Clergy sexual abuse has become a significant concern. Legal processes and practices have been put in place so that there are protections for leadership and requirements for self-disclosure of any previous issues by ministers who are updating their profiles. Clauses in the profile of a minister ask about previous losses of positions, charges, or court cases. Failure to disclose allegations, arrests, or convictions put the minister in legal jeopardy. The conference now has a legal responsibility to share what is known to protect the congregations. And there are many helpful processes and types of support for congregations going through this kind of turmoil.

For over a year the church moderator had managed to keep things within the congregation from blowing up. She did consult with the conference minister, and he shared what wisdom he had. After I had been functioning for several months the conference minister told me that moderator had done the job of moderator as well as any person had ever done any job. That was a strong compliment for lay leadership during a crisis.

The following summer the moderator's daughter interned in the church office for a month. She was a college student. I told her the story of what I had been told of her mom's leadership and the conference minister's powerful compliment. Molly paused for a moment and said, "Naw, she's just my mom."

I had had no previous experience with this situation when I said yes to the call from the church. My best strategy, best I could think of, was to say, "Hey, it's a new day, I'm the new guy. We're moving ahead into the future, and you'll have to run to keep up." But there were many conversations along the way that helped the healing process.

Looking back over my eight years, this seemed to work out okay. The only moment of worry occurred a year after I had moved to Madison, Wisconsin. I read a column in the weekly church newsletter from Santa Barbara in which the interim minister had concluded that there had been other clergy sexual abuse in the past. Since I was now one of those past ministers, I worried that I was fair game for speculation. If charged, how might I possibly defend myself? My record was clear, but one man or woman's claim could potentially bring down a career. I was relieved when that investigation was concluded without involving me.

Rusty Pastoral Leadership

Having not practiced the art and craft of local church pastoral leadership for sixteen years, I had many questions for which I should have had answers as the leader of the congregation. Ann, a member of the search committee, was chair of the worship committee. After I was on the job for two weeks, she came to visit my office with a notepad and sharpened pencil. She said, "We're about to plan the Advent season. What are your plans? We'll build around that."

I had no clue, hadn't given it a moment's thought but felt the weight of having to give leadership to justify her vote on the search committee. I should have been straight with her. That's the best policy. But I see that in hindsight. My response, almost quickly enough that I don't think she noticed the panic, "I don't want to introduce new things too quickly so tell me what you did last year." That saved my day, and we worked out a good plan for Advent. It looked pretty much like last year but with different leadership. We were comfortable for my introducing new ideas the following Advent.

Rebuilding the Staff

As in most places where I have given leadership to a staff in ministry settings, I did not ask for resignations of current staff. I accepted what was given and evaluated what we had. And then I developed a picture of what we needed to do the job as well as it could be done. Changes were always necessary. I rated the music and support staff high and the associate minister with Christian education responsibilities low. I found he had not earned much respect in his two years of work. I asked for and accepted his resignation.

We did a nationwide search to find the best Christian education candidates available. That approach was a morale boost, just saying we're going after the best in the country made folks have a new appreciation for the program.

We called a warm, idealistic, well-educated seminary graduate who, after a year and a half, decided this work did not match her skills and interest. She went back for more graduate work. We searched again.

We called a recent graduate of Harvard Divinity School, a woman who grew up in New Hampshire in a wonderful church with deep roots in the congregational tradition. She brought rich experience as well as a solid education. Janet Hatfield joined our staff. She was ordained at her home church in New Hampshire and settled in for the several years that her fiancé, Jeff Legro, had remaining in his PhD program at UCLA.

Staff meetings were lively. Janet felt free to challenge director of music Steven Townsend on program areas where the music program and youth program intersected, especially scheduling Sunday evening programs where the junior and senior high groups switched choir practice with social and educational program. They challenged me. Planning worship and programs was a rich experience and I always looked forward to our times together. Their debates were serious, funny, and substantive about ministry. Having a colleague Janet and a wife Janet often caused confusion. I had to remember to ask which Janet had left a message for me.

We enjoyed working together and sharing an evening meal at our home together. When wife Janet and I started this evening meal effort we asked for food and drink preferences. Gradually it came out that there were scotch and bourbon preferences for drinks. Sounded good to us. When we circulated for a date for the dinner, we got in the practice of putting in all our calendars "hard liquor party at Paul and Janet's."

Colleague Janet, working to set a date for a committee, opened her calendar for the chair of the committee to see so they could pick a good date. And there it was for the following Friday: "hard liquor party at Janet and Paul's." Maybe you can remember the time when hard liquor was not generally expected to be served by the minister and wife to the staff. For these dinners we included Julie Lyons, our office manager. We enjoyed her company, and she brought wonderful homemade peanut brittle.

Preaching

Before I left Washington, I had focused on the idea that I was going to be preaching every Sunday. When I listened to sermons from other preachers, unless I was completely brought into the flow of the preacher, I would sit there composing how I would handle that biblical text. I had a bunch of ideas about sermons I would preach. It took me about three weeks in the Santa Barbara pulpit to realize that those ideas belonged back in Washington, a very different context, not here in Santa Barbara with these people. As I became aware of these folks, I let go of the Washington questions and issues and embedded myself in my new pastoral life and context.

As a pastor I studied, worked, and fussed over my Sunday sermons constantly during the week. The creative process was never far from my consciousness. After church there was a half day of not thinking about a sermon. Then came Monday and the look at the lectionary lessons for next Sunday. I could never write my sermons ahead of the week of the service. I knew a pastor who took a summer month at the family cabin and wrote all the sermons for the coming year. And they were good sermons. I had to be in the week, in the moment, processing what was happening around me, to hear what needed to be said.

Another word about my preaching. I studied the texts and commentaries for the key idea around which to build the sermon. My dear friend, Mary Lou, sitting in the fifth pew on the preacher's right, was listening for the feeling that brought renewal for her. She was always apologetic after church but, nonetheless, persistent to complain that she felt little in my ideas.

I came to realize that she was right, I was not going for feelings. I was going for ideas. And I wanted to bring the love, forgiveness and renewal that is in the gospel. I wanted Mary Lou to feel it. So, I tried adding Mary Lou's insights to my creative process. But that did not work. My mind could not create in that way. I finally decided that the way for me to go was to write the sermon in the way that creativity worked for me and then do a "Mary Lou scan" to find where stories fit and ensure the stories carried feeling. I found that this strengthened my sermons and brought a new round of positive comments after church.

Roy wanted me to know that he was never satisfied. With a warm handshake at the door after church, with a twinkle in his eye, he regularly told me, "That was a good sermon, pastor, but like my Daddy used to say, I sure saw a lot of stop'n places."

I found significant support in the newly published *Book of Worship* by the UCC.[1] It is a lectionary-based resource for an enriched liturgy for every occasion: the seasons of the church year, baptisms, weddings, memorial services. The *Book of Worship* dropped the male-based language throughout the liturgical resources it provided.

Breaking new ground, it had a service for "Order for Recognition of the End of a Marriage." After a civil divorce is granted, in a brief service with the family, children, and friends, the minister announces that a husband and wife have decided to dissolve their marriage "after much effort, pain and anger."[2] And the once married couple recite words of regret and respect. This recognition of divorce brought this powerful, painful moment in people's lives into a liturgical setting, to bring an affirmative blessing and conclusion to the end of a hard story.

The *Book of Worship* was published in 1986, two years after I became a local church pastor again and I remain enormously grateful for it. It guided, taught, and grounded me in the Christian faith again.

Bible Study

In 1986, *The Christian Century* advertised a book I was interested in called *Jesus before Christianity* by Albert Nolan.[3] It was a good introduction to liberation theology, about serving the poor, spiritual growth, and taking sides. He presents an account of Jesus's radical involvement in the struggle for full humanity in the context of first-century Judea: he challenged the rich to identify in solidarity with the poor. Nolan was a South African Roman Catholic priest. He introduced the kind of biblical criticism more familiar in Protestant traditions. His quick review of this treatment of the Bible was clear and understandable.

The logic of the title *Jesus before Christianity* is that before there was Christianity, there was a Jewish Jesus, who was the incarnated Jesus. And this Jesus acted upon the world in the conflict between good and evil. The book retains the biblical themes of the kingdom of God and the good news. Nolan was presenting the gospel per se as the liberating event.

I put out a call for an evening adult Bible study. Ten signed up. After we read the book and read many of the biblical references, the group was drawn in by new insights about Christianity, about how to read the Bible as a liberation document, and about the life and work of Jesus. At the end

1. Sheares, *Book of Worship*.
2. Sheares, *Book of Worship*, 289.
3. Nolan, *Jesus before Christianity*.

of our six evening sessions one woman looked at me with angry eyes and asked, "Why have you clergy been keeping this from us all these years?" Liberation indeed.

In Christmas notes for years after, I was thanked for that class and the intellectual and spiritual doors it opened. All my Bible study classes through the years were based on providing tools that lay people could use to make sense of it. I introduced critical methods, *The Interpreter's Bible*, and Nolan's book as the most helpful way into examining the four Gospels, seeing their similarities, contradictions, radically different versions of stories, different communities of origin, and contextual issues. That had been empowering to participants. Of course, the Bible is the primary source of the Christian faith and is filled with total mystery, unlikely miracles, a confusing jumble of accounts, lists of rules, shaggy dog stories, and impenetrable texts. I enjoyed an occasional gentle critique of my handling of a text in a sermon by one of those class members.

Christmas Eve

Christmas Eves in this church were wonderful and exhausting experiences. We had identical services at 7:00, 9:00 and 11:00 p.m. Our choir sang several special anthems in all three services. We always looked forward to the end of each service. The sanctuary light was lowered. Then we passed the lighted candle through the congregation, lighting the candles each person held while we sang the familiar memory-bank Christmas hymns and lifted the candles into the air, shouting in the brightly lit sanctuary, "Merry Christmas!" And we processed outside to surround the church with our candles while singing "Silent Night" into the night. Of course, after doing this three times in one evening, I was always ready to put "Silent Night" to rest for a year.

The time between the seven and nine o'clock services and the nine and eleven o'clock services provided a challenge to our kids to provide unusual refreshments to the staff to keep us nourished through the rest of the services.

At home after the last service, my deepest desire was for all the youthful visitors to be silent and go to bed and for me to have a glass of Bailey's in silence.

Easter Sunrise Service

Not since Pacoima had I led an Easter Sunrise service. There is something in the Easter story that lends itself for telling at sunrise on a hilltop overlooking the ocean. A special opportunity arose in my third year in Santa Barbara. The Elings family had made a major grant to the city for the purpose of purchasing a large plot of land that included a 2,500-foot high ridge overlooking the city and the channel. The family had a longtime relationship to our church and their son was in the high school youth group.

Eling's Park included several baseball fields, a soccer field, and picnic areas along the top of the ridge. From there one could look down on the city, the beach, and boats and on out to the islands. The experience was spectacular. The administrator of the park called and asked if our church would be interested in sponsoring and leading a sunrise service in the open-air theater at the top of the ridge. "Yes" was my immediate reply. We planned a service and hosted it for five years before other churches had put on enough pressure to move it to an ecumenical service. Our ads in the newspaper drew scores of other people.

Three Easters stick in my memory. Always wanting to exploit the theatrical opportunities in the liturgy, I envisioned a massive bunch of balloons being released with the proclamation, "Christ is risen!" So, members with theater experience took that idea and placed helium filled balloons under nets out of sight just over the edge of the low wall around the back edge of the stage. With the shout of the proclamation the balloons were released into the blue sky and bright sunlight just peeking over the horizon. It was breathtaking, as that proclamation should be.

The third year we worshiped under a heavy marine layer. The thick gray fog sat just about ten yards over our heads at the top of the hill. So, the release of the balloons was only briefly enjoyed. They rose quickly up out of sight into the fog. For some odd reason I pictured a small plane flying over the fog and suddenly witnessing a cloud of colorful balloons rising above the ground fog.

The fourth year we had learned that gas-filled balloons would float out over the ocean and eventually drop into the water and attract fish and birds looking for lunch. The rubber film choked the animals. Warnings went out over the environmental networks to ban release of gas-filled balloons. Major bummer. More people came for the balloons than listening to my release of hot air.

I challenged the balloon group to come up with something equally exciting for next Easter. It became obvious they had come up with an idea that tickled them. They wanted it to be a surprise to everyone. As the service unfolded, it held suspense for me, too. When the proclamation, "Christ is risen!" was pronounced, there arose from the same area where the balloons had been hidden a giant sound of wings flapping and up rose thirty homing pigeons who looked to me exactly like doves.

Their rise was much noisier than the balloons and they stayed in sight a lot longer. As the owner of the pigeons later told me, they must gain a lot of altitude before they find their GPS system and head home. So, they circled round and round to gain altitude, flapping loudly. At about thousand feet up, they headed off to their home some forty miles away.

The Easter experience and the Easter message had congruence.

Middle of the Night Phone Calls

When my phone rang in the middle of the night, I felt a surge of dread and assumed that an important opportunity for pastoral care was called for. Somebody was in deep trouble. There are a certain range of crises where clergy are first responders, not with flashing lights, sirens, badges, and guns or fire hoses, but with a calming presence to reassure people that they are loved by God.

One such caller asked me to come immediately. I responded as requested, wondering all the way up to their home what the nature of the crisis was. Husband and wife welcomed me both looking pale and shaken. They had received a phone call from their adult daughter who accused her father of sexual abuse when she was a child. The daughter said she had been going to therapy and discovered this forgotten memory. There is no defense for this accusation. She accused, he denied. We talked. They needed me to believe them which I did, having just read about the discredited "false memory" syndrome that some therapists were having some so-called success with. Their emotions ran strong with fear. What if this got out in the family or neighborhood?

They identified some work they thought they should do the next day to get their heads around the false memory therapy and they needed to keep talking about the fear they felt. And they felt they needed to be in touch with their adult son who was supportive of them. This was all much more complicated that I am free to report. It took years to sort this out and then more years to reestablish a working relationship with their daughter. Every minute of those years was heavy with fear. But a level of reconciliation has occurred through very hard work with a therapist.

For me this was one of the most perplexing counseling situations I have ever given myself to. It was hard to know for sure at first who was telling the truth. Based on several years of experience I had great doubts that the father would have behaved as his daughter accused. On the other hand, I know that it takes great courage for those who have been abused to come forward. But my job was not to sort out the truth but to provide support to the parents since they asked me to help. Thankfully in this case, my trust in the parents' story was well-placed.

Another urgent call requested that both Janet and I come immediately. All the way to their home we wondered what the call might mean. The husband and wife had five adult children. Their urgent news was that their middle son, the architect, had just announced to them that he was gay.

The next words were from Janet, "Oh good." Having long ago resolved that same sex orientation was a normal feature in animal and plant life, she was expressing support for Ben and his courage to seek a deeper honesty with his parents. They were not prepared for that perspective. They had shared jokes about gays in the past. They loved and affirmed their son and knew that now the courage had to be theirs as they came to wrestle with this new situation in their lives.

Eventually, the father was a primary organizer of the Santa Barbara chapter of Parents and Friends of Lesbians and Gays (PFLAG). And the mother, a trained therapist, expanded her work to include support for those who were in the process of coming of the closet.

The son stayed active in the church and helped a lot of people come to terms with homosexuality. And he continued to be one of our most successful youth leaders. The church recognized him with an annual award for the person who contributed the most to the Christian education program of the church. I had a lump in my throat on the Sunday that award was given, watching him stride with pride up the center aisle of the sanctuary. And I was aware how many smiles were in the congregation, happy for all the help he had given to people to get over one of the most difficult hurdles of that generation.

A Stranger Walks In

A man I did not recognize walked into church one Sunday morning. He stood in line after church to give me the opportunity to greet him and chat for just a moment. He seemed embarrassed or frightened or something. I sensed something uneasy about him. I asked if he would welcome a visit from me. He warmed a bit and said he would. I got his address and midweek I drove to Montecito to visit.

He served me tea and told me his story. Until a few months previous, he had been the highly respected vice president of a large corporation in Chicago. He had made a lot of money and worked to fit in to the high-end social life in the north shore area. He was married and had two daughters.

He had gradually become prepared to reveal he was gay. He did not share that with anyone except with a series of one-night partners during his frequent travel responsibilities. Sharing it, he felt, would blow up his life and ruin the lives of his family. He came to the point of decision. He could no longer continue this charade.

After the family reached two milestones, the daughters' completion of college and the big community celebration of the twenty-fifth anniversary of his marriage, he knew he had to act. He was being generous, he felt, in setting up a financial trust to allow his wife to live comfortably as she had become accustomed. He set up trust funds for his daughters. He had these prepared confidentially before he disappeared.

He put his letter of resignation from his position at the corporation on the president's desk. No explanation was given for his action. He packed a small suitcase, got on a plane, and flew to California, drove to Santa Barbara, walked into a Montecito real estate office, and bought a house, the one I was visiting. He was evolving.

As we talked his story came tumbling out like a long-dormant volcano. The emotion seemed to be an urgency to let go of the secret. I listened. It was an amazing story and an enormous confession. He had been in that home for a couple months before he showed up in church. He also was lonely.

I asked if his daughters now knew who and where he was. He then told an amazing episode, one filled with deep power. He had asked his daughters to come to visit. He had wanted to tell them his story. He was frightened to tell it to them, but he desperately needed some connection to them, felt he owed them an explanation. They had come in anger to deal with the shock of his sudden abandonment of them and their mother. They were without a clue about this part of their father.

He had sat with them in the comfortable living room where he and I were talking. He had told them he needed to share what he was certain would be devastating news about himself.

They waited as he summoned his last bit of courage. He said, "I'm gay."

There had been a moment of shocked silence before one of the daughters jumped up from her chair and rushed over to give him an enormous hug and to shed tears.

She said, "Oh Daddy, I am so relieved. I thought you had cancer."

It was hard for me to imagine what her response meant to him, after all these years of keeping his secret. The acceptance, forgiveness, affirmation, and love that that daughter gave him in that moment was at the core of my faith.

Of course, I asked about the other daughter, and he said it didn't go so easily at first but that they were working on it.

He had been a member of a UCC church in the Chicago area and knew that he was likely to be welcomed in our church. He was but he was not then seeking church life. He wanted to tell God his story. I was an empathetic pastor who might help the story get delivered. I was moved and honored to be available to him at that time.

I walked out of his home feeling like I had performed a miracle that afternoon. All I did was drink tea and listen and soak it up, his story and all the powerful emotion that carried the story. I thanked him, gave him a hug, and assured him God loved him. It was a while before I saw him again.

I figured he was busy reinventing his life and opening his personality, exploring a future and life free of the secret, and reconnecting to at least one member of his family. As I said, he was evolving. He did get involved in the church for a while serving on a finance committee. And he did show up one Sunday with a friend.

His former wife's response to the outing of his secret was to feel deep hurt and betrayal expressed by lots of yelling and massive flows of tears. He had lied to her all these years. She found the lie especially embarrassing in the context of the big twenty-fifth anniversary party. She didn't know how to face her friends.

I counseled him that her hurt and anger were completely understandable. And, I suggested, there was not a thing he could do to ease her pain or help her work her way through it and to find a new future. That was her work and he'd better stay out of it. He said, "I guess my job is to accept responsibility for causing that pain, to know there is nothing I can ever do to relieve her of it, and to try to live a life based on fundamental truth at its core from now on."

Transition House: Shelter and Meals for People

Trinity Episcopal Church, a few blocks down State Street, began to take in people who were homeless for overnight shelter. Then they added a meal at night and a morning take-away meal as people departed for the day. The need for shelter increased way beyond what the church by itself could manage. The Trinity program team called a meeting of leaders of several congregations they thought would respond to their proposal. We were included.

Soon a rotating shelter system was set up with each participating church providing hospitality for two weeks at a time.

This experience challenged all of us at the church to face our prejudice and ignorance about homelessness. Who were these people? Why were they homeless? Why didn't they get a job like the rest of us? Many images, full of fear and prejudice, filled our imaginations. Taking steps that would bring us together took courage and willingness to risk for our church folks.

There are in Santa Barbara several very large, gracious, and beautiful Morton Bay fig trees near the train station. They were worth including in the driving tour for visiting friends and relatives. First, the Mission, then East Beach, the fig trees, Hendry's Beach, and a drive through Hope Ranch and Montecito. We learned that the big fig trees were a landmark for the itinerant homeless. Many itinerant homeless travelers knew, maybe chatting in Salt Lake City, what it meant to say, "Meet you at the fig tree." There was a substantial encampment under the widespread sheltering limbs of the tree. In registering to vote, one had to have a legitimate address on the application. For a period, a judge ruled that it was permissible to name the fig tree as an address after someone put up a mailbox under the tree.

When it was our church's turn to provide dinner and all-night proctors, the shelter was at the Lutheran church further up State Street. Janet and I took a night. We alternated with each other sleeping and staying awake. As Janet tells the story she reports that she felt basically safe. Later she and our friend Mary Lou agreed to be the proctors. That night felt different. She says scenarios of what could go wrong floated through her imagination. The clearest one was what to do if a drunk and violent husband came looking for his sheltered wife. The proctor's responsibility was to keep the shelter a safe place.

The police had agreed to drive by frequently. The list of what might happen was a long one. Drugs, alcohol, acting out, fights, weapons, sorting out men, women, and children were all real possibilities. Several of the scariest "might happen" items were mitigated by a screening process of who was welcomed into the shelter. Several social workers agreed to develop a screening protocol and to do the screening at 5:00 p.m. every evening. Guns and drugs were not allowed.

Our folks, aware of what might happen, became comfortable in the routine of serving their turns at Transition House. We began to know the names of some of the regular clients and their stories and they learned our names and greeted us by name when we saw each other, sometimes on the street during the day. Several of them began to take responsibility for keeping the place tidy and safe and helping sort out troublesome guests.

After a year another meeting was called to think about finding and opening a permanent overnight accommodation with services for those who were homeless. Janet wrote a first draft of the articles of incorporation. After several years of sheltering people in the churches, a piece of property by the freeway was identified and successfully secured for what was to be called "Transition House." This signaled not a permanent housing solution but temporary voluntary effort of the congregations while something permanent could be worked out and the various kinds of support could be organized.

After years of experience and the development of a funding strategy Transition House is staffed and many services are provided. It still relies on the churches in the community taking their turn for providing food, hot dinners and take-out breakfasts. The churches have honored this commitment for over thirty years, providing meals hospitality, financial, and other support. First Congregational UCC regularly participates.

After two years living next to the church Janet and I bought a condo to take advantage of the upward rise in real estate values. In under two years we sold it at a very nice price and bought a small two-bedroom adobe in the San Roque section of town. Three years later, in the depth of a down market, as we were moving to the Upper Midwest, we sold it for the same price we paid, which meant after we paid the closing costs, we lost money. I'd be glad to give you my autograph as the only person you know who lost money in real estate in Santa Barbara.

After renting the manse for a couple of years, the church decided to repurpose it as a childcare center, the Storyteller, for the children of the homeless parents. When parents went out looking for jobs or working when they found jobs, there was a childcare problem, which was solved by this specialized care facility.

AIDS: What Do I Do with What I Know?

In 1986 a young single woman I will call Pam joined the church. She had a young daughter named Annie. After she joined, Pam told me their story. Annie was the child of Pam's sister. The sister had died of AIDS. Pam, in an act of love, agreed to be surrogate mother to Annie. Annie was HIV positive. I had not encountered all this before. I was ignorant except to know that there was a general panic in the population about this devastating disease. Rumors on how it was transmitted made living in the same county with an HIV positive person seem dangerous. I was not sure what to do with this information. I had given Pam my assurance of confidentiality. She told me that all the medical personnel had assured her that Annie would not pose a danger to others. Annie was in the Sunday School every Sunday.

Two days later I had lunch at the Brown Pelican at Hendry's Beach with a cardiologist who had just established a practice in Santa Barbara and was looking for a new church for his family. He was checking us out. He did not have much church experience and had questions about what we believe, what we practiced, what we cost, etc. At the end of our conversation, I decided to ask him about AIDS and HIV. I told him I was very uninformed and maybe would need to know down the line. He shared all the new protocols that were being developed in medical practice to protect against the spread of this disease. I took the risk asking how he would feel if his two young daughters were assigned to a class in their school that had an HIV positive student in it. He said he'd yank them out of that school.

Now I really didn't know what to do with what I knew. One of his daughters was in the same Sunday school class as Annie.

I spent the next two days getting as smart as I could, reading, and interviewing medical sources about HIV/AIDS and an attorney about legal issues. After these conversations I felt enough confidence in how the disease was spread to decide that the best path to honor my confidentiality agreement about Annie was to proceed with things as normal. I was nervous but this decision turned out to be a good decision. If children in that class had contracted AIDS from Annie I would have been in a lot of legal trouble.

Annie was in her early twenties when she finally succumbed to the disease. Our church had provided a wonderful experience for Annie and her "Mom" in the years in between.

The Choir

Before departing from Washington to begin a new ministry in Santa Barbara, I had several lunches with DC area UCC pastors just to talk shop about pastoring. One insight stuck in my memory. One pastor told me, "Beware the choir. They are the war department in the church." He explained. "They gather every week to rehearse and perform every Sunday. They spend a lot of time together. They spend decades together. They bond like no other group in the church. They defend the music budget with high levels of self-interest. They highly prefer that nothing ever changes."

This was not the case in Santa Barbara.

Every Sunday, the time in the service when I worshiped was when the choir sang. The music they gave us touched my soul. It "happied me up," as my granddaughter would say. By listening carefully to what they sang I got a music education in the eight years I was there.

The chancel choir was about forty voices and was relatively young for church choirs in my experience. I learned that Steve required an audition to get into that choir. The director of music did not choose everyone who auditioned. He was looking for a certain sound. He wanted to hear a flute rather than reeds in their tones. He was seeking the English boy choir sound. That requires singing without vibrato! Not everyone qualified. This made singing in the choir even more important. He actively recruited voices that fit what he was trying to create.

The deal Steven and I made was that each month when we were taking new members into the church, wife Janet and I would host a meal for the those joining the following Sunday. Steve would attend. Before eating we would sing grace. Steve would play the piano and lead us in some familiar simple song. No one suspected that this was an audition. Before the evening was over, he often had recruited some new voices. Not every time, but often. He recruited Janet. He convinced her that her singing was important to his vision.

Rehearsals were held from 7:00 to 9:00 p.m. on Thursdays. Not sitting in your assigned seat at 7:00 was unacceptable. Steve assigned seats with an ear to balancing voices. Certain voices blend and others do not. He tuned the choir like one tuned a violin.

One Thursday evening we were entertaining guests for dinner. Our windup clock with Westminster chimes began chiming the 7 o'clock hour. Janet stopped in mid-story and was in her seat in the choir next door at the church before the seventh chime struck. I mean this was discipline.

I wondered why these people worked so hard and with so much dedication on their music. Several told me that they knew Steve was striving to make this music sound the best it could ever be sung by anybody. One said she knew it was the best church choir in the area and she wanted to keep it so. A psychotherapist joined the church, and I asked him why the choir members put so much of themselves into this activity. He suggested two things. One is that they are singing to heal themselves. The second is that they probably have no other thing they do in their lives that can produce this level of excellence. Steve did strive for excellence, and they wanted to give it to him and to the rest of us.

The choir director specialized in contemporary settings of text. In addition to the usual file of church music, they sang the music of Howells, Sowerby, Rutter, Duruffle, and Tavener. This is not easy stuff.

For me the anthem and any other incidental service music sung by the choir in the Sunday worship service was my time to forget I was the worship leader and to open my hungry soul to some healing. And it still works. Listening to recordings they made renews me.

The Peace Mission: Singing in East and West Germany

I stayed active in the national UCC-EKU Working Group of the United Church of Christ. I asked at a meeting of the UCC-EKU Working Group if we might consider a modest cultural visit. I suggested our choir in Santa Barbara. They all thought that would add to the continued knitting together of these church bodies fighting against the restrictions laid down by the East German socialist government. There were many problems to be solved. The main one was that in socialism, the state controlled cultural events. A choir from the West would have to submit a proposal to the German Democratic Republic (DDR, East Germany) for approval. East Germany was starved for hard currency like US dollars. So, the choir would have to be booked into the most expensive hotels and eat at expensive restaurants and ride fancy buses. We could not afford that. We would need to develop another approach.

There were no such problems in the West. The choir would easily be booked into eight congregations across northern Germany with home stays included.

Our partner committees in Germany gave us the green light to proceed with planning. It was time for me to put the idea to Steve and the choir.

When I returned to Santa Barbara, I walked into Steve's office. I said I had an idea. He was sometimes enthusiastic about my ideas about the choir. The ideas he didn't like he would say, "We'll see." I quickly came to recognize that meant "no way in hell, preacher." We were on great terms and enjoyed the sparring around. I told him that I had broken the code on his language.

I told him my idea, that the choir was so good that we ought to find a way to put them on the road to be enjoyed by others. He brightened up and said he was thinking the same thing. I asked, "How about to Germany?" He said, "I was thinking of Fullerton."

Steve put the proposal to the choir, and they responded with huge interest but a million questions. The church would have to finance the trip, ten days on the road. Most meals would be provided either in private homes or at church dinners. Nights would be spent in the homes of families providing rich opportunities for conversation and connection. The EKU provided the bus and driver who stayed with us the whole trip. Our traveling group numbered forty: thirty-five singers, a director, an organist, a trumpet player, a helper who was the mother of one of the younger women, and me. Janet sang in the choir.

I wrote a four-page paper for our traveling choir members and for church members who were interested. I laid out some history of the divided Germany they would encounter and why we were calling this a peace mission rather than a concert tour. I wrote that we were a church traveling to visit other churches to share our faith and our lives with them, seeking to share love and hope with them and to experience their lives and concerns.

I told the choir to expect questions like I had encountered in my 1981 trip, questions about the thousands of cruise missiles the US Army had placed in German farmland along the border with East Germany and how the Soviet Union, in retaliation, had placed SS-20 missiles on the other side of that border. Cruise missiles are "designed to deliver large warheads over long distances with high precision" a pastor had told me in my previous visit. And they could be nuclear armed. Soviet short-range missiles were certainly targeted on the cruise missile silos. Thus, the farmers would be the first to know when the war broke out. How would we talk with them about that?

Choir members should expect, since our hosts were church people, that conversations about church life and conversations about the peace issues would be related to their Christian faith. Our singers did not absorb much of what I wrote because for them what was most at stake was the excellence of their singing. Their rehearsals were hard work given the quality of performance they set for themselves. But the church leadership in Germany with whom I was working made sure my paper was translated and widely circulated among our hosts.

I had briefed our folks about how hospitality would probably occur. One key lesson I learned is that it is standard practice in a German home for the bathroom door to remain closed at all times. If you need to use it you knocked on the door. Last trip I had sat one evening forever waiting for whoever was in the bathroom to come out. A small house gift was appropriate. And we were a church group which carried meaning in terms of prayer at mealtime, etc. One of our tenors trying to appropriate all this said, "I've never gone anywhere as a Christian before."

Each traveler had a prayer partner, someone in the church in Santa Barbara with whom they worked out ways of praying for each other at the same time every day.

Before we left Santa Barbara, I heard a lot of griping from our travelers because the Germans did not provide detailed itineraries like the choir members received from tourist travel companies. People wanted to know where we were having lunch each day and what bed they would sleep in. When we boarded the plane, except the first night in Hamburg, we had no advance travel itinerary. I told them that our journey had been planned by people who cared deeply that we were coming to be with them on this peace mission, that they would provide us with every need we may have, and that a plan was in good hands. All would be revealed when we got there. All we needed to do was trust them and me. There were anxiety and thin layers of trust.

After landing in Hamburg, the odd experience of seeing fire trucks speeding along on both sides of our plane after wheels hit the runway was explained. We'd had a fire in one engine. Hadn't noticed.

When the bus delivered us to our first church where the choir would sing the next day, we were, as one traveler put it, "auctioned off" to host families. Each name was called. A person or family on the ground would step forward and we got off the bus to be matched with them. We went off to their car for a ride to their home for the evening.

One man in the choir had expressed great reluctance to going on this trip. Jack's voice and personality were important. We had talked for a while, and he had finally shared his reluctance. Jack had served as a bombardier on B-17s dropping tons of bombs on industrial sites in Germany during WWII. He feared that by going to Germany he would be hated by our hosts if they found out or that he would find out that it was the wrong thing to have dropped those bombs that surely meant the death of many. He felt the potential of feeling shame for what he had done for his country as a young man. But, gathering courage, he came with us.

I was very curious to see him the morning after our first night in Hamburg. I wanted to know how it went for him. I was hoping for a good experience for him. When he was delivered back to the church that morning, he came directly over to me and asked that we step aside for his story. He said he decided to share with his host as they had a predinner drink at the fireplace that he had dropped bombs on Germany. The host paused a few moments and reported that he had served in WWII in the German Navy as a U-boat captain. His job was to sink American troop ships. Such relief I have rarely seen. He said they sat up most of the night in front of the fireplace, drinking Brandy, and sharing stories about how strangely history worked, given how they once risked their lives seeking to kill each other and now engaged in this intimate sharing and caring. Jack said they also talked about the current threat to peace, the Soviet Union. It was a deeply affirming and healing evening.

The time in East Germany, because of the limitations, took on a different character. We could not stay overnight. We could not move around as a big group. So, the Sunday in Berlin started with small groups of the tourists crossing on foot at Checkpoint Charlie and walking to the Bartolomäuskirche. Our folks were not that keen about walking the streets of

East Germany with a piece of paper their only guidance. One couple had immigrated from Basel, Switzerland, and spoke fluent German. I matched the most insecure with them.

Our hosts there were eagerly looking for our arrival. On arrival we were ushered to pews in the sanctuary joining about fifty locals. The service was in German, of course, meaning only three in our group were able to follow along. When it came time for the music, our choir gathered in front around the communion table facing the congregation. They sang beautifully. The organ was in great shape according to our organist. It had been maintained with great care. The acoustics were spectacular. The choir sang four anthems, two in German. I felt a thrill that representatives of our modest congregation in Santa Barbara, California, were here in a local church in East Germany sharing the beauty of choral music.

The care that was being given to that old building and the organ, the warmth of our welcome, the awkward dinners in peoples' homes, the eager search for language to share our stories with each other all pointed us to the words of one of the anthems: "Surely, the Lord is in this place. . . . This is none other but the house of God" (Gen 28:16–17). As liberation theology proclaims, God's work is being done wherever one might go. It might not be called church or mission, or even Christianity, but where the hungry are fed and the prisoners visited, Christ is there. At Bartolomäuskirche it was a Christianity we could recognize and experience. We were in an authentic congregation, not that we could understand all the words, but there was no doubt about the tears and hugs at the end of that brief sojourn in socialism. Christ was in that place, and we felt it.

In my preparation paper I alerted our travelers that in West Germany the second language taught in school was English. But in East Germany the second language was Russian. Some students might be able to talk a little English but only as a third language. And in the East the government had drilled into them that America was their enemy and Americans should be feared. We would probably be the first Americans they have met. A lot rested in our sensitivity to this. We would be participating in new levels of experience on both sides. After the service and a lot of awkward efforts at communication, we were matched up with hosts who walked us to their homes for a meal and conversation. We strolled back to the church in late afternoon and back out of East Berlin as we had come in.

The impact of the peace mission on those choir members was deep and profound. The experience of love and warmth and eating at various dining room tables and sharing stories created a global connection within the life of the church. They found that saying the Lord's Prayer in American English and German simultaneously had a similar rhythm and the commas were about in the same places. The idea of the church had many new dimensions.

A year later, several of our host families came to visit, hosted by our folks who had stayed in their homes. This included the U-boat captain and his wife. They were greeted with warmth and appreciation.

Kristallnacht, Fiftieth Anniversary

During a major renovation of the church in 1988, the rabbi of Congregation Bnai Brith, Jonathan Kendall, invited our church to worship at the synagogue on summer Sunday mornings while we had to vacate our building. The rabbi, at my invitation, walked us through their shabbat service on Sunday morning in place of our usual service. In return for their hospitality, twenty members of our church volunteered one Saturday to work with members of their congregation to carry their pews out of the synagogue so it could be renovated.

In October 1998 Rabbi Kendall phoned with a proposal. He suggested our two congregations cosponsor a commemoration of Kristallnacht on the fiftieth anniversary of that terrible moment in history. "The Night of Broken Glass" had taken place on November 9–10, 1938, in Nazi Germany. I agreed. Then he proposed that our church host the service. Great idea, I thought. Our people were more likely to participate in familiar space. Our leadership, after some study, decided to drape the cross in black as recognition of the German Christian complicity during the Hitler years.

I suggested that our congregations put a full-page ad in the *Santa Barbara News Press* inviting the public. The sanctuary at First Congregational Church was full that evening. It was a quiet, somber service with elements of both of our traditions. It felt to me, as I listened, as I spoke, as we prayed, as the rabbi spoke, a very deep opening to God's presence. After the service Rabbi Kendall and I expressed our thanks to each other. Between us, we could only identify about half of the worshipers as being members of our two congregations. Half were strangers to us.

A week later he called with thanks for our experience together with our congregations. He also reported that he believed our Kristallnacht service was the only one held in a Christian church.

The 1990 Painted Cave Fire

The biggest traumatic disaster in our time in Santa Barbara was the Painted Cave Fire in 1990. It was started by an angry rancher up near the top of

Highway 154 at four-thousand-foot elevation. He was having an argument with a neighbor on the ranch below. It was hot weather, up in the triple digits in the backcountry on the inland side of the mountains. This produced a several thousand-foot tower of heated air which was held away from the ocean side of the mountains by the onshore breeze that typically kept us cool in hot weather. But typically, in late afternoons, the breeze stopped, and that tower of hot air collapsed spilling over the coastal mountains and down toward the ocean. Winds that afternoon were sixty to seventy miles an hour. It fanned the flames and expanded then drove them downhill toward the ocean, creating an inferno in its path. Burning leaves, paper, and embers skipped house to house, ridge to ridge downhill. Most homes had untreated wood shake shingle roofs which easily were set aflame. Flames easily leaped across the six-lane freeway, Highway 101, and on down toward the beach. It covered five miles in less than an hour, burning 440 homes, twenty-eight apartment complexes, and thirty other buildings.

Our neighborhood was only a half mile from the main path of the fire. We felt the wind and experienced fire debris, burned paper, falling from the sky. The sky was a weird color—ashen orange, I call it. The smoke driven by the wind was in turmoil and choking.

As sun set, the winds died down. The fires eventually gave out with the gentle breeze coming on shore. Residents who fled for their safety could not get back into the fire area until the next morning. Overnight they did not know if their homes had survived. One friend had come to our home for the night, slept on the floor, and returned to his home the next morning. He found that his home was destroyed, burned to the ground and smoldering ashes.

A church family's home also burned. She was a bass player for the Santa Barbara symphony and lost two prize instruments. Even the silverware was melted by the heat of the fire. He was an aerospace engineer and a good jazz guitarist. He lost both valuable computers with project files and guitars. He was on the East Coast the day of the fire. She left their home to pick up processed photos and was not able to return until the next day. Never saw that home again. There had been no fire visible when she left home.

Most families had good insurance and were able to rebuild on the same site but with far more precautions in design and building materials. One told me some years later that the fire really helped solve several problems. Both of their widowed mothers had died within two years before the fires. The garage was full of furniture from both sides of the family. What to do with it? The fire solved that dilemma. While the loss was heartbreaking and tragic, it did open some opportunities. The redesigned and rebuilt home was a big upgrade.

Another family lost everything and rebuilt after the fire. They never found such perspective. They talk about the fire as a disaster and that they are victims. The list of what they lost was still the important thing about their story of the fire. Interesting how different people respond to the same circumstances in such different ways.

One of the families who checked in with us the morning after the fire got a call that they would be permitted to enter Hope Ranch to see if their home survived. They left after a quick breakfast to see what if anything was left of their home.

We drove another couple to look at their home. They were lucky. The fire did not take their home. We drove back to our house.

As I drove along Madrona Drive toward our home, Jack, whose home was the one in Hope Ranch, was standing in our driveway. When he saw us, he sent a signal about what he found where their home was located. He bent over at the waist and extended both his arms downward, palm facing down, moving them back and forth like he was polishing something.

Janet said, "Oh, his house burned to the ground."

I said, "That's a baseball umpire's call. Safe." I, in this rare moment, was right of course.

Men's Work and Robert Bly

With the urging of Mark, an avocado ranch manager who was active in the church, I joined him for a week in forest near Mendocino. We were in a program hosted by Robert Bly, the poet, and a team including Michael Meade, an Irish storyteller and drummer; John Stokes, an Australian tracker; and James Hillman, a Jungian therapist and author.

To get to this remote camp I drove from Santa Barbara to San Francisco and took California Highway 1 along the coast to Mendocino. Then I followed the map that had been sent to us. It was twenty miles along a single-lane dirt road, winding through thick, second growth redwoods. I found the clearing where we were asked to leave our cars and I hiked, carrying my sleeping bag, clothing, and a drum, for a mile farther under those tall trees.

Eventually I found the small logging camp that was serviceable with water, small cabins with cots, and mess hall. We ate at picnic tables outside so group gatherings could be held sitting on benches in the one larger room.

There was no way to communicate with the world, no cell phones or landlines. The outside world did not exist. There were only the one hundred of us, all men. Cooks had been hired to plan and serve meals. We were assigned randomly to the small, scattered cabins for sleeping. There were outhouses and sinks with running cold water.

There was only one hard rule for our life together: absolutely no violence allowed. In the late afternoon we sat at the picnic tables in front of the kitchen. As recommended, most of us had drums. I bought one at the folk music store in Santa Barbara. It had been crafted on a nearby Indian reservation.

As was the practice in those gatherings, we beat our drums with our hands. There was no leader to the patterns of drumming. It was herd behavior guided by, it seemed, a mysterious spirit. Our drumming was a series of rhythms in which we all joined. It was loud and energetic or quiet. It seemed to me to a unifying feeling. In this drumming we were becoming one. It felt mysterious, beautiful, eerie, even a bit scary. The energy being expressed revealed a lot of power. Sometimes angry, sometimes sweet. I had never experienced drumming before. But we drummed every evening, while waiting for the bell calling us to the picnic tables for a meal. Often small groups would go further into the woods and drum together for hours. I entered this week knowing that drumming was involved but I was very skeptical about its value. It did have an impact on me. It is difficult to say exactly what that impact was. I already said that the drumming did create a sense of being a connected to one another. We were all doing something while together creating rhythmic sounds in a remote setting. The rhythm made our bodies move together as though dancing while sitting with our drums.

All the activities during this week were invitational, not required. If you weren't comfortable doing it, no dishonor sitting out. That made it a very free space for me. I have a strong, counterdependent reaction when I am told what I must do. Being invited with the freedom to refuse made it a lot more likely I would participate. I went into this men's gathering fearing I would be struggling with a lot of required activities. Because the activities were entirely invitational, I did everything.

One afternoon we were instructed to pick up some small rocks and gather at the creek that ran through our camp. We needed as many rocks as we had men in the direct line of our ancestry on our father's side, male ancestors whose first names we knew. We stood along the edge of the stream and were instructed to throw a stone into the water and shout the first name of our father. It was a big yell and splash. Then we were told to throw the next rock and shout our grandfather's name. A big shout. Then to throw and the shout of the name of our grandfather's father. A big shout. I could go that far. My middle name is Louis, my father's name is Louis, my grandfather's name is Louis, and his father's name is Louis. He's the one who fled Germany to avoid the military draft of the Kaiser and settled on a farm in

Leavenworth, Kansas. He was a farmer and a skilled cabinet maker. So, I threw three rocks into the water shouting Louis.

That third time it seems like maybe only half of the men threw rocks and shouted. When we got to the grandfather of our grandfather, three rocks flew and names were shouted. I felt like a had kind of a puny hold on my ancestry, and I admired those who were still in the game. When it came to names of our grandfather's grandfather's father, there was one guy who threw and shouted. And he went one more. We walked back to camp and shared our experience of how far back we got and how it felt. I was disappointed that I knew the names of such a short list of my ancestors on my father's side. At home later, looking at my mother's side, it was even shorter. I knew the name of my grandfather. My mother was the youngest of three sisters and the only one born after her family immigrated from Croatia to the US.

Another evening we were randomly divided up into four groups, twenty-five in each. We were separated into the four corners of the hall. We had team-against-team competitions. Team A decided which team they wanted to challenge. The rule was that there could not be any physical contact in the competition. So, teams had to figure out what they thought they could do better than the team they challenged. The winning team challenged another team but had to name a different competition. Each round the teams named a different representative to go into the ring for them.

My team had an athlete who could, from a flat stand, jump a backward summersault landing on his feet. That was our first challenge. The team we challenged could not find a representative to enter that challenge. We won. We had a guy who was a champion tap dancer so that was our next challenge. But the team we challenged had a guy who turned out to be an even better tap dancer. At the end of the evening, they tap danced in competition with the drummers for an hour challenging each other back and forth.

The most fun came from a team who said the challenge was to be the best at cursing. Going to college was a poor training ground for this competition. Growing up in urban streets was way better preparation. Never had I seen fabulous cursing as a value.

The sense of competition was fierce all evening. It was interesting to see how the teams created structure so they could make fast decisions, what game to play, who to represent them, etc. There was a heavy lesson that if you have an idea, you either get your idea in early before others got one or learn to shout with authority if your idea came in late.

On the first evening of our week together we were introduced to our resource leaders. Each spoke a bit. During the week they each worked with a smaller group and rotated to a new group the next day. Robert Bly took an evening to tell the "Iron John" story and invited us to interpret the story, seeking to help us learn to use story to help us find more about ourselves.

On that first evening, Bly said that the most stable cultures and societies in history all honored their elders. Elders represented the wisdom of years and experience. He said we should do the same. He asked how many of us were over fifty-five. There were eight out of a hundred. Bly asked the young men in the front benches to find seating elsewhere to sit and invited the eight of us to come sit in these honored seats in front and to sit in these seats the rest of the week. He said we elders are going to anchor this community. I felt strangely important as I stood to step over several benches to get up front. And the men broke out in applause and shouts. I first felt these guys had no clue who I was. This was weird. Then the thought came to me, "but I know who I am, and I do have wisdom and I do belong up front in an honored wisdom seat as an honored elder!"

Several times during the week, young men approached me saying something like, "You're one of the elders, right?" Yup. And then some question was asked, and a great conversation usually followed. I felt a responsibility to respond in a deep, serious way. It was a conversation between an elder and a searcher.

Surprisingly, an afternoon with Stokes, the tracker, made the biggest impression. He took five of us deep into the forest and found a place where he pointed out there had been an animal fight. We spent three hours on our hands and knees trying to answer the powerful question: What happened here? Why was this branch broken? Was this blood? What kind of animals would bleed like this? The grass was flattened out along the west side. Why? Learning to read the clues left behind and reconstructing the most likely narrative takes enormous skill, intuition, and learning such things as animal habits. You look at the same dent in the mud from different angles and at different positions of the sun to pull from it what you can.

I often now walk into a room and ask myself, "What happened here?" With the information I see in the room I construct a narrative that best suits the clues. Go back when the sun has moved and look again. Learning the skills of a tracker was fascinating.

This week gave me time to reflect on my strong sense of counterdependence. If you told me what is the proper thing to do, what I should do, I would choose its opposite. I have fought that all my life. I discovered that sometimes the direction someone gives me is actually what I should do but I seem to need to find the options for myself and choose.

I could override the call to do the opposite that arose in me, but I could not overcome the feeling that I will not be controlled, that I needed to demonstrate my freedom. I keep my freedom as I enter into community. I also know that doing the opposite of what I'm told I should do is not freedom. Doing what I choose to do or choosing to follow a community discipline are both acts of freedom. Following orders is tough for me.

I could not join a creedal church. When I finally found myself in a congregational church, I found that we did not have a creed, nor does the United Church of Christ. We do have a statement of faith which we sometimes read together in worship, but it is not expected that everyone believes everything in those words. Janet was startled, having grown up in a Lutheran tradition, to hear me make that claim. It was a little unnerving. We do gather as a church led by Jesus Christ. We find and evolve how we state our own faith, but we don't talk about it that much. We think our faith is expressed in our work for justice and peace and providing shelter for the poor and visiting prisons.

At the men's gathering that week there was never a moment when I felt my counterdependence. I was not required to be or do something that raised that reaction. Each step was carried by an invitation and respect if it was refused.

I did come away from that time in the tall trees with valuable perspectives. The experience of the mysteries of drumming. The storytelling by Bly and Meade, often accompanied by drumming, moved from rational to mythical reflection. It helped consider one's life as a story with themes, related events, and the necessary work to do in a particular sequence. Hillman's notion of the soul having a code that can guide one to a much more meaningful and joyful life has been a valuable resource through the years. Bly's use of the "Iron John" story to explore the male softness, passivity, and immaturity felt profound.

I had promised Janet that I would be in touch during that week not knowing that it would take half a day round trip to make a phone call. I did not honor my commitment to be in touch. That was hard on both of us.

My Conversation with Jesus

I had almost nothing to offer those who sought a deepened spirituality. I had little experience of, and I might even say not much hunger for, such practices. I had no problem that others found meaning in these disciplines except when it made them too occupied to show up for the picket line I was organizing. But I do have one experience to offer, one that has meaning for me.

I was for a year a client of a Jungian therapist. Remembering dreams, writing them down, talking about them, trying to find points of contact between the dreams and my own feelings about my experience, that's what

I was doing. I was interested in the exploration, but it was not why I was doing therapy. I had issues. I wanted solutions. Instead, we explored my dreams. Seemed we never got around to my issues, but my issues were only what I was conscious of, not, according to him, what was really going on. Okay, so that's worth some exploring to see if he's right.

I was also doing some reading in the field. In one of John A. Sanford's books, he described forms of self-guided exploration of one's own unconscious world.[4] He described a question-and-answer format. I ask a question that is fundamental to my anxiety. And then, in the quiet, I listen for the answer and, he claimed, it would come. It was almost like the exercise of two chairs. You sit in one to ask and switch to the other, becoming another persona, and seek to answer.

One afternoon after a session of sermon preparation, I heard my two staff colleagues, Music Director Steve Townsend and Associate Minister Janet Hatfield Legro, engaged in lively conversation. I decided to take a break and to wander down the hall to join in.

When I got near their offices, I discovered that they were both on phone calls to different people. No way I could find some fellowship with that arrangement. So, I walked into the sanctuary, walked midway up the center aisle, and sat. It was quiet, very quiet. I was alone. I remembered what I had read of Sanford and decided I would bring my three biggest anxiety laden questions at that moment to this exercise. But I needed at least an image of the foil, the person to whom I was asking my questions. I thought, well maybe Jesus was the partner I was seeking. I always thought that Jesus looked a lot more like Jimmy Durante than the head of Christ that Warner Salman had painted. So, I imagined my Jimmy Durante Jesus walking in the same door I had entered and him following me down the aisle, pausing at the pew where I was seated. I moved over so there was room for him to sit. He sat. He was quiet and waiting.

My first question was this: Was Janet going to survive the breast cancer for which she was in radiation treatment?

I listened. "She will prosper," I heard.

After a few moments feeling the deep relief that that response gave me, I asked my second question: "What is the future of my own employment?" I was feeling the need to enter the search process but thought perhaps staying longer here was my real challenge. I felt stuck.

I listened. "It will unfold in a way that you will be happy," I heard. I can't say I heard a voice. The words just came clear in my mind.

---

4. Sanford, *Healing*.

Again, I felt I could let go of a big bag of stress and tension for which I was grateful.

I cannot now remember the specifics of the third question, but I know that it also was answered in a way that lifted tension from me.

I said "thank you" and watched as he stood and walked back down the aisle and out the door without looking back.

I exited the sanctuary full of new energy. It was wonderful. Both responses above were exactly right for me at the time and true to my experience. I have no idea if that was a ten-minute or a sixty-minute experience.

That was so awesome that I have never tried to repeat the experience. Many times, I would have welcomed the stress reduction of that moment in the sanctuary but did not do it again.

While many of my friends practice forms of meditation, have Zen practices, or other regular prayer disciplines, I have none. At least I don't have any like those. I guess it is better to say I have none. But I felt deepened and learned skills in the year of Jungian therapy. So, dreams became a canvas to explore for meaning. Rather than talk about the "problem" for which I was seeking solutions, we talked about my dreams. There was no connection to what brought me to this appointment that I could see, but it was enormously interesting. Roaring trains in my dreams became surges of energy in my psyche. They needed attention in my consciousness. Falling became losing control somewhere in my psychological life. Again, I had to sort that out.

I read an occasional book on this Jungian approach and how it has been adapted in various areas. I especially found much to explore in myself and occasionally in men's groups. The proposals in a book by Robert Moore and Douglass Gillette, *King, Warrior, Magician, Lover,* gave me a Jungian introduction to the psychological foundation of a mature, authentic, and revitalized masculinity. Redefining age-old concepts of masculinity, Jungian analysts Moore and Gillette make the argument that mature masculinity is not abusive or domineering, but generative, creative, and empowering of the self and others. Moore and Gillette clearly describe the four mature male archetypes that stand out through myth and literature across history: the king (the energy of just and creative ordering), the warrior (the energy of aggressive but nonviolent action), the magician (the energy of initiation and transformation), and the lover (the energy that connects one to others and the world).[5]

I find myself referring to those archetypes in reflecting on my own or other's behavior. Starting with a viewing a video called "A Gathering of

5. Moore and Gillette, *King, Warrior, Magician, Lover.*

Men" featuring poet Robert Bly,[6] I led a very productive men's group in Santa Barbara. Such questions as these were asked: How was being a man now different than when my father (or grandfather) was my age? How was life better for men now that women, including our wives, were in the workplace? How did a boy in these days become a man? What were the necessary markers along the way? How did you know when you became a man? We worked on these and other questions.

Projects and Programs that Strengthen the Ministry

My eight years as senior minister for the First Congregational Church UCC in Santa Barbara turned out to be the second longest tenure of any previous minister. For me it was a test, a big test about whether, having spent sixteen years out of local church ministry, I still had the stuff and the passion to retool myself, to be transformed into a very different calling and life. It was a risk for both the church and for me. I am grateful that they were able to give me space to figure things out, to try my wings. I'm certain we came out of it in pretty good condition.

When I look back, I ask, "Was the institution stronger and better equipped to carry out the ministry given to it by Jesus?" And I ask, "Was it engaged in that ministry?" Several projects that the church took on during my ministry, which satisfy my own answer to these questions, are these.

1. FCCSB was one of the founding congregations of the homeless program called Transition House. This ministry has developed major funding sources so that a permanent sixty-bed facility near the ocean and other transitional housing has been created with professional staff and services available. The supporting congregations still provide a warm evening meal and a carry away sack breakfast for guests.

2. The church provided facilities for and supporting Storyteller, a day care program for the children of homeless persons so that they could seek employment, training, and housing. The three-bedroom house next to the church that we had lived in was transformed for this ministry.

3. The church completed the process of voting itself an Open and Affirming Congregation, publicly declaring itself as welcoming to persons in the LGBTQ community. I began this education and policy study process, familiar to many in the UCC, by approaching the gay and lesbian persons I had identified, most long-term members. Two women,

6. Bly, "Gathering of Men."

very active in many roles in the church, shared a residence and life for forty years. Several lifelong unmarried men were active. But to activate questions about homosexuality would eventually lead to new realizations about what has been before our eyes but never saw. I did not want to out anybody but knew once we began to open people's awareness that new questions would be asked. I called together a committee to carry the process forward. We met and, using the materials provided by the UCC, we began the study process.

We knew that, at the end of the process, there would be a vote of the congregation on the question of making a public statement of welcome to the LGBT community. The work continued to its completion after I departed for my call to the Madison church. The process was completed, and the vote was affirmative by a very high margin. It was one of the earliest congregations in Santa Barbara to make this declaration. And the church has been served by both lesbian and gay pastors.

4. The Sunday morning services at 9:30 and 11:00 a.m. had a combined average attendance of three hundred. The staff included a senior minister; a full-time minister of music with two adult choirs, three children and youth choirs, and a bell choir; a full-time ordained associate minister; a part-time ordained minister for ministry to seniors; and support staff. The church was always just over the edge of its budget and income but that was as it should be. There was always more to do than we were willing to support. A successful capital fund drive was completed. It supported physical renewal to the facilities—resurfaced parking lot, new roof, inside and out painting, reconfigured sanctuary, reconfigured pews, newly constructed chancel, relocated organ, removal of a stairway, and creation of a larger hallway.

5. There continued an energizing connection to churches and persons in churches in East and West Germany, including various visits by Germans to Santa Barbara and by our folks to Germany, continued conversations about our experiences and responsibilities during WWII, and discussions about the Cold War, about the Berlin Wall, about the role of the church in shaping national conversations on the big questions before society, and about the vitality of the local congregation. These gave this church an international connection that helped shape new perspectives on local church life and wider understanding of the work of the church in other places in the world.

Personal Events

Janet decided not to practice law in the tradition of an opening or joining a law practice but to offer her administrative and legal training to nonprofit organizations. She first worked for the Santa Barbara Community Clinics Association that offered health care on a sliding fee scale. Then she was hired by the dean of students as director of the Women's Center at the University of California at Santa Barbara. Under her leadership the center expanded its rape prevention work, its art gallery and library, and the visiting lecture program bringing visiting scholars and leaders in women's studies. This laid the groundwork for establishing a women's studies academic department. She was appointed assistant vice chancellor for Student Affairs responsible for nonacademic student support programming for the campus. At the University of California system level, she led a team to draft the University of California statewide system policies on sexual harassment.

I had surgery for further repair of my left leg putting me back on crutches for three months. It improved the function of the repaired leg. The first day back in the pulpit, after I moved from a walker to a cane, I held the cane up and claimed, "Cane and able." Fewer chuckles than I thought.

Janet was diagnosed with breast cancer and treated by surgery and radiation. The literature said that her chances of survival were less than five years. That was in 1990.

What's Next?

After seven years in Santa Barbara, I began to realize that I was repeating myself, that I was no longer on the edge of learning and experimenting. I experience myself as one who thrives on being lost and trying to find my way. Moving into the ghetto with my family was moving into a world in which, at first, I felt lost and gradually found my way. Moving to lobbying work in Washington was moving into a new landscape, an unfamiliar language, into the midst of a very smart and ambitious bunch of people, and eventually I found my place there.

After sixteen years of ministry not pastoring a local church, I was back and worked hard to relearn what I had forgotten and learned for the first time what I needed to know and do.

In 1991 in Santa Barbara, I felt that all the creativity I could bring to that ministry had been given. The next phase was managing what was created. I was feeling the desire to get lost again and the challenge to find what's next. There were a variety of other things that supported the notion that it was time to move on but getting lost again was primary.

I went through the process of application and interviewed for several conference minister positions. None produced a new position for me.

While attending a meeting of the UCC-EKU Working Group at Wesley Seminary in Washington, DC, the UCC Wisconsin Conference minister Frederick Trost invited a conversation about my status in Santa Barbara. It was in February 1992. Did my need to get lost again show on my face? I shared that with him, and we got to the point of his question. "There is a church in Madison, a sleeping giant on the edge of the campus for the University of Wisconsin, that could use your pastoral gifts. Might you be interested?"

Just that little bit of information hit just the right notes. Seemed like a great place to get lost again.

The hard point was that Janet was assistant vice chancellor for Student Affairs at UCSB, responsible for programs she was most interested working with. She also had a compatible group of colleagues. And there were interesting new projects to be done. She does not like to be lost. When we talk about these dynamics she says, "I'm a rut person. I like to get in a rut and go back and forth wearing it smoother and smoother." This was a very difficult set of issues we had to sort out.

She could not discuss it with her most trusted friends at work nor could I in my situation. We needed a safe space with sensitive, skillful friends who were able to keep confidentiality, to help us. We immediately agreed on who fit the job description: Ann Jaqua and David Griffin. Ann was an active lay leader at Trinity Episcopal Church. David was a professor of theology at the Claremont School of Theology. They agreed immediately to our request to walk with us through this difficult and complex decision. They invited us to their home in Isla Vista for some good wine, a pleasant dinner, and hard conversation. I can't imagine anyone who could do any job better than they did walking us through this struggle. It was resolved in that one hard evening. I shudder to try to imagine what might have happened if Ann and David had not been available, had not been who they are. And we remain grateful.

Chapter 10

Serving in Madison 1992–1999: LGBT Affirmation and Pigsty in Chiapas

THE PEOPLE AT FIRST Congregational UCC in Madison, Wisconsin, needed to be loved, to have their imaginations awakened to new directions for the ministry and justice work, said Wisconsin Conference minister Frederick Trost. They were ready for what God was calling them to be and do.

His approach to me about this open position came out of the blue. I had pretty much abandoned the possibility of another location for ministry after several frustrating efforts for conference minister positions. Going to another church was not on my agenda. But I must confess, my heart jumped at the thought of another place to take my wares and get lost again, to start over again. This would be a major challenge in an historic big liberal church in the Upper Midwest.

This eight years (1992–1999) at the end of my time as a full-time minister was full of very interesting experiences for me. I met some fascinating people as one always does, challenged the church to some forms of ministry they had not experienced before, and was the first senior minister to resign or retire under relatively happy circumstances since the Rev. Alfred Swan's retirement in 1965.

The Church is a Sleeping Giant

The church building occupied a visible, prominent location. It was architecturally notable, an example of American Georgian Revival: tall, red brick, white trim, six tall columns in front, and two steeples. It was built in 1928, the third location since the church's founding in 1840. The sanctuary was designed to seat a thousand. The view of the stately church is sufficiently treasured in Madison that a major, new UW College of Engineering building, built in 2000, across the street has a curved front to avoid blocking the view of the tall towers and front of the church.

As I prepared for the opportunity to interview with the search committee, I found one major worry arise in me: the prospect of a church with an enormous sanctuary and with only a handful of worshipers. I had a few times visited and led worship at the First Congregational Church in Pasadena. It was a different architectural style but a sanctuary of similar size. As the congregation declined through the seventies and eighties, the preacher's experience was of leading in worship thirty people occupying the space for one thousand people. How could one not feel the sense of declining Christianity? If I were invited to serve that congregation, I'm sure I would not have looked eagerly to face Sunday mornings and all those empty pews from that pulpit. In fact, this was serious enough that it could be a deal-breaker for me.

Telephone interviews went well. Janet and I were invited to come to Madison to meet with the search committee and tour the church and community. It was the summer of 1992.

The critical conversation with the search committee took place in the student lounge of the church. It had a large fireplace, lounge furniture, and a high ceiling with decorative architectural features. The conversation went way too long because we were all were having an enjoyable time. I had as many questions as they did.

They were aware of the trend lines and shared the concern but were convinced there was reason, with the right leadership, to stop the decline and to turn the things around. I asked when the last time was that the membership roll had been updated. No one knew. So, the number of listed members had to been viewed with serious suspicion.

The committee was hopeful about what was possible and responded with energy to some ideas. I was also listening for their resistance to change. They seemed eager to find a vision. We discussed the "Dr. Swan problem." Given his declining health, I was less likely to experience the constant reminders of the great days of the church under his leadership during the fifties. This had been an issue for clergy who had served since Swan retired.

I tested the idea of employing a full-time music director. In Madison the music program was led by a series of part-time people, some of them very good. But my sense was that a full-time person whose entire reputation rests on the program at the church would produce so much more than part-time people who had full-time day jobs and led a church choir to supplement their incomes. The current part-time staff were appreciated and loved so I knew then that there was going to be resistance to that change.

They described several lay-led services and justice-oriented programs already in place so more in that direction would not generate resistance.

As we moved to the end of that time together, I was energized, and they seemed to be also. Then I shared my concern about a remnant congregation in an almost empty sanctuary.

We seemed ready to move onto some serious detail about the possibility of becoming their candidate to propose to the congregation. In the back of my mind was the nagging question about the sanctuary based on my Pasadena experience. I said that before we shift the conversation into serious and necessary detail, I needed to be shown the sanctuary.

It was 9:00 p.m. Several of us entered the dark sanctuary and the lights were switched on. Wow. No problem here. My first impression was that though it was a large room, it was very warm, and the pulpit was very near the front row of pews.

Ron Bowen, the architect who designed the transformation of the sanctuary, later showed me that they had taken out the three rows of pews across the back thus creating hospitality space, allowing enjoyment of a cup of coffee in the sanctuary after the service where it was warm and protected from the wind and open doors. The only problem was that the large coffee urns in the back of the sanctuary began brewing about the time of the sermon. The delectable smell of freshly brewed coffee wafted through the pews. I was told, usually with a smile, that the sermon was the thing that stood between them and a much-desired cup of coffee.

Ron showed me that the plan he had developed also removed three rows of pews from the front of the sanctuary and built a platform thrusting out from the chancel stairs into the empty space. The pulpit was cut down from its imposing tower and, in its shorter form, brought forward and placed on the platform along with a large, handsome communion table. The walls were decorated with stained oak paneling. The front of the balcony was similar. The warmth of the wood created the effect that a smaller congregation comfortably filled the new space. That room was one of the most beautiful, warm, and welcoming worship spaces I had known. It had both large size and intimacy. The beautiful sanctuary removed a major barrier to my consideration of the call. I could easily envision myself entering this room Sunday after Sunday to greet the congregation and lead our worship together.

This church was a sleeping giant in that its physical location and its historical prominence in Madison gave promise to revival for the future. While the size of the congregation had slowly come down, it still had a strong lay leadership core. In my view, in the period since Dr. Swan's retirement some thirty-four years previous, the ensuing three ministries were so compromised by Swan's continuing presence and meddling that a clear vision for the future had never been allowed to develop. Thinking was moored in the past. Long term members were always referring backwards.

The task for me, as I understood it from conversations with leaders in the church and several conference staff, was to point our eyes to the future, to what needed to happen so there would be a future to this congregation.

On Christmas Eve in my first year, ushers had to add folding chairs to accommodate the numbers of worshipers. When they were opening folding chairs in the middle of the service, I said to the congregation that the most beautiful sound a preacher can ever hear is the sound of opening folding chairs.

I discovered that the member records included their dates of birth. When I found we had that information I asked the office manager to develop the correlation between birth year and value of pledges in five-year increments. Turned out that 60 percent of annual pledges was given by people aged eighty and older. One simply had to look down the road five years to see what we were facing. That one piece of information shifted the conversation.

The sleeping giant needed to awaken.

The University of Wisconsin across the Street

The University of Wisconsin dominated all life in Madison including the churches. There was your calendar hanging on the refrigerator door. There was the church calendar with Advent, Christmas, Easter, etc. There was the University of Wisconsin calendar, and, of course, the Badger's football schedule. The last one was the most important. Ask anyone the date of Easter and get a blank stare. But they all knew when the Iowa Hawkeyes were playing the Badgers at Camp Randall Stadium.

The congregations of many churches were filled with deans, associate deans, tenured professors, research assistants, etc. At First Congregational, seven presidents and chancellors of the university had been members. And, over time, a diminishing number of students.

The Swan Legacy

The most prominent reality influencing the life of that congregation was the very much alive memory of the epic ministry of the Rev. Dr. Alfred A. Swan, 1930–1965, thirty-five years.

He built on the reputation for the church as a liberal cathedral. I searched for archives in the church eager to read some of Dr. Swan's sermons. I heard old-timers tell me about them. One title that many remember was "Why We Must Bring Red China into the United Nations."

And nobody ever referred to him in any other way than "Dr. Swan." I was the new minister in "Dr. Swan's church." He had retired in 1965. He and Mrs. Swan were in church every Sunday thereafter.

I met him. He and Mrs. Swan were present for my sermon when I was presented as a candidate for the senior minister position. He voted yes on the question of calling me to be his successor. He died during the period after he voted for me and before I arrived to take up my duties. So, I stepped into a position that had been difficult for the last three senior ministers. My sense was that many members were aware that things had not gone well for clergy since Swan. The search committee shared with me the question being asked by some, that "maybe the problem is us." There were some other issues but the primary one was the continuing presence of the much admired and loved previous pastor.

Swan's death cleared the deck of whatever problems arose from his lingering need for affirmation from "his" people and a reluctance by them to support changes that lead further away from his days of leadership. There weren't that many of his people around anymore.

There was no doubt inside or outside the church that this was a church that had the social gospel at the center of its understanding of the gospel. Swan had continued that path and is remembered for the boldness of his vision, the intellectual work of analyzing the human situation, and building a vision based on liberal understanding of the Christian faith. The groundwork he had laid for the mission work of the church was deeply entrenched.

I do regret not having been able to have conversation with him about those tumultuous years between 1930 and 1965.

Being Lost and Loving It

I remember my first trip to the grocery store in Madison. We bought a house in Madison and sold our Santa Barbara house. We shipped my car on a car carrier scheduled to arrive the same day my plane arrived. I had arranged for the car to be delivered to a hotel where I would be staying. The manager of the hotel at the front desk had signed for the car when it was delivered, and it was waiting. The moving van arrived in Madison the next evening.

During that day awaiting the moving van, I had work to do at the house. All my tools were in the van, so I needed to find a hardware store.

And I needed food so finding a grocery store was required. I was lost and had no idea where these stores were to be found. I was on it. I headed west on University Avenue and saw a hardware store. I was conscious of the fact that I had an out-of-state driver's license and checkbook. Credit cards were not yet commonly accepted in hardware and grocery stores. Coming from California, I assumed I would run into identity problems when writing a check. I assembled the tools and stuff that I needed, put them on the check-out counter, and went into a long speech about just arriving, not having time to get the new driver's license or open a checking account, how the moving van was about to arrive, and hoping that he would be able to take my California check. The cashier watched me squirm, then reached his hand across the counter, shook my hand, and said with a big warm smile, "Welcome to Wisconsin." No issue cashing a check for my groceries either. I was remembering the Midwest hospitality in which I grew up.

After the moving van departed, I still needed to assemble the bed frame and put the mattress on. All the furniture and boxes were awaiting the move-in work. I had a dinner date, but I was so tired and my legs hurt so much from all the carrying that I'm sure I was not good company.

Existing Mission Projects

I explored and evaluated the various forms of ministry that were functioning. In addition to worship, social groups, and strong financial support, three major mission projects were working well. Lay leadership was strong and volunteer staffing was in place. People were happy to be working together.

What really impressed me was that in most churches these kinds of projects were led by clergy. At FCC Madison, all three were envisioned and organized by lay leaders. These were a great sign of a moral vision, of a willingness to work to fulfill the vision and a level of confidence that lay leadership was sufficient alone to make the gospel move from word to deed. It also reflected the absence of resistance within the congregation, the kind of resistance that puts a drag on initiative, that loads the discussion with the question of how many members we will lose if we do this. Swan had cleared the way long ago. This division did not exist here.

Thanksgiving Meal

One lively mission project was the annual Thanksgiving meal shared with the wider community. Those who came for generous helpings of the traditional Thanksgiving fare were students who didn't go home for the Thanksgiving break, foreign students whose residence hall didn't provide meals during the break, church members, discerning neighbors who enjoyed the food and social interaction, and homeless people. In retirement, Clarence had found in himself the desire to feed people and organized this major event. Many responded to help him with great joy and enthusiasm. Thirty frozen turkeys were delivered to the narthex during worship the Sunday before Thanksgiving. Those who had signed up took home a turkey to roast for the meal.

Because of the commotion in the narthex as the boxes of frozen turkey were being delivered, I always had a hard time keeping everyone's focus. One time I said we'd arrange next year to have live turkeys delivered.

On Turkey Day the church kitchen was busy from 5:00 a.m. There was a general sense that we were not just serving the visitors but sharing in a common meal. We ate our Thanksgiving meal communally, scattering ourselves around for conversations with strangers whom we hoped would not stay strangers. The meal served several hundred people.

Clarence was also a deacon and took responsibility for the communion services in worship, further fulfilling his call to feed people, this time spiritual food.

Shelter for Women

The second ongoing mission project was a shelter for women. Several congregations worked together to organize a shelter for women. The criteria for hosting a women's shelter included that it be monitored by women; that it be behind secure doors locked from the inside with an outside entrance, so guests did not have to wander through the church when they arrived; that there be bathroom facilities; and that it be heated and available from 5:00 p.m. through 8:00 a.m. seven nights a week. It was difficult for churches to provide that kind of space. Women from our church led by Mari figured out that our narthex could fit the criteria. It was a large space with sturdy, lockable doors. There was also storage space for cots and blankets. Monitors were easily recruited within the congregation. And there were bathrooms accessible from the shelter space.

Every night homeless women, including those who fled a violent relationship, came up the front steps, were screened, and welcomed into a secure, warm, temporary shelter for the night. Social workers who helped with the screening each evening provided professional support for the guests.

The only catch was Christmas Eve when we held a 5:00 p.m. family service and an 11:00 p.m. service. How about announcing that there would be no room at the inn for homeless women on Christmas Eve? Special arrangements were made for use of another room in the church for the shelter.

Vote to Declare Itself an Open and Affirming Church

The third project was the vote to become an Open and Affirming Congregation, the UCC's designation that a congregation actively welcomes LGBT participation, membership, and leadership, both lay and professional. The successful study of educational materials and congregation-wide discussions had been completed during the interim and a congregational meeting was called to debate and vote. The meeting was held about a month before I arrived.

I'm told that when the congregation assembled to debate and vote on whether to become an Open and Affirming Church, Betty Smith, local realtor and active Republican, was the last speaker and urged the congregation to vote yes. She explained that real estate law in Madison prohibited discrimination against gay and lesbian people and that she hoped the church would not be worse than the real estate industry. It was an almost unanimous affirmative vote.

These two projects and the Opening and Affirming vote were signs of an active lay leadership who were familiar with the concept of the church's mission. The lay leadership had been working to improve what fit the current vision. And they were very effective. It had been a while since a pastor had worked to develop a longer-term vision that could be used to measure the significance of program and staffing. Part of my responsibility was to open discussion about long-term vision, which potentially meant running into many points of resistance with what lay leaders were already doing.

As I reflect on my experience in Madison, I am grateful for the seriousness with which the society took the role of the church. This point is easily illustrated by the story Janet tells of the difference in Monday morning conversations between her staffs at the University of California in Santa Barbara and at the University of Wisconsin Madison. The conversations in Santa Barbara were typically about the adventures of the weekend. In Madison it was regularly how the different pastors in the churches attended by staff members used the lectionary lesson in their sermons.

Another difference that I appreciated was the community openness to concerns that clergy brought to political life. For example, the city of Madison contracted with a company that organized city-sponsored marathons, which typically generated major income for the business community. The geographic layout of Madison is shaped like a bow tie. Two major lakes,

Monona and Mendota, are separated by a mile-wide isthmus. The State Capitol is on the isthmus as is downtown Madison. The race started and ended in the isthmus. A 26.2-mile marathon route had to be run partly on the east side and partly on the west side, thus running through the isthmus twice and looping around sections on both sides. The marathon was on Sunday of a three-day weekend to accommodate travel for the runners. Great fun except all the important roads people used to go to church were full-time or part-time blocked for the race. The race started at 7:00 a.m. and concluded around 1:00 p.m. The big churches had less than half the usual attendance. The half that did not get to church sat in their cars for long periods of time keeping the race route clear and safe.

The clergy had a hot clergy association meeting the following week and authorized me to call Paul Soglin, the mayor, for a meeting. He set up an appointment right away. We elected the Baptist minister to raise our questions. The Baptists historically have fought the church-state issues most often. We had cumulative attendance data and the decrease in pledge and plate offering contrasted to the same Sunday the year before. Thirteen of us were present. The mayor got our issue immediately and said they would alter the route and timing with awareness of the church issues. And they did make modifications that helped.

Scouting Out Wisconsin: Brats, Beer, Eagles, and Ice Fishing

On a below-zero Saturday morning, Janet and I would sometimes fill a thermos with hot chocolate and some brandy, pick up some pastries at a fabulous bakery, and drive out into the countryside to a dam on the Sauk River just above the town of Sauk Prairie. The action of the water released through the dam created a churning that kept the river from freezing just below the dam. The bald eagles gathered in the tall trees on the ridge top and, when hungry enough, would take flight with a great awkward flapping of ten-foot tip-to-tip wings, gain elevation, circle around, and then swoop down with talons out to pluck a large fish from the water. It was for them a great breakfast feast and for us very dramatic entertainment.

Many locals in Wisconsin claimed that winter was their favorite season, that there was no such thing as bad weather, only bad clothing. They claimed that there was so much more to do in winter: ice fishing, deer hunting, skiing, and racing through the snowy fields and woods with snow mobiles.

Speaking of winter, it was always easy to get our far-flung children to come to Santa Barbara for Christmas. Opening gifts in the morning and going to the beach in the afternoon had a nice flow to it. The first Christmas in Madison they all came. They usually needed a day or two shopping locally to get gifts for under the tree. In Santa Barbara a leisurely stroll down State Street was in order. But in Madison, also shopping on State Street, it was so cold that they stopped at every store along the three blocks because it was too cold to be outside for the length of more than one store.

Research shows more brandy is imbibed per person in Wisconsin than any other state. Unfortunately, it is an all-seasons problem, not just antifreeze. Brandy-fed bravery has led many a local to drive a snow mobile onto the various frozen lakes, out far enough to find the ice too thin to carry the load. A few were lost each winter that way. As were a few autos and deer lost each winter by running into deer crossing the road. Drivers didn't seem to honor the "Danger: Deer Crossing" signs and many deer didn't either. The coldest non-windchill temperature during our seven years in Madison was seventeen below zero, far from a record. On that Saturday I led a men's retreat at my house. All thirteen men who signed up were present.

Since neither Janet nor I knew Wisconsin, it became a project to get our heads and hearts around this new venue in our lives. I confessed our ignorance in the weekly church newsletter and invited suggestions for the best place to get good hamburgers, fries, dessert, brats, and beer and to see art, hike, enjoy live music, etc. And we followed many of the suggestions. Best and tallest lemon meringue pie at the Norske Nook in Osseo. Best brats to buy at the grocery were Usinger's. Best brats and beer served were at the Brat House Tavern in Milwaukee. This deserved a special drive over there. I ordered the traditional bratwurst, potato salad, and a local beer. Janet ordered the brat and hot tea. My first reaction was to slink away in shame. Suggestions sent us to many places that were favorites of actual residents of Wisconsin. We benefited from the suggestions and the sense of connection that arose from this small project.

We lived three blocks from the University of Wisconsin Field House where the Badgers played basketball and from the Camp Randall Football Stadium where they hosted Big Ten football. We bought season tickets to both and the next year we bought season tickets to the women's basketball season. The first women's game we saw was with the University of Tennessee team, coached by the best women's coach in the country, Pat Summit. Janet discovered that the price of our tickets for that mid-season game also bought us season tickets. Several women in the church were avid fans. New levels of relationship opened up because we became fans of women's basketball. One of those women had not missed a St. Louis Cardinals baseball opening day in fifty years. She was blown away by the fact that I had for several years mowed Stan Musial's lawn. She said she had to resist the urge to ask me for my autograph.

The football team won two Rose Bowl games, 1994 and 1999, during our time in Madison. On Saturdays when the Badgers hosted home football games, we saw about forty thousand of our best friends walk down the street in front of our home toward Camp Randall Stadium. The other forty thousand came from other directions. And the church could not schedule weddings or memorial services on those Saturdays. More than one bride's mother's heart was broken by our rigidity on the matter. No place to park within miles. The church owned parking lots that could handle about sixty cars, so the tradition was that each home game parking was hosted by different groups in the church. They staffed the parking, collected twenty dollars per car and kept the funds for their own programming. For several years the ESPN and network sports broadcasters parked their staff buses and equipment trucks in one of our lots. After the 1994 Rose Bowl victory, the UW Foundation became the largest public university foundation in the country. Alumni pride turned into alumni generosity.

Roots of Progressive Policy: Bascom, LaFollette

To experience a sense of being grounded in communities in which I served, I often found an historical event or person to learn more about. In Madison it included John Bascom, the sixth President of the University. I was enthralled by the story of Bascom, a former president of the University of Wisconsin (1874–1887) and active member of this church. His roots in the New England Social Gospel movement shaped his thinking about the role of the university in society and his leadership completely changed how the university and the state interacted. The "Wisconsin Idea" and the Progressive Party, Robert LaFollette, and the start of New Deal economics were all stimulating history of Wisconsin. The anti-Vietnam War bomb blast of the Army Math Center in Sterling Hall at the University in 1970 was the largest nonmilitary explosion in the US until the bombing of the Murrah Federal Building in Oklahoma City in April, 1994. Both were fertilizer truck bombs. One was killed in the Madison bombing, 168 in the Oklahoma City bombing. The truck loaded with six barrels of fertilizer in Madison belonged to a church member who had reported it stolen a few days earlier. Windows in the church were blown out. Many remembered it. During our time in Madison, Karl Armstrong, the leader of the New Year's Gang that did the bombing and had served prison time for the act, was by his cart every Saturday at the Farmer's market on the Capitol Square. As a veteran of the anti-war movement, I remembered the bombing. I was interested in what drove this small group to that violent act of resistance. I've been close to something like that in myself, that level of frustration when it seemed my own government was the enemy of our vision of a peaceful world.

Ushers Playing Basketball

Serving as pastor of this church with its storied liberal social gospel, prominence in the community, and reputation as one of the larger membership churches in the denomination back in the prewar time held many challenges and opportunities. After six months I invited the members of the search committee over for coffee on a Sunday afternoon. I told them I was seeking feedback from them. They were the committee that made the fateful decision to recommend me to the congregation for leadership of the church and I wondered how they felt, what they heard, and what needed to be looked at.

My vulnerability seemed to surprise them. Criticizing and/or praising the pastor is usually relegated to the conversation in the parking lot, not in the pastor's living room. After a pause the chair of the search committee said, "I hear two things from the congregation. One is that you seem to be glad you're here. The other is that you seem to like us." Those two observations were true, I was glad to be there, and I did like them. But I still wonder why that seemed such a surprise to them. What did they experience from previous pastors?

I've had the sense that some pastors and laity think of the church as a hospital with the mission of healing the broken people one by one. I've had the sense that the church is a boot camp preparing and leading teams of Christians into the world to find Jesus at work healing and building a just and peaceful world. The Madison church seemed more like both. There was stuff that needed to be done and it was up to us to join the battle. When Janet and I were married in 1981 you'd probably not be surprised that I wanted the congregation to sing as the closing hymn "Onward Christian Soldiers." The kind of army I was trying to create was like those marching across the Edmund Pettus Bridge. The other side carried guns, clubs, and badges. We carried love, outrage at injustice, and willingness to sacrifice.

Many traditions of worship within the wide family of Christianity have different practices. Gathering in the sanctuary for worship takes on very different moods. In Episcopal churches I have known, the people gather in quiet piety, making their spirits open to the presence of the Holy Spirit. Some bend their knees briefly, cross themselves, and sit quietly, praying. One Sunday in Madison I watched, as I usually did, how our congregation gathered. It was a noisy affair. Our tradition was for the worship leaders to enter from a side door and move to chairs on the platform as worship was about to begin. My spirit was always lifted by the sounds of the big tracker organ for the prelude. The choir processed up the center aisle with the opening hymn. I saw the joyful faces as friends greet each other. I saw the suffering on some faces, some I knew why, others I noted to follow up. I saw the widow sitting in the same pew where she sat decades ago with her young family, now sitting alone. In her imagination, her husband and family gathered with her every Sunday in that pew. There was no genuflecting or crossing and not much sign that people entered personal prayers as they sat.

One Sunday, through the entire organ prelude, two ushers, both avid UW basketball fans, stood in the center aisle near the front of the sanctuary, each holding a stack of worship bulletins, trading stories about the great game the men's basketball team played at the field house the night before. I saw hook shots, fancy dribbling, and dunks. I'm not sure anyone else even saw them as I did. It was who we were. A joyful spirit connected us to one another, bringing us energy and enthusiasm. To life!

I was comfortable in both traditions of gathering of God's people.

I poked fun without judgment at the guys for reliving the basketball game. They promised me that they were going to a UW hockey game next Saturday night; I should prepare myself.

I enjoyed an easy back-and-forth connection with the congregation during announcements and sermons. On the Sunday before Advent one year, I was using the announcement time to encourage families to come in the afternoon to help decorate the sanctuary for Advent. I said, "Come help us this afternoon. We're going to be hanging the greens for Advent." The Green family, sitting four pews back on my right started loudly clearing their throats. I apologized. I said I misspoke. "We will be decking the halls." And the Hall family sitting in row three on my left started making similar sounds. This congregation seemed to welcome my wit, such as it was, and politely gave it right back.

Since it had been such a moving experience in Santa Barbara, we sang "Silent Night" at the close of Christmas Eve services at the Madison church. The Christmas Eve temperature regularly hovered around zero degrees. We formed a circle inside around the inside walls of the sanctuary. Almost as good.

Several initiatives were undertaken during my time, all building on the work FCC Madison members were already doing. There were two trips to Chiapas, Mexico, two capital fund drives, the hosting of the Agenda for a Prophetic Faith program, and a major push statewide on LGBT rights led by our church.

Police Chief in My Office

The Agenda for a Prophetic Faith was a well-established annual program in Madison. Each year a major speaker was invited focusing on a theme of interest usually in the realm of public policy and the role of the church. Local officials were included as responders. The venue shifted among the large churches in Madison. It was all very impressive. The primary organizer was the Rev. Vern Visick, the Presbyterian campus minister, with the help of Mark Thomas, a member of our church. They invited me to join them in the planning stages having weekly breakfasts together.

The year our church hosted, the theme was the future of the city, and the speaker was a widely known futurist in urban planning. In the audience at our invitation were the mayor, the police chief, the fire chief, the public school superintendent, a vice chancellor of the university whose responsibilities including planning, the president of the technical college, and a representative of our congressman.

At the end of the talk, the people were offered the opportunity to sit with one of these public officials to discuss the implications of the new city planning ideas on the various institutions present. As host pastor, I toured around the building to all the breakout spaces where the conversations were taking place. Having spent all my previous pastoral work in California, it was very impressive to me to see Mayor Paul Soglin sitting in the middle of the Fellowship Hall talking with fifteen people, to see the police chief in my office with eight people including two city council members, and the other groups. It was a form of public policy engagement, face-to-face seeking common ground, that seemed unique and wonderful. The New England town meeting comes to mind. I sat in for a few minutes to listen to the new police chief, wanting to get a fix on him. Someone described how University Avenue was so massively clogged up with students at the times when classes ended and asked what the chief might do about it. He said, "You see students. I see violators." But everyone agreed there was little that could be done except for drivers to be patient.

Raising Money

The church learns a lot about itself in capital fund drives. There are unintended consequences, usually good ones. New leadership is discovered, ties to the church are reflected on, and its value is established by each person. Bonding among participants occurs, and major projects determining a lot about the future of this ministry are established. Goals are set.

The first of my capital fund drives in Madison was to make the church more accessible. Fifteen years earlier an elevator had been built to allow people to go to the second and third floors. But the elevator did not make the sanctuary accessible. Our job was to have the elevator redesigned so that there were both front and back doors making it possible to handle passengers at the sanctuary level. There were massive stairs to climb to enter the front of the church and one could not enter the sanctuary in a wheelchair. This project enabled access from the parking lot.

The church hosted a highly respected childcare program that dated back to the sixties. It was a great location for university employees. I included the director of the childcare center in the weekly construction meetings because it was important to protect the center during construction. The contractor announced at one meeting that a massive rock layer had to be dynamited so rock could be excavated allowing the elevator shaft to extend down another five feet. The childcare director raised three feet off her chair. After hearing a careful description of the project and all the safety measures that would provide protection it was agreed, under the condition that there would be "no dynamiting during nap time." Lots of careful negotiating skills were used to get to that agreement. It all worked out fine.

The second capital fund drive was focused on exterior painting issues and protecting the massive glass windows in the sanctuary. Both drives were successful and the work done well.

The church had organized a foundation but had not determined its purpose. I challenged the leadership to establish a focus for it and to continue to educate the congregation of the need to raise support for it and to have wise leadership.

Chiapas and Guatemala: Refugee Resettlement 1996

In 1996 I noted in the United Church of Christ Wisconsin Conference newsletter a notice that a team was being formed for another two-week journey to Chiapas, Mexico. In the background was a decade of building of partnership between our conference and the Diocese of San Cristobal de las Casas and Bishop Samuel Ruiz. In years past, teams from our conference had traveled to extend the connections and provide critical support for projects of the diocese.

The previous summer, the team had joined in the accompaniment of Guatemalan campesinos from the refugee camps along the border just inside Chiapas to new villages created with the help of the UN Commissioner for Refugees inside Guatemala. It was still not totally clear that the paramilitary forces of the oppressive Guatemalan government would honor the peace agreements.

Having experienced the impact of the immersion in the city, in East Germany, and in the Santa Barbara Peace Mission, I signed up for the 1996 team of eleven Wisconsin UCC lay members and clergy. I liked churches that had foreign policy. Our team was driven by our families to the Chicago O'Hare Airport, and we flew United to Mexico City airport and then, via Mexicana airline, to Tuxtla Gutierrez in Chiapas. We were met by several vans and cars sent by the diocesan office and transported up the winding, steep seven-thousand-foot climb to San Cristobal. After a day of orientation, we boarded a charter bus to be transported to the Guatemalan border. We were accompanied by Bud Moore, a UCC missionary working with his wife, the Rev. Paula Bidel. Bud was eager for us to immerse ourselves in the realities of residents' lives, not the tourist experience of the society. Bud's idea for transportation from the Mexico-Guatemala border to the remote new village of Chacula, Guatemala, in the mountains, was by a class 3 bus. It was loaded, like some old movies I'd seen, with farmers, pigs, and chickens, with half the people sitting with luggage on top of the bus. Folks were very polite to the group of eleven gringos, giving us their seats while they stood, hung on the outside, or joined the crowd on the roof. We headed up a rough dirt road winding and climbing, moving about eight miles per hour with the old engine moaning and groaning. A heavy rain squall came along soaking everything and everybody on the roof and most of us inside. Around one turn, we faced a large pool of water and mud. Through the mud was the only option for the driver. It was not possible to see how deep it was, so the driver stopped, told everyone to get off the bus and carry animals and heavy items and walk around the pool. We then watched as the driver revved up the engine and sped, so to speak, across the pool and bogging down in the deepest place. He revved the engine and the wheels spun spraying great arcs of mud out the back and, of course, the bus sank lower in the pool.

I was thinking that there was no phone service within walking distance and no means of communication. No McDonalds to grab a Big Mac or a cup of coffee. We were alone together to solve our situation. There was no way to summon help. Only the strength and resourcefulness of the community of travelers provided hope. Turned out that there was enough strength with all of us pulling, pushing, lifting, and praying to move that old bus out of the mud and across the water. Seemed almost like a biblical moment. How do you sing the doxology in Spanish or whatever dialect of the Mayan ancestors' tongue was appropriate? Smiles all around.

After seven hours of travel covering thirty miles on that rough dirt road climbing ever higher and further, our team was deposited alongside the road at the new village. Maybe forty small houses lay scattered around the hills. Apart from the building made of concrete block, rough timber, and corrugated metal being used as a community center, all the homes were constructed of sticks and blue plastic tarps. Two church workers greeted us and took us to the building where we could choose a space to roll out our sleeping bags on the floor. We had a brief orientation and a bowl of soup and went to bed. Everything was wet but lying down was a great idea.

The next two days we visited with people in the village, which seemed not very productive since they did not, except for a few, speak Spanish. They were a mixture of people from remote areas in the mountains of Guatemala who did not even speak the same dialects of the various Mayan languages. We saw the beginnings of an additional permanent building that would eventually hold a health clinic and other services. This was financed and built by the United Nations.

Several women in our group saw some beautiful hand embroidered huipils and belts and suggested that women hold a cooperative sale of their work. Since the women of the village did not know each other, our brief visit may have created a knitting together of people, a joint venture in which they would become acquainted. And maybe not.

I was invited to one of these stick and tarp homes for an evening meal. Each of us went to a different home. We sat on the dirt floor, a woman, her sister, and me. In the candlelight I looked around. They had fled from their villages in panic a year earlier. The government ordered a paramilitary force to forage through the mountains and kill as many indigenous citizens as possible. The government assumption was that communist revolutionaries were being supported by these remote mountain villages.

The food they served included a Guatemalan tortilla, some corn in a warm liquid, and coffee. I'm sure it was a feast compared to their usual fare. We could find no common word except *niños* (children). She had six who were nowhere to be seen. I had four in faraway places.

A thought crossed my mind while I sat there in the awkward silences: I will never again be this far from civilization as I know it, this remote from all familiar forms of communication, from health care, and from my own culture. The only luxury that woman offered me was a cup of coffee. It was instant but it was clearly a major gift celebrating my presence in that home. And it was in a cup with a nice handle. I saw there was a logo on the cup. It read, "First Congregational Church UCC Washington, DC" and had a small image of the church located at Tenth and G Street NW. I was stunned.

That's the church where Janet and I were married some seventeen years before. I knew immediately how that cup got to that far-off, isolated place. The Rev. Barbara Gerlach was copastor of the First Congregational Church

UCC of Washington, DC, with her husband the Rev. John Mack. I knew that she had made numerous trips to Latin America to various trouble spots. I knew right away that she must have carried coffee cups when she came to participate in one of the accompaniment trips. I confirmed that with her in recent years. It blew me away and totally ruined my sense of isolation.

After several days we packed up to reverse the trip back to San Cristobal de las Casas. Before dawn, our team waited alongside the dirt road hoping the bus on its return trip would come sometime on the day it was scheduled to take us downhill back to the border and to our charter bus for transport back to San Cristobal. It came eventually and took us away. I was left wondering why pigs and chickens rode both ways on the bus.

While we drew many benefits from this exposure, the primary goal was to have international teams visit as many of these new settlements as possible. The government-controlled paramilitary groups would likely refrain from attacks. Killing church people from Madison would have been bad press for the Guatemalan government.

Chiapas 1998: Digging the Foundation for the Pigsty, Facing Deportation

Of course, this conference-wide trip created another idea. Such a journey with a team from our church would be transforming for them and for the church. I had seen that happen in Santa Barbara.

The conference hoped to send a team in the summer of 1998, and I suggested the First Congregational UCC Madison take that challenge. The conference committee said, "Give it a try."

The church responded with sufficient enthusiasm and a team was formed. We began to hold orientation and planning sessions in our living room. Bud and Paula were back in Minneapolis, their home, on furlough and Bud agreed to come to Madison a couple times to help orient our team.

He had worked with a priest in the small town of Las Margaritas, creating a project for us. We would travel to Chiapas and help build a pigsty for use by several families working together. The campesinos had caught Bud's vision to begin a cooperative together instead of each of them working on a small plot for their own sustenance.

A faculty member from the School of Business at UW immediately wanted to see the business plan and the architectural drawings. It took both Bud and me a while to get our folks, mostly professors and grad students, to see that they were common labor, that they were not managers of this project. "When Jorge says, 'move this rock from here to there' it would be our task not to ask why, but to move the rock," Bud insisted.

Las Margaritas was a community in central Chiapas. The project was jointly planned by the diocese and the UCC missionaries, Paula and Bud. The project was supported by Bishop Ruiz and assigned to the parish, so we had guidance and hospitality from the priest and the nun of the local parish. Bud was our guide and principal translator if Spanish were the other language. Mayan dialects were another story. He had worked out many details with Padre Mauricio, the priest, and Sister Soccora, the parish nun, prior to our arrival. They arranged for us to be housed in a U-shaped vacant home with four bedrooms, an open courtyard that served as living and dining room, and a kitchen. There was a single entrance from the street in a hallway between two of the bedrooms. We were transported to the worksite each morning by an old Toyota pickup truck Bud had borrowed and were supervised by the local men who oversaw construction. Of course, they argued about design, priorities, and materials through the process. We were told where to dig trenches and where rock and concrete foundations would be placed. And we spent six days digging with pickaxes, shovels, and our hands, mixing concrete on the ground and moving concrete and big rocks around in a wheelbarrow.

Half our team were women and we all understood that they would share the labor on the worksite. Our women wore work pants. That was a cultural shock to the folks in Las Margaritas. Men did manual labor. Women, wearing embroidered dresses, tended to the children, tended open fires on tables in their kitchens, made tortillas, and carried lunch out to the worksite for the men.

They all stood and watched in amazement as our women lifted rocks into the wheelbarrow, took picks and dug big rocks out of the soil, and mixed concrete on the ground. The local women invited our women to the small church nearby for a conversation. There was enough Spanish translation in the group for adequate communication. The question of the women's role in the co-op was discussed and finally an idea was settled on. The Las Margaritas women wanted to create a tienda, a small store, so that each family would not have to walk three miles to the tienda in the next village.

Scholars have written about the unintended consequences of Americans coming south to do good and damaging the social fabric of communities. Ivan Illich set up an international training center in Cuernavaca, Mexico, to sensitize missionaries and hopefully prevent this damage. I believed that questions about the role of women on the jobsite, wielding shovels and pickaxes instead of preparing a meal over an open fire at home as our host families were doing, were raised in their minds. They watched us closely. I have wondered how destructive we were in addition to laying a pigsty foundation with them. That we dropped in out of somewhere, raised some questions that imposed our values in their context, and then disappeared into thin air without experiencing the consequences made me wonder about unintended consequences.

A second important point is that our team became a pawn in an ongoing battle between the Mexican government and the Zapatista revolutionary army in the mountains of Chiapas just south and east from Las Margaritas. The entire time we were there, the smoke from fires in the mountains clouded our vision and brought tears to our eyes. The army had set the fires to burn out the Zapatistas. Bishop Ruiz was the last liberation theology advocate serving as bishop in Latin America. Thus, he basically supported the Zapatistas.

The first night our team went to a restaurant for supper. Five uniformed and armed deputies from La Migra, the immigration police, came into the restaurant and collected from us our passports. It felt really threatening to have the police take away our passports and give no indication when or if they might return. After a nervous hour, the police returned the passports.

The next day an article appeared in the newspaper reporting that our team had been invited by the bishop to bring arms into Chiapas to give to the Zapatistas and to provide training for their use.[1] This was a new experience for us middle-class, white citizens from the Upper Midwest. From that point on, we were never without an unfriendly escort provided by La Migra. And at a rate of about every other day, our passports were collected and kept for periods of time.

Bud contacted the diocese office, and they arranged an attorney from a church-sponsored legal services program to brief us. It was clear to that attorney that we would likely be detained and deported. The process, he told us, usually meant long hours in the La Migra office in San Cristobal, buses to the airport, flights to the US in whatever numbers of opens seats were available, and flying to whatever US city that flight was scheduled for. Our passports would be returned along with our IDs, usually Wisconsin drivers licenses, when we found our seat on the plane. Our money would be confiscated. So, we would arrive in various cities in the US without money and would have to find our way back to Madison. Many did not see the adventure in that.

When we completed our work on the pigsty in Las Margaritas with two extra days before our scheduled return flights home, the diocesan attorney asked us to spend a day visiting a mountain encampment which was

1. Herrera, "Agentes del INM."

under threat from government paramilitary forces. We would simply walk three miles into the village and spend time with the people learning as much of their story as possible. Our presence would send a message to the paramilitary that their actions were being monitored.

In El Bosque on Pentecost Sunday, we gathered with campesinos at their church. In their tradition there were no pews. People stood for the mass. The problem presented itself when an army transport truck pulled into the street in sight of the church. The priest was alarmed. Seemed like the rumors were true. This village had resisted the army building new camps in the forest. The army seemed prepared to punish them. The priest asked our group to gather in the chancel area. He then invited all the elders of the village to step forward and stand in a row along the front of the other worshipers. And he asked most of our group to file down from the chancel and form a line behind the elders.

He asked me to preach the sermon. At Pentecost, Christians believe through the outpouring of the Holy Spirit, people from every tongue, race, and nation are brought together in Jesus Christ. We reenacted it. I spoke in English. After a quick search the only person available who could translate English to Spanish was a Dutch missionary. Then one of the villagers was asked to translate Spanish to Tojolabal, the local Mayan dialect. I spoke briefly, saying essentially that we are made one in Christ, but who knows what the people heard after being twice translated.

When the worship concluded, the army trucks had pulled away. The priest told me that the reason our people had been asked to form a line behind the elders was to protect them from gunfire.

As we returned to Las Margaritas from that visit, we were informed that the next day we were to report to the La Migra office in San Cristobal for the purpose of deportation.

One of the men in our group agreed to go with me to see if we could find someone with a phone and make some calls back to the US. A Baptist missionary's home was within walking distance nearby. We were welcomed and given free use of two phone lines for international calls. The missionary said that we could be deported given the circumstances.

I first called my daughter in Washington, DC. She worked for the State Department in the US Agency for International Development. I described our situation and asked her to use her network of government contacts to see what pressure might be put on the Mexican officials. I phoned our Wisconsin conference minister Fred Trost and laid it out for him. He activated the national church officials and various Wisconsin-based religious leaders asking their help. Fred called the office of our congressman who was in his district office in Madison and recruited his help. What all this generated we didn't know.

Our experience was that we showed up at the La Migra office and surrendered our passports and sat in the waiting room for many hours. One by one we were interviewed in Spanish. Several buses pulled up outside and waited. We were told that the buses were for us, to take us to the airport and ship us on the next planes flying north.

My thoughts were running along the line that this situation was a great opportunity to generate news about the deportation of a US church group who had spent their own money to dig ditches for a pigsty in Chiapas. We could bring more attention to the military oppression in the forested mountains in Chiapas and the brutal effort to defeat the Zapatista army seeking to push the government out of control of southern Mexico. Most of our group were frightened and just hoping to return safely to Madison.

We heard the La Migra director in his office receive many phone calls. We didn't know what, if anything, that had to do with us. After about five hours he came out and gave us our passports and told us we could leave.

I can't say I was fully happy with that outcome. Part of me wanted them to ship us back to whatever cities we landed in and we would have to use our clever problem-solving skills to find our way back to Madison. We were nonetheless welcomed back as heroes and had many opportunities to tell our story.

I am aware that teams from the church organized followed-up visits to Las Margaritas. I have photos of the enormous pigs that were housed in our pigsty. I heard that the co-op however fell apart because of issues among the men and the project eventually failed.

One final note. We had a simple prayer service each day before we went to the worksite. One of the men, a professor at Madison Area Technical College, about halfway through our immersion in Chiapas said to us that he had felt for a very long time that his soul was a parched field and dying. "Now, here in Las Margaritas, I feel it is raining on that field and my soul is happy."

Homosexuality is Neither Sickness nor Sin

The role our church played in advancing the pastoral and justice conversation about lesbian, gay, bisexual, and transgender (LGBT) issues and the publishing of "The Madison Affirmation" were, for me, the most significant project during my time in Madison.

Bill Coffin called me to say he was accepting an invitation from Lawrence University in Appleton, Wisconsin, to spend a year as guest lecturer. Lawrence would provide him with a comfortable home on campus. The furnishings were to include a big grand piano that he would use to restore some of his own broken places. He would meet with classes and students as invited. He was confident they would make good use of him. He said he was available to come down to Madison any time and for anything I wanted him to do.

He had shared the story of how he led the Riverside Church in New York through a process leading to their public support for LGBT concerns including welcome to participation, membership, and employment at the church. It had been hard work. First Congregational, Madison, had already crossed that bridge and the only other Madison congregation beginning to talk was the First Baptist Church led by the Rev. Mark Clinger. I thought that this was the issue for which I wanted to provide public push. This meant getting the issue on the agenda of the city and its churches. The other Madison clergy needed a nudge also.

I invited the senior clergy leadership in all the so-called downtown churches to a conversation on what we might organize. I said to this group that Coffin had agreed that LGBT issues and the role of the church were to be the focus of his visit. They were all thrilled to have a close-up experience with Coffin and thus willing to take some risks to get it. They agreed to serve as the planning committee for a Sunday afternoon event at First Congregational. We needed six weeks to get publicity going. We envisioned that the announcement would be clear about the issue focus and that the wider community would be invited. And the group agreed to be listed personally as sponsors on the flyer and advertisements. This meant that they would all be publicly identified with LGBT justice, no longer sitting on the fence. Their churches were also listed "for identification only." I cleared the date and general plan with Bill. He suggested his title, "Homosexuality, the Last Prejudice."

I also asked the six-member clergy planning committee to serve as a panel to respond to Coffin's address. That put them on the chancel platform close to the podium. I was envisioning media photo possibilities. I sent press announcements to the city desk of the two Madison newspapers, papers in nearby communities, and to the TV and radio stations. And we published a half-page paid advertisement of the program and speaker. We invited interested people to come. We challenged churches to welcome LGBT people.

Coffin loved the format of having designated responders whom he thought would generate a deeper level of conversation. The panel was so thrilled and intimidated that there were no serious challenges from them on the positions Coffin took in his address.

My role, as I understood the role of a community organizer, was to find the leadership and the issue that needed to be talked about but that was still taboo. My notion of the organizer was to not be the star of events but in the background. To move the LGBT agenda on to the public agenda was, for me, to show as many clergy as possible to be public leaders on the issue. That concentrated their minds on becoming clear toward what they believed and what needed to be done.

The topic brought a large crowd of approximately 450 to the church on that Sunday afternoon. After welcoming those who came for the talk, I offered a brief introduction of Coffin and the clergy panel members. Then I wandered around in the rear of the sanctuary listening to the program and wondering who all these people were. I later asked the other clergy how many from their own congregations attended. My conclusion was that probably half were not members of any of our congregations but drawn in by the subject. My clergy colleagues, happy to have had the opportunity to share the stage with Coffin, were ready to take on whatever issues were going to arise in their churches because of their public role in this event. And they became national go-to leaders in their own denominations as the conversation in the church about LGBT people spread.

I also planned several events in addition to the Sunday afternoon talk. Bill preached the sermon at our church on Sunday morning and spoke at the adult education forum. The dean of the College of Letters and Science, Dr. Philip R. Certain, scheduled an invitational reception for Coffin at the university. Coffin offered opening remarks about discrimination against LGBT students, faculty, and staff in higher education and opened some new areas of conversation among those in the room. Janet and I also had a reception and a dinner at our home for friends to meet Coffin. I was shocked how many people didn't have a clue who Bill Coffin was. In my world he was famous.

To help keep the conversation alive in the UCC, I signed up to do speaking engagements in UCC churches all over southwest Wisconsin. They were all rural, largely agricultural congregations. And on LGBT issues they were difficult groups to talk to. My most treasured event took place one night in a UCC church in Platteville, Wisconsin. This was a group of farm families. There was one very large farmer standing in the back of the fellowship hall, away from the conversation happening in a circle of chairs. Suntan from the eyes down, white from eyes up. Sunburned forearms and hands. He did not look happy during my talk. I kept my eye on him, wondering what questions or other things he was planning to throw at me. My last point was to report on research that the same-sex reality occurs in all animals. After a few questions, my farmer friend in the back walked up to the chair circle, close to where I was standing, and said, "I'm with you all the way, pastor. I lost ten thousand dollars last year at an auction. I bought a goddamned gay bull."

The next stage of this story took place soon after the Coffin weekend. I called the Rev. Mel White, founder of Soul Force. I was not familiar with either White or his organization. I learned that he and his husband, Gary Nixon, had traveled across the country, speaking on university campuses, teaching the "soul force" principles of Gandhi and King, organizing people of faith to do justice, and confronting religious leaders whose antigay rhetoric, White believed, "leads to the suffering and death of God's lesbian and gay children."[2]

I made him aware of our session with Coffin and the widening conversations. He was in the Midwest and wondered if I would call together that same group of pastors for a workshop with him, searching for more follow-up. At that point it was easy to gather a group of clergy. On a weekday morning two weeks later, eighteen clergy gathered in the student lounge for a workshop with White.

The workshop connected our thinking about the LGBT conversation with the nonviolent work of Gandhi and King and showed us a path for much clearer analysis of the issue and bolder action. And it provided a clearer picture of the suffering brought about by the church. When asked for more specific suggestions for what might be done next in our context, he suggested a statement be drafted and signed by our group. Such a statement could be widely circulated.

A team of five volunteered to meet and draft a statement. I got a call from the chair of the drafting group. They had not been able to draft a statement, not because of disagreement, but because none of them had been able to find the right language to state the case. We were just learning how to talk about this issue. I phoned White and reported this problem and asked if he could send us a draft. He agreed and just before the second meeting I was able to circulate his proposed language to the drafting committee. They changed two words and brought it to the meeting with full recommendation. We all felt that the statement said what we wanted to say to and for our congregations.

We were ready to put our names on it as supporters and go public with it. I suggested we post "The Madison Affirmation" as a paid ad in the *Wisconsin State Journal*, which would mean it would be read across the state.

2. "Mel and Gary's Story," para. 1.

Again, agreement. A suggestion was made that we post it in two weeks and use the time to gather additional signatures from clergy in our denominations across the state. All those names with denominations listed "for information only" were printed in the piece.

When it was published as a full-page ad, we had under the statement the names of clergy as follows: three American Baptist, five Episcopal, nine Evangelical Lutheran Church in America, one Society of Friends, one Religious Science, one Moravian, ten United Methodist, fifteen Presbyterian USA, twenty-six United Church of Christ, four Unitarians, eleven lay Roman Catholics, and a few other lay signers, a total of ninety-nine statewide. They all pitched in to pay for the ad.

The opening paragraph read:

> Jesus Christ calls us to love God and our neighbor as ourselves. As Christian clergy we embrace gay and lesbian persons as our neighbors. From our reading of scripture and from our pastoral experiences, we believe there is sufficient evidence to conclude that homosexuality is neither sickness nor sin. For too long, homosexual persons have been condemned and mistreated by the followers of Jesus Christ. Sadly, the Bible has been misused in support of this condemnation. This abuse of scripture must end. Heterosexual and homosexual persons are children of God, created in God's image. We invite Christians to prayerfully reexamine scripture and their consciences for any vestiges of hatred or prejudice against their homosexual brothers and sisters.[3]

The Open and Affirming public decision made clear that LGBT folks were welcome at First Congregational. We experienced a significant growth in participation in the life of the church. The church treasurer Rich was a bank vice president and openly gay at the church. He assured us that as the church became known to welcome gays and lesbians, we would be surprised how many were hungering for such a church.

Rich, Janet, and I measured this phenomenon in the following way. On Sunday, Janet and Rich sat together. The following week, a visitor named Dave arrived. Janet, Rich, and Dave sat together for worship. Janet, being the preacher's wife, carried assurance of his welcome. Dave felt the fear of rejection that had been his personal history as an out gay man. Sitting with Rich and Janet, he found safety. They called it "the Row." In a few months after the founding of the Row, one of Janet's lesbian colleagues came to visit and joined them. Soon a gay friend of Janet's started attending. Before too long, they needed a second row to accommodate the LGBT folks. After that

---

3. *Wisconsin State Journal*, "Madison Affirmation."

there was no longer the need for unspoken dedicated space for them. They claimed the entire place as a safe and sacred space where they found welcome. Our church was the first to enter a curb-to-curb bright banner with our name in the pride parade.

One couple, both with Roman Catholic backgrounds, joined the church. As lesbians they had done their best to find a safe place in their church. They heard the word on the street that our church would welcome them. They introduced themselves on their first visit and were in tears with their experience walking into the church. A couple months later I performed their wedding. One was a retired police officer, the other a radiologist at University Hospital. They shared with me that they were working on in vitro fertilization and had six months of frustration. They finally concluded that their best choice was the adoption of a child from China. After all the paperwork and arrangements, one of them went to China to bring home their baby. A month later I baptized the child, a great festive occasion for all the church. After church that morning they whispered to me that the in vitro had worked and a pregnancy had been achieved. Seven months later their family expanded by two. Twins. From two to five in eleven months.

And yet they said, even with all the warmth and welcome, all the support and participation of the whole church in their rapidly expanding family story, walking up the steps into the church was still the hardest thing they had to do every week. That historic pain of rejection carries a long time.

How the Clergy Keep Each Other Healthy

Clergy need support, regular conversations where we can tell horror stories about people in our churches, where we can describe a situation and ask for help on strategy development, and where we can share victory stories and know that all that was shared was locked up never to see the light of day. We need other kinds of enrichment for those engaged in local church ministry. In Santa Barbara we could look forward to twice a year half-day retreats with other clergy in our association. We had a small UCC sister church in Santa Barbara. The next closest UCC church was in Ventura to the south and Lompoc to the north, at least a forty-five-minute drive. Our UCC churches and clergy colleagues were scattered.

In Madison there were eight UCC churches in the metropolitan area and more in the little towns that dotted the countryside. There were lots of colleagues. The Association, covering the southwest quadrant of Wisconsin, had full-time staff and a wonderful enrichment program including lots of intellectual conversation and pastoral care. I was invited to join a study group reading Karl Barth theology, liberation theology, feminist theology, and a twice a month theology study group with papers by members of the group that were published at the end of each year. It was not possible to work full-time and belong to all these groups, so we each selected ones we thought most valuable.

I joined a clergy support group that met for two hours twice a month. The format was set so that the first hour was for a case study and conversation and the second hour for updating previous situations that had been shared. We took our turns bringing a case study, some actual situation we were facing in the parish, and inviting the group to help us think it through to consider ways of dealing with things, people, complaints, and temptations. This was a very helpful conversation and I looked forward to driving over to McFarland where those conversations took place. I deepened my appreciation of the pastoral task, the courage and insights of my colleagues, and felt completely free to talk of some the most difficult issues, even those I thought I should know how to deal with and didn't.

About a year after I retired and moved to Pilgrim Place, I had reason to talk with Rev. Bob Mutton, the staff person for the Southwest Association in Wisconsin. I told him how important all the support options were to me and especially the clergy support group. He said it took them six months to deal with my absence from the group. I did not know what he meant. He shared that I had a powerful way of saying to people sinking into despair, "Get over it!" It is true, I am uncomfortable with colleagues who experience themselves as victims and powerless. Bob said they took turns saying it when needed.

Another form of support was dear friendships we developed in Madison. Out of the Ministerial Association, I formed a connection with the rector of Grace Episcopal Church on the Square across from the State Capitol, John Fetterman, and the pastor of the Luther Memorial Church down University Avenue a few blocks, Harvey Peters. We met for lunch on occasion and decided to have dinner together with our spouses. Janet and I invited them to our home. Turns out all three women were avid quilters. We continued to meet and found a lot that bound us together in our theological and political views as well as our quilting adventures.

We met for dinner at the Fettermans' one evening. Janet had been held up in a meeting and arrived almost an hour late. She was amazed we already had three empty bottles of good red wine on the table.

In 1998 the three couples decided to go to Italy together for a couple weeks. The Peters had done a Road Scholar (formally Elderhostel) tour the year before and wanted to go back on their own schedule. John Fetterman had studied for the Roman Catholic priesthood in Rome and had been ordained in the St. Peter's Cathedral. He spoke some Italian so we felt we could make our way around. We spent a week in Rome and a week on a farm in the middle of an olive grove in Tuscany. Except for pickpockets trying to steal money from me, it all worked out great.

One of the commonalities we discovered at one of our dinners was a weariness of the closed groups in Madison. We all experienced a widely shared attitude that making it in Madison was an exceptional honor, that only the worthiest people gathered in that small but exceptional city. We each had lived in other exceptional places like Los Angeles; New York; Washington, DC; St. Louis; Chicago; Santa Barbara; Pittsburgh; and Mount Pulaski, Illinois. We didn't get it. We also experienced that there were few open groups. Most groups, even in church, were closed, no room for new people. Janet suggested to a couple women in our church that they get together for lunch. One of the women said, "I don't have time for new friends." We all envisioned retirement from our three churches and being eager to move on somewhere else. That would be blasphemy in Madison.

I liked Madison and did my best to get to know its history, its wonderful university, its activist political life, and its Big Ten sports. I even enjoyed a friend describing Madison as "the People's Republic of Madison completely surrounded by reality."

Personal Side of the Madison Years

During our seven years in Madison, we were able to be present to several family crises and celebrations. Both Janet's father, Wilford Herschel Vandevender (born 1915) in Fayetteville, Arkansas, and mine, Louis William Kittlaus (born 1904) in St. Louis, died in 1994. Those locations were close enough for us to be present with our families during these hard times.

Janet's mother, Mildred Hazel Jelken Eberle Vandevender, gradually disappeared into dementia and died in 1999. Mildred's illness required switching around among care facilities all over the state of Illinois. At that point the medical field had not yet developed care facilities that could accommodate all the various stages and forms of Alzheimer's. Janet was able to join her three sisters in making medical decisions.

Our son Adam was engaged and married to Pam Lord in a ceremony in Carmel Valley, California. Ann was engaged and married to Jay Byrne in Silver Spring, Maryland. I was both proud father and presiding minister for these joy-filled weddings.

And on Easter 1998 Ann gave birth to our first grandchild, Erin Leitner Byrne.

Janet was appointed associate dean in the College of Letters and Science at the University of Wisconsin in Madison. In that college there were 15,500 undergraduate students and 900 faculty. In addition to being on the management team for the college, she was responsible for academic support for these students and for students in several campuswide programs. She supervised two hundred combined faculty, staff, and students in a wide variety of programs. My favorite administrative dilemma for her occurred when the football coach came to her to find a way to change a grade for a star running back who otherwise would be academically ineligible to play in the Rose Bowl. She refused to budge. She referred that major exception to standing policy to the faculty and highest levels of administration for final decision.

Nice Ending for a Switch

When I approached my sixty-fourth birthday, we began to think seriously about retirement. I intended to retire at sixty-five, which was April 1999. When I arrived in San Diego for my first ministry in 1959 all the Congregational and UCC pastors I met talked of retiring at Pilgrim Place in Claremont, California. That's what we do! Janet and I had visited Pilgrim Place several times. We felt aware of what it offered. I never had another thought about going anywhere else.

We met with our financial advisor to look at finances for retirement. It occurred to me then that I never thought about funding my retirement. I had been since 1959 putting money into the UCC Pension Fund and that was it. And Social Security, of course. I did not have any idea what together these two funds would generate for my retirement. I never had training in personal finances. Money showed up because of my work and I spent it. If earned more, I spent more. No discipline whatever. In her last two positions at the two universities, Janet earned considerably more than I did. That was good. She had pensions, an IRA, and Social Security. Retirement was financially feasible.

Again, as in Santa Barbara, we had to be careful where and to whom we could talk about this major transition. People from the church were all over the university and university people were all over the church. My retirement meant Janet's resignation and vice versa. We chose to have lunch with Rev. Bob Mutton to begin a wider circle. He was very supportive and observed that it had been more than thirty years since First Congregational Church had had a good ending to a ministry. He proposed that a nice event be planned so the church could feel more confident about itself. He agreed that when the retirement decision was public, he would work with the planning committee for whatever the event would be.

Jerry was chair of the retirement party planning committee and made sure that the scope of the planning was well beyond a church potluck in the basement, even though those can be spectacular, too.

My retirement dinner was held in the Monona Terrace, the Frank Lloyd Wright–designed conference center built during our years in Madison. The buildings were beautiful and reflected the Wright Prairie style. It is located on the south side of downtown Madison on the edge of Lake Monona. It was an excellent dinner at a spectacular location.

I was given a hard time by a trustee who thought two capital fund drives in seven years was a bit much. Some very nice tributes were offered. And we had a great deal of fun. Gifts included cash, which we used to purchase two nice Trek bicycles to use in California to help us recover from the effects of so much Wisconsin butter fat. They presented me with a piece of original artwork, a beautiful calligraphy by Linda Hancock with the Oliver Wendell Holmes Jr. statement: "As life is action and passion it is required of us that we should share in the action and passion of our time at peril of being judged not to have lived." The church, to honor my years of ministry, commissioned a new hymn text by Brian Wren entitled "In Christ We Live."[4]

Janet and I commissioned a new organ prelude by Emma Lou Diemer, a composer we knew in Santa Barbara. The prelude was variations based on a favorite hymn for the congregation, "Bring Many Names."[5] We did this to honor First Congregational Church United Church of Christ, Madison.

This was a sweet ending and entirely proper liturgy for bringing a positive end to my work there and releasing me to retirement.

I realized what retirement meant on Thursday September 1, 1999, in California. I woke up realizing that on that day, by electronic funds transfer, my pension and Social Security funds had been deposited in my bank account. I didn't necessarily have to get up.

Retiring to Pilgrim Place in Claremont was a wise choice. We have thrived here. Twenty-four years and still looking for more. Justice church, I believe, is still what needs to happen. The church must engage in our new moments of history or we continue down the path to irrelevance.

4. For the full text of this hymn, see appendix.

5. Crawford et al., *New Century Hymnal*, no. 11.

Chapter 11

Exploring Possibilities of Justice Church

ALONG THIS WAY, I found colleagues, clergy, and lay people who shared a vision of the church being an active agent for social change. They wanted to become involved in a church working for justice, a church programmed to engage in the issues of their moment in history, under skilled leadership, working in coalition with other justice-seeking groups to make serious change in society.

When I say justice, I remind you, I'm not primarily talking about food banks and charity. I'm talking about working out understandings of why vast numbers of people are poor and hungry and then working out strategies for changing the conditions leading to hunger and poverty. I'm talking about getting a local congregation engaged in community analysis, and empowering people to build a better life for themselves and their families. And I'm talking about the role of government on behalf of us all maintaining a safety net to protect the poor. The social safety net consists of assistance existing to improve lives of vulnerable families and individuals experiencing poverty and destitution.

Most seminaries offer courses and some a degree program in pastoral care, to heal the wounded and comfort the afflicted. Not many offer degree programs in social change. A justice church orientation will require new thinking and new skills in action planning and in community organizing. Seminaries will have to create new curricula and new teaching positions. Tearing down the walls of hostility of racism, poverty, and other such conditions require skills that are available.

Schools of social work offer programs in community organizing. The archives of the old urban training centers contain rich resources for this kind of work. Several organizations offer community organizing workshops

235

and consulting for specific projects. I am aware of PICO, a community organizing network; Industrial Areas Foundation (IAF) founded by Saul Alinsky in 1940; and Community Change (formerly Center for Community Change), a national organization that builds power from the ground up.

We need leaders to free the captives, to empower the blind to see their oppression, to proclaim the year of the Lord, to tear down the walls of hostility, and to beat swords into plowshares and their spears into pruning hooks.

I suggest we put resources to address the following questions: Why are people in this nation (in this community) of so many rich people without food, shelter, education, and jobs? What needs to be changed? How do we transform the church into engaged justice-seeking communities working for needed changes?

It is tempting to give to charity and feel we've met our responsibility. Though these acts of charity are lifesaving, the next step is opening ourselves to see the conditions which lock people in poverty. Most of our members easily accept the walls that separate them from the poor. "Yet, millions and millions of Christians are not close to the poor and do not want to get close."[1]

I came into awareness that the primary focus of the churches' work was ministry to the members of the church.[2] I saw the typical organization of the church council consisted of the deacons (worship), trustees (finances), the building committee (the buildings and grounds), and the Christian education committee (church school and youth programs). In some churches there was also a social action committee whose job it was to distribute the mission budget to worthy groups. Nowhere was there a group responsible for developing program for our "parish."

I was interested in developing another focus, namely, with the people outside the church who were suffering from hunger, homelessness, unemployment, and the various other sources, causes, and symptoms of poverty. Many of the stories are about how I improvised projects to engage members of the church in reaching out to the parish. These stories are about primarily single congregations exploring justice ministry.

Rector Ed Bacon, in a sermon at All Saints Church in Pasadena, said that it's not that the members of All Saints live better lives because they are members of the church. It is crucial that the poor in this part of Pasadena live better lives because of the members of All Saints.

Reading the Herzog book, my imagination is stimulated about what might happen if several American denominations were to commit major

---

1. Herzog, *Justice Church*, 26.
2. Herzog, *Justice Church*, 14.

resources to adopt "liberating the poor" as a new ministry or function, as Herzog calls it, how seminary curriculum would be adapted to include a theology to support and guide the new clergy and how church school curricula would be written to include this understanding of the mission of the church. I wonder how an organizer could work with several congregations to develop programs to address the issues in a citywide effort. How could debate about civic issues be enriched by perspectives rooted in a biblical understanding of justice? Could a group of congregations come together and present to a city council a new issue that cries out for public attention? Could churches across the country come together like we did in the "The Poor Have Suffered Enough" campaign and seek legislative remedies to poverty?

We have moved from the individual to communities and institutions that have potential for justice church engagement.

This is way outside-the-box thinking. There will be enormous resistance. It will take sizable risks to work on this vision.

In my own experience I found that there are people looking for the church to engage in its moment of history. While some members will depart from the fellowship, I know others are there to take their place. I know God is out there at work bringing healing and justice.

As Herzog claims, "It has to be understood at this point that God is fighting the battle. Human beings are asked to join God. We will never be able to accomplish much while assuming it is we who are battling for others."[3]

I watch and listen for signs in the churches of an awareness of the new task, liberating the poor. Are people engaging in connection with the poor?

There are a lot of reasons why I loved my mother-in-law. Mildred Vandevender provided one of the clearest signs of justice church consciousness. At her memorial service a minister who had been a candidate for the Good Shephard Lutheran Church in Fayetteville, Arkansas, said Mildred was responsible for giving the candidates a tour of the city. When they got in the car for the tour, Mildred said, "Any minister of our church must first know where the poor people live."

3. Herzog, *Justice Church*, 117.

Appendix

In Christ We Live

Hymn text by Brian Wren commissioned by
First Congregational Church United Church of Christ, Madison, Wisconsin,
to honor the ministry of Rev. Paul Kittlaus, senior minister 1992–1999.
Meter: 8.8.8.8.—LONG METER. Season: Easter Sunday

Words by Brian Wren

1. In Christ we live, whose life was more
than teaching love and doing good.
In Christ we meet, whose trust in God
derision, fear, and hate withstood.

2. In Christ we hope, whose death exposed
the evil bent, the tragic flaw
in leaders, followers, and friends,
religion, government, and law.

3. In Christ we grieve the trampled lives
of people shunned, abused, oppressed.
In Christ we vow to serve the weak
and lobby for the dispossessed.

4. And if we find out how and when
to show them they are not alone,
we will not proudly be their voice,
but humbly help them find their own.

5. Their kindness, anger, or distrust
   are angels, calling us to see
   the fear, the need to have and hold,
   that frame our own captivity.

6. In Christ we live, and life is more
   than learning love and doing good,
   so praise, and pray, and trust in God
   who makes the earth our neighborhood.

Bibliography

131 Cong. Rec. H820 (bound ed. Jan 22, 1985; Ted Weiss, "Statement on Abortion").

Bly, Robert. "A Gathering of Men." YouTube, May 4, 2012. https://www.youtube.com/watch?v=TP3HWLIL1Aw.

———. *Iron John: A Book about Men.* New York: Da Capo, 2004.

Buechner, Frederick. *Wishful Thinking: A Theological ABC.* New York: Harper & Row, 1973.

Buttrick, George Arthur, et al., eds. *The Interpreter's Bible.* 12 vols. New York: Abingdon-Cokesbury, 1952.

Cox, Harvey. *The Secular City: Secularization and Urbanization in Theological Perspective.* Princeton: Princeton University Press, 2013.

Crawford, James W., et al., eds. *The New Century Hymnal.* Cleveland: Pilgrim, 1995.

Davis, Charles. "Folk Singer Refuses to Take Loyalty Oath." *San Diego Union,* May 14, 1960.

Doxiadis, Konstantinos. *Dynapolis, the City of the Future.* Athens: Athens Center of Ekistics, 1966.

Freire, Paulo. *Pedagogy of the Oppressed.* New York: Bloomsbury, 1960.

Friedan, Betty. *The Feminine Mystique.* New York: W. W. Norton, 1963.

Friedenberg, Edgar D. *Coming of Age in America: Growth and Acquiescence.* New York: Vintage, 1963.

———. *The Vanishing Adolecent.* Boston: Beacon, 1959.

Hall, Mitchell K. *Because of Their Faith: CALCAV and the Religious Opposition to the Vietnam War.* New York: Columbia University Press, 1990.

Handel, George F. "George Frideric Handel: *Messiah* Oratorio Libretto with Scripture Links." The Tabernacle Choir. https://www.thetabernaclechoir.org/messiah/libretto-with-scripture-links.html.

Hearing before the Subcommittee on Rural Development, Oversight, and Investigations of the Committee on Agriculture, Nutrition, and Forestry United States Senate. 98th Cong. 56–63, 139–144 (Mar 14, 1983; Paul Kittlaus, "Statement of Interreligious Taskforce on U.S. Food Policy").

Herrera, Carlos. "Agentes del INM Investigans Actividades de Extranjeros." *Cuarto Poder,* May 23, 1980.

Herzog, Frederick. *Justice Church: The New Function of the Church in North American Christianity.* Eugene, OR: Wipf & Stock, 2005.

Hoeveler, J. David. *John Bascom and the Origins of the Wisconsin Idea.* Madison: University of Wisconsin Press, 2016.

Holmes, Oliver Wendell. *Speeches by Oliver Wendell Holmes*. Boston: Little, Brown, and Company, 1896. https://archive.org/details/cu31924014419547/mode/2up?q =passion.

Hough, Joseph C. *Black Power and White Protestants: A Christian Response to the New Negro Pluralism*. New York: Oxford University Press,1968.

Illich, Ivan. *Deschooling Society*. New York: Harper & Row, 1971.

Kennedy, John F. "Ask Not What Your Country Can Do for You." US History. https:// www.ushistory.org/documents/ask-not.htm.

Kittlaus, Paul. "Evaluation and Proposal for the Washington Offices of Denominations." Unpublished paper, United Presbyterian Church USA, 1981.

Leas, Speed B., and Paul Kittlaus. *Church Fights: Managing Conflict in the Local Church*. Louisville: Westminster John Knox, 1973.

———. *The Pastoral Counselor in Social Action*. Minneapolis: Fortress, 1981.

Loftus, James. Title unavailable. *The New York Times*, Sep 28, 1967.

Los Angeles Times. "Church Gets Funds for Youth Work." Aug 15, 1967.

———. "Citizen Silences Klan Loudspeaker, Sets Off Chase." Sep 15, 1966.

———. "EYOA Will Seek Change in Veto of Pacoima Project." Jul 9, 1968.

———. "Robbery Arrest Perils Poverty Unit." Sep 13, 1967.

"Medellin Document: Poverty of the Church." Poverty Studies, Sep 6, 1968. http:// www.povertystudies.org/TeachingPages/EDS_PDFs4WEB/Medellin%20 Document-%20Poverty%20of%20the%20Church.pdf.

Meeks, M. Douglas. *God the Economist: The Doctrine of God and the Political Economy*. Minneapolis: Augsburg Fortress, 1989.

"Mel and Gary's Story." Mel White. https://melwhite.org/mel-garys-story/.

Moore, Ralph. *Breakout*. New York: Friendship, 1968.

Moore, Robert, and Douglas Gillette. *King, Warrior, Magician, Lover: Rediscovering the Archetypes of the Mature Masculine*. New York: HarperCollins, 1991.

Nolan, Albert. *Jesus before Christianity: The Gospel of Liberation*. Cape Town: David Philip, 1976.

Pear, Robert. "Kennedy, Assailing Reagan, Urges New Drive on Hunger." *New York Times*, Dec 23, 1983.

Prokosch, Eric. *The Simple Art of Murder: Antipersonnel Weapons and Their Developers*. Philadelphia: American Friends Service Committee, 1972.

Redman, Eric. *The Dance of Legislation*. New York: Simon & Schuster, 1975.

Robert, Henry M., III, et al. *Robert's Rules of Order Newly Revised, 12th Edition*. New York: PublicAffairs, 2020.

Roszak, Theodore. *The Making of a Counter Culture: Reflections on the Technocratic Society and Its Youthful Opposition*. New York: Anchor Doubleday, 1969.

Rowan, Carl T. "Reagan's War on Poverty." *Syracuse Herald-Journal*, Feb 16, 1983.

Sanford, John A. *Healing and Wholeness*. New York: Paulist, 1977.

Sheares, Reuben A., et al., eds. *Book of Worship: United Church of Christ*. New York: Office of Church Life and Leadership, 1968.

Sweeney, Joan. "Unit Formed to Coordinate Quake Plans." *Los Angeles Times*, Feb 8, 1981.

Thistlethwaite, Susan, ed. *A Just Peace Church*. New York: United Church, 1986.

Valley News. "Anti-Poverty Worker Faces Liquor Store Holdup Charge." Sep 12, 1967.

———. "Valley Pastor Joins Civil Rights Demonstration." Mar 18, 1965.

Weber, Hans-Rudi. *Salty Christians*. New York: Seabury, 1963.

Williams, Colin. *Faith in a Secular Age.* New York: Harper & Row, 1966.

———. *What in the World?* London: Epworth, 1965.

———. *Where in the World?* London: Epworth, 1966.

Winter, Gibson. *The New Creation as Metropolis.* New York: Macmillan, 1963.

———. *The Suburban Captivity of the Churches: An Analysis of Protestant Responsibility in an Expanding Metropolis.* Garden City, New York: Doubleday, 1961.

Wisconsin State Journal. "The Madison Affirmation." Oct 11, 1997.

World Council of Churches Department on Studies in Evangelism North American Working Group. *The Church for Others and the Church for the World: A Quest for Structures for Missionary Congregation.* Geneva: World Council of Churches, 1967.

Wren, Brian. "In Christ We Live." Hope Publishing Company, 1999. https://www.hope publishing.com/find-hymns-hw/hw197.aspx.